# WHY DECISIONS FAIL

# WHY DECISIONS FAIL

avoiding the blunders and traps

that lead to debacles

## Paul C. Nutt

BERRETT-KOEHLER PUBLISHERS, INC.
San Francisco

Berrett-Koehler Publishers, Inc.

235 Montgomery Street, Suite 650

San Francisco, CA 94104-2916

Tel: (415) 288-0260 Fax: (415) 362-2512 www.bkconnection.com

**Ordering Information**

*Quantity sales.* Special discounts are available on quantity purchases by corporations, associations, and others. For details, contact the "Special Sales Department" at the Berrett-Koehler address above.

*Individual sales.* Berrett-Koehler publications are available through most bookstores. They can also be ordered direct from Berrett-Koehler: Tel: (800) 929-2929; Fax: (802) 864-7626; www.bkconnection.com

*Orders for college textbook/course adoption use.* Please contact Berrett-Koehler: Tel: (800) 929-2929; Fax: (802) 864-7626.

*Orders by U.S. trade bookstores and wholesalers.* Please contact Publishers Group West, 1700 Fourth Street, Berkeley, CA 94710. Tel: (510) 528-1444; Fax: (510) 528-3444.

Berrett-Koehler and the BK logo are registered trademarks of Berrett-Koehler Publishers, Inc.

**Printed in the United States of America**

Berrett-Koehler books are printed on long-lasting acid-free paper. When it is available, we choose paper that has been manufactured by environmentally responsible processes. These may include using trees grown in sustainable forests, incorporating recycled paper, minimizing chlorine in bleaching, or recycling the energy produced at the paper mill.

**Library of Congress Cataloging-in-Publication Data**

Nutt, Paul C.

    Why decisions fail : avoiding the blunders and traps that lead to debacles / Paul C. Nutt.

       p. cm.

    Includes bibliographical references and index.

    ISBN-10: 1-57675-150-3; ISBN-13: 978-1-57675-150-3

    1. Decision making. I. Title.

HD30.23 .N883 2002

658.4'03—dc21                         2001043678

**First Edition**

10 09 08 07 06                  10 9 8 7 6 5 4 3 2

Interior Design & Illustration: Gopa Design & Illustration

Copy Editor: Kay Mikel, WordWorks

Proofreader: Henrietta Bensussen

Indexer: Paula C. Durbin-Westby

Production: Linda Jupiter, Jupiter Productions

For Frank, Margaret, Charles E.,
Isabel, Nancy, Richard, Suzi,
Charles A., and Tim

# Contents

# Preface

People fear a decision that can turn into a debacle—a decision riddled with poor practices producing big losses that become public. This book reveals how a decision can turn into a fiasco and how to prevent this from happening.

For more than twenty years I have been studying how decisions are made, writing about what works, what doesn't, and why. The key finding is startling—decisions fail *half* of the time. Vast sums are spent without realizing any benefits for the organization. Failures are traced to three blunders and seven traps that ensnare decision makers. Avoiding these blunders and the traps that they set will cut the failure rate significantly. Thoughtful managers, students of management, and others providing advice and services to managers should find the lessons derived from my two-decade-long research effort useful. The book is directed toward a practitioner audience of midlevel to upper level managers in for-profit and nonprofit organizations, those who aspire to these positions, and others who serve these groups. Those in executive education and master's of management programs, such as MBA, MHA, MPA, may also find the book useful.

The book is very different from those found in the market today. The scope of the research effort that stands behind the recommendations is unprecedented. To draw conclusions, four hundred decisions made by top managers in private, public, and nonprofit organizations across the United States, Canada, and Europe were collected and analyzed over a period of twenty years. Appendix 1 provides a description of this research effort along with a list of the papers drawn upon to fashion my recommendations. To ensure that the list of things to do and things to avoid are both real and compelling, my research is limited to important decisions top managers frequently encounter. The research spotlights decisions made by real people who experience real consequences for their actions. The decisions involve choices top managers often face—what to do about products or services, pricing and markets, internal operations, personnel policy, technology acquisition, reorganizations that stem from mergers and acquisitions, and control systems. Fifteen decision debacles, costly decisions that went very wrong and became public, are pulled from my database to illustrate key points. The debacles provide vivid illustrations of what went wrong and what could have been done to turn things around. A list of the debacles follows the preface.

Some of the myths about decision making that have crept into the folklore of management are dispelled. Failure cannot be put at the doorstep of events we cannot control, such as fickle customers who are constantly changing their buying habits. Failure stems from blunders that point unsuspecting decision makers toward traps that ensnare them. A key blunder is using failure-prone decision-making practices, called tactics. Failure-prone tactics are used in two of every three decisions. Some decision makers do quite well, and the tactics they apply provide exemplars that argue against some well-accepted decision-making practices, such as problem solving. Best practice tactics and how these tactics can be substituted for commonly used tactics that have a poor track record are offered. Failure also stems from the order in which these tactics are used and which is emphasized. Most decision makers stress economic rationality in the tactics they employ—what things cost—and some stress political rationality, putting a positive spin on things. The book will show you how tactics that stress logical rationality and ethical rationality can be added to the mix, how to blend political considerations with logical and ethical ones, when economics misleads you, and how to include economics in useful ways.

Each chapter describes the tactics that are used in one process stage. The stages follow the sequence found to work best in my research. Chapters begin with the description of a debacle, followed by a discussion of what went wrong and why, probing to find causes and remedies. Then tactics that have a good track record are offered, documenting their success and how to apply them to decision making.

Chapter 1 presents the three blunders found in all debacles: rushing to judgment, misusing resources, and applying failure-prone tactics. Each blunder is illustrates with five decision debacles: EuroDisney's location, the new Denver International Airport, Nestle's marketing of infant formula,

Ford's unwillingness to recall the Pinto, and BeechNut's misrepresentation of its apple juice product.

Chapter 2 shows how the three blunders set traps that unsuccessful decision makers fell into and successful ones dodged. The EuroDisney, DIA, Nestle, Pinto, and BeechNut debacles are drawn upon to show how the seven traps waylaid decision makers. Each of the seven traps is discussed in a subsequent chapter.

Chapter 3 illustrates two decision-making processes—one that points toward success and one toward failure. An "idea-driven" process is prone to failure. A "discovery-driven" process will increase the chance of success by 50 percent. The five debacles are used to show how decision makers make blunders and get caught in traps that push them from a discovery process to an idea-imposition process and how difficult it is to get out of the clutches of the idea-driven process once decision makers are caught in it.

Chapter 4 is devoted to the trap sprung by misleading claims. Shell's disposal of the Brent Spar and the Waco siege show how misleading claims identify a failure-prone decision's topic or "arena of action." Every decision has a number of plausible arenas in which to act. Savvy decision makers find an arena of action with a base of support that can avoid political and ethical traps.

Chapter 5 identifies the trap set by social and political forces that erect barriers to action, illustrated by Quaker's acquisition of Snapple and the building of Nationwide arena to attract a major-league sports team. With careful implementation, decision makers can dodge this trap by selecting tactics that manage social and political forces stirred up by a decision.

Chapter 6 deals with a subtle and often misunderstood trap involving logic: a lack of direction. A major university's decision to join a telescope consortium illustrates the dangers of failing to be clear about the results that are wanted. Tactics that help you find a direction for your decision-making effort are offered.

Chapter 7 uses the AmeriFlora debacle to illustrate the trap set by limited search and no innovation. The chapter provides tactics that help you deal with zealots and expand on their pet ideas with your own search effort.

Chapter 8 deals with the trap set by misusing evaluation and ignoring risk that leads to shoddy practices. The New York City blackout shows how evaluation is misused and risk ignored when making tough decisions. This and the other debacles are used to show how to estimate the risk in your choices and to make useful evaluations.

Chapter 9 deals with the trap set by ignoring ethical issues. Mass transit with light rail illustrates the dilemma of ethics—a misalignment among who pays, who benefits, and who gets to decide. Tactics that provide a way around the dilemmas in "right wrong" and "right right" choices that pose ethical dilemmas are offered.

Chapter 10 presents the trap that arises from learning failures and how to avoid them. The Barings Bank scandal shows some of the impediments to learning, how they can arise, and what to do to cope. Tactics are offered that break down the defensive culture many organizations unwittingly create, which inhibits learning.

Chapter 11 offers a summative look at the lessons found in previous chapters and notes eight steps that you can take to increase the prospect of success for your next decision-making effort.

Appendix 1 provides a brief summary of the research project, the factors studied, and the research approaches used. A partial list of the decisions in the database is also provided along with citations to my research by chapter, which identifies the studies drawn upon to reach the conclusions offered. Appendix 2 provides a more complete treatment of the steps taken to measure risk in Chapter 8. Appendix 3 provides the citations used to construct "the story behind the story" for each debacle. References are cited sparingly throughout the book. Readers can refer to the Reference and Selected Readings to pursue topics of interest.

My hope is to help leaders, and budding leaders, improve their chance of being successful when making decisions. To realize this aim, the book must find its way to the executive's desk as well as to graduate seminars, executive education, and university classrooms.

## Acknowledgments

I am indebted to many people who have helped with this vast project. The ideas offered build upon a foundation constructed by many people who have become intrigued with the study of decision making and mounted long-term efforts to investigate and explore how decision making is done and how it can be improved. The decisions in my database were collected with the assistance of literally hundreds of my students over the years. I am indebted to their hard work and insights and to their careful application of the ideas in *Making Tough Decisions* (Nutt, 1989), which this book builds upon. I regret that the many student contributors are too numerous to mention here. I hope to make a list of all the people who contributed to the research project and add them to my Web site in the near future. Steven Piersanti and the staff at Berrett-Koehler were very helpful, as were the reviewers. I'm particularly grateful to Kathleen Epperson who offered many useful ways to clarify my message. Bob Backoff helped me over my conceptual blind spots with many useful suggestions as the book was being written. Mark Koewler typed the first drafts and did the tables and figures, a task that I was happy to avoid. Suzanne Jenks and Charles Nutt provided critiques of the contents of the book and how the content could be shaped to reach my audience. The book is dedicated to my growing family, including those no longer with us, giving age the priority.

Paul C. Nutt
Columbus, Ohio
March 2002

# The Decision Debacles

| SUBJECT | DECISION TO (CHAPTER) |
|---|---|
| ▼ The New York City Blackout | ▼ Shed load (Chapter 8) |
| ▼ EuroDisney | ▼ Locate a theme park near Paris (Chapter 1) |
| ▼ Ford Pinto | ▼ Not fix hazardous gas tank (Chapter 1) |
| ▼ BeechNut Baby Food Scandal | ▼ Mislabel the contents of apple juice products (Chapter 1) |
| ▼ Nestle Infant Formula | ▼ Market infant formula to third world countries (Chapter 1) |
| ▼ *Challenger* | ▼ Make a low-temperature launch (Chapter 10) |
| ▼ Telescope Consortium (Chicago, ASU, OSU) | ▼ Join the consortium (Chapter 6) |
| ▼ AmeriFlora | ▼ Hold the event (Chapter 7) |
| ▼ Denver International Airport | ▼ Build a new airport (Chapter 1) |
| ▼ Shell Oil Platform Disposal | ▼ Dispose of the Brent Spar in a deep sea location(Chapter 4) |
| ▼ Quaker Acquisition of Snapple | ▼ Purchase Snapple (Chapter 5) |
| ▼ WACO Siege | ▼ Attack the compound (Chapter 4) |
| ▼ Barings Bank | ▼ Allow unsupervised commodity trading (Chapter 10) |
| ▼ Arena for Major League Sports | ▼ Seek tax support for arena (Chapter 5) |
| ▼ Light Rail | ▼ Propose tax support for mass transit (Chapter 9) |

# Blunders That Launch
# a Decision Debacle

CHAPTER ONE

The overpriced and rarely visited Millennium Dome in London and Firestone's botched tire recall spotlight decision debacles. The dome opened January 1, 2000, ushering in the new millennium with promises of a futuristic, flashy, high-tech experience for people willing to ante up the price of admission. Controversy soon quelled the hype. Championed by the previous conservative government, Labor Prime Minister Blair embraced the dome as he took office, calling it "a triumph of confidence over cynicism, boldness over blandness." Others saw it differently, and the dome became a national embarrassment within weeks of its opening. Tories and Laborites pointed fingers and argued over whom to blame. Critics were downright hostile, calling it, among other things, vain, vapid, patronizing, and, with its twenty-five pound admission fee, grossly overpriced. The dome's sixteen zones offered a blend of theme exhibits, interactive technology, and live shows that, according to the critics, failed to work together and lacked the promised "wow" factor. Worst of all, no one came. Twelve million visitors were forecasted, but fewer than 4.5 million, many with cut-price tickets, paid to get in. The Labor government put 785 million pounds into the project and had to infuse it with an additional 175 million pounds to keep it afloat. Heads rolled. Blair and the dome's other champions, including the former head of British Air and major bank and local television executives, took hits on their reputations. The dome closed a year to the day from its opening, awash in red ink, with still another overhyped celebration, this time to mark the actual date of the new millennium. Bidders on the bankrupt dome plan to bulldoze the building and build something else at its picturesque site on the river Thames.

After 1,100 incidents, 57 lawsuits, and 119 deaths, Firestone recalled 6.5 million of its best-selling radial tires. "What took them so long?" critics in Congress and elsewhere ask. In one of the first lawsuits to come to trial, Firestone incurred $9,000 in fines before handing over documents describing test results and employee depositions about them. The documents show that the tires, widely used on Ford's hot-selling Suburban sport utility vehicles, or SUVs, have treads that peel off like skin from a banana causing an SUV to veer and roll over. Hot weather, high speeds, and under inflation of the tires increase the hazard. Ford, the biggest user of the tires, and its long-time alliance partner, Firestone, soon began finger-pointing. Ford officials conceded that the company had been aware of tread separation incidents in South America but claimed Firestone delayed the recall. Firestone officials admit that the tires were mislabeled as having an extra nylon strap but say that they built them according to Ford's specifications. Firestone officials also pointed out that the Ford Explorer and Expedition manuals recommend tire pressures below those suggested by Firestone, to soften the ride, and that this contributed to the tire's failure. As the accident toll swelled to more than 6,000, with 174 deaths and 700 injuries, the Ford-Firestone feud became bitter, and very public. To preempt action by Ford, Firestone severed its nearly century-long supplier relationship with Ford. Ford responded the next day, announcing the recall of an additional 13 million vehicles equipped with Firestone tires at a cost of $3 billion. Critics fault the National Highway Transportation Safety Administration (NHTSA) as well as Ford and Firestone for not acting before so many lives were lost. Trial lawyers and industry observers claim that Firestone faces a $50 billion loss in lawsuits and lost sales. The CEO of Bridgestone, Firestone's parent, was called to testify before Congress about the recall failure and subsequently resigned. To squash the controversy, Ford is settling accident claims out of court. The recall situation gets worse and worse for Firestone. The NHTSA has expanded the tire recall to include Mercury Mountaineers, a related sports utility vehicle, calling for 3.5 million more tires to be included in the recall. In an attempt to head off still another recall, Firestone officials claim that 40,000 jobs are at stake.

Are these debacles isolated incidents? Everyday experience suggests otherwise. But what is the evidence, and are debacles preventable? Can the risks taken and the magnitude of the losses in a debacle be foreseen and headed off with a midcourse correction? The answers may surprise you.

Like many big-ticket undertakings born of hype and bloated expectations, the Millennium Dome used public dollars for an obscure aim. Watch as your city vies for the next Olympic Games, a sports team, or a World's Fair and see if you can spot the similarities. Also, watch as blame is spread around with little reflection about what went wrong and why. Recall snafus are hardly new to the automobile industry, or to Ford and Firestone.

Few decisions have the visibility of the Millennium Dome and the Firestone tire recall fiascoes. What about the rest—the failed decisions with big losses that evade public attention? After all, a debacle is merely a botched decision that attracts attention and gets a public airing. As we shall see, debacles such as the Millennium Dome and the Firestone tire recall have much in common with the rest—the failed decisions that no one hears about. My research shows that half of the decisions made in business and related organizations fail. The true failure rate may be higher because failed decisions that avoid a public airing are apt to be covered up.

Considering the vast sums spent on these decisions and the benefits forgone, finding ways to avoid failure is vital. This motivated my research into decision making. In my studies, stretching back over twenty years, I have looked at more than four hundred decisions to uncover and evaluate decision-making practices, accounting for the situation confronted and measuring success. The decisions involve new products, equipment purchases, staffing, pricing, marketing, and locating operations—the kinds of decisions made with regularity in organizations across the planet. By considering real decisions in real organizations made by real people, my research got me close to the action so the consequences of a decision, in which responsible people bore burdens or reaped benefits, were revealed. Linking decision-making practices to their consequences, both good and bad, provides a telling appraisal of the practices used by people to make decisions. The decisions also provide a rich description of events that allowed me to probe for why some practices work and others do not, looking for ways to improve the chances of being successful. This book reports on these conclusions and the lessons each suggests. Appendix 1 provides additional detail about my twenty-year research effort along with citations to my work drawn upon in each chapter.

## The Blunders

The startling rate of failure prompts questions. Why is there so much failure? What causes the failure? Is corrective action possible? Answers can be found in three blunders: failure-prone decision-making practices, premature commitments, and time and money spent on the wrong things. Bad practice, rush to judgment, and poor allocation are called blunders because they are made so often, with so little reflection. The chain of events that leads to failure begins with one of these blunders, which points decision makers toward traps that ambush them. (The traps are considered in Chapter 2, showing how each trap arises and what to do to avoid it.) To begin our journey, let's see how the blunders arise and set the stage for failure.

### 1. Failure-Prone Practices

Two of every three decisions use failure-prone practices. Decision makers seem oblivious to the poor track record of these practices. Top managers can recall their decision-making successes, and their failures, but they seldom, if ever, systematically study them. Lacking this analysis, the connections of decision-making practices to results are apt to be misunderstood. Perfectly good ways of making decisions are discarded, and others with a poor track record continue to be used. People spend little time thinking about how to make a decision. Without help in identifying what does and does not work, the widespread use of failure-prone practices will continue. There are several reasons for this. Let's consider a few.

Decision-making practices with a good track record are commonly known, but uncommonly practiced. Nearly everyone knows that participation prompts acceptance, but participation is rarely used. We will explore why participation and other practices with good track records are not used and how to encourage their use. There are subtleties. Managers often look for the cause of a jump in cost. Telling people what is wanted as a result, such as lower cost, produces better results than seeking the cause of the cost increase. Managers drawn to finding and removing problems elicit blame. The problem, such as labeling costs as unacceptably high, alerts people that blame will be dispensed and prompts them to take defensive action. Energy is directed away from finding answers and funneled toward protecting one's back. Managers that indicate what is wanted (lower costs) liberate subordinates to look for answers. We will explore some of the reasons blame and other subtleties arise and what can be done to avoid them.

Failure is often placed at the doorstep of things beyond a manager's control: draconian regulations imposed by government, unexpected budget cuts by higher ups, or loss of market share due to fickle customers. Failures can result when regulations run up costs, when budget flexibility is lost, and when customer preferences shift and wreck a marketing plan. But the decision-making practices followed, such as issuing an edict or using a self-managed group, are more important. Contingency theory, as it is called in the management literature, argues for the selection among decision-making practices when certain situations arise, such as using an edict to take rapid action in a crisis. But is best practice contingent upon the decision situation such as decisions that prove to be difficult, rushed, or particularly weighty? In a word: No. Best practices work regardless of the situation being faced. We will explore why top managers blunder so often in their selection of decision-making practices.

## 2. Premature Commitments

Decision makers often jump on the first idea that comes along and then spend years trying to make it work. This is a key cause of failure, which decision makers fail to see that they fail to see. Decision makers, like most people, fear the unknown and seek self-gratification. Decision making can be a lonely endeavor in which a longing to meet one's responsibilities and the failure to do so elicits fear. When answers are not readily available, grabbing onto the first thing that seems to offer relief is a natural impulse. This helps one set aside fears but encourages a rush to judgment. Self-gratification is fed by ego, lust for power, and greed. This push from fear and pull toward a reward make it difficult for a decision maker to step into the unknown and to remain there until insight emerges. These urges mount as time pressure increases. Decision makers take shortcuts when this pressure gets intense. Looking for a good idea is set aside for homilies, such as,

"Why rediscover the wheel when someone may have done it for you?" One response is to copy the practices of a respected organization to "get on with it." This is rationalized as being timely and pragmatic. But shortcuts lead to unanticipated delays as decision makers attempt to convince onlookers that the company's interests, not their own, are being served and as retrofits are made. A rush to judgment is seductive and deadly and can be headed off.

### 3. Wrong-Headed Investments

Blunders are made when decision makers use their time and money for costly evaluations and little else. To make matters worse, these evaluations are often defensive—carried out to support an idea someone is wedded to, trying to show that it will work. The urge to demonstrate the value of your idea can get intense. Expensive evaluations are then needed to show that your idea is useful or doable or both, stressing economics. Critics see such evaluations as pointless, carried out to sanctify what you want to do or must do to satisfy others. This creates an impression that your motives are less than pristine. Others, suspecting a hidden agenda, become suspicious. The appearance of a vested interest, even if there is none, raises questions. To fend off these questions, evaluation expenditures increase as more justification is demanded. This persists even when the defensive evaluation is avoided. Decision makers spend vast sums to uncover the cost of an idea, but little on anything else. Little time or money is spent to investigate claims, set objectives, search for ideas, measure benefits and risk, or manage social and political forces that can derail a decision. Decision makers blunder when they fail to see any of this as a worthy undertaking.

### Illustrating the Blunders

In a medium-sized firm with strong growth over a ten-year period, key managers focused on sustaining this growth and spent little on their internal systems designed during an earlier, simpler time. Customer complaints about tardy shipments, caused by items that were out of stock, were dismissed as "growing pains." This changed when a vice president received a phone call from an important customer blasting the company for its lax attitude toward filling orders. The caller claimed that a well-run company would have an up-to-date production planning system and that such systems never have stock-outs. The vice president, stunned by a respected customer being so dissatisfied, became a missionary for this type of system. After some lobbying, the CEO asked for a briefing and the VP sold the idea to the CEO. Both saw the vehemence expressed as demanding action. The CEO suggested that someone outside the company be hired as soon as possible to revamp the ordering system, and this directive was given to the VP. To act quickly, the VP contacted the complaining customer and asked for a recommendation about whom to recruit. The recommended individual was hired the same day, at a very competitive wage, and named "manager of production planning." The new hire received a generous budget to set up a new department and make the needed changes. The new manager analyzed the current system to uncover problems and solved each problem by adapting business practices that he had used successfully in his prior job. The new manager then wrote memos to people telling them what to do to make the plan work. Despite all this, the stock-outs continued. The CEO was furious about the lack of results, the cost incurred, and the disruption that the company had endured.

Further study revealed that stock-outs were caused by delays in the flow of information due to unnecessary hand-offs between layers of management when filling orders, which slowed down order filling and increased the chance of error. What could have been done to uncover this and find a corrective action? Company officials failed to investigate the claim prompting action. Lingering here to look for the causes of the stock-outs, company officials could have discovered that inefficient and unneeded steps were causing delays and errors in the flow of information—a very different arena of action from that selected. What about setting objectives? No targets were set. "No stock-outs" was believed to be an inherent part of an up-to-date system. Note the subtlety here. Decision makers thought they were clear about what they wanted as a result, but they were not. A single complaining customer had prompted action. Note the premature commitment. Artificial time pressure got the best of company managers, and they rushed to make a judgment. As pressure appeared to mount, behavior became even more bizarre. The need for a quick fix by hiring someone new was never questioned. Was there a better way to get an up-to-date system? How about a vendor search? Decision makers knew about this but went for the quick fix instead. Commonly known, uncommonly practiced.

The new hire used his newfound power to tell people what to do. He knew about participation but saw things as too urgent to have committees sitting about when things needed to be done. This actually slowed things down. His use of an edict to take action prompted resentment that derailed the adoption of his ideas. Through it all, little time or money was spent on anything but trying to make the customer's idea work.

## Why Study Debacles?

Debacles highlight blunders. They offer insights into how a decision can go wrong, why it went wrong, and what changes in decision-making practices could improve the chance of success. When we analyze the actions that lead to debacles, we can look for how things could have been done differently. Consider RCA and its failure in the digital videodisk or DVD market. RCA abandoned its DVD product and took a $175 million tax write-off after years of intense effort. A short time later, the DVD player became a staple in a surround sound system, with a substantial and growing market. Failures of this magnitude are called debacles—if they become public. The tax write-off by RCA signaled a failure. Business media watchdogs, smelling a juicy exposé, pointed out errors of commission or omission and looked for someone to shoulder the blame for RCA's premature market entry and untimely exit. This book addresses a key question that such an exposé overlooks. Was RCA's decision to enter and exit the digital video market caused by bad luck or by careless and clumsy moves that prompted mistakes? Was RCA's premature entry and untimely exit foreseeable if the blunders of bad practice, premature commitment, and misused resources had been avoided?

This book deals with "tough decisions"—frequently occurring and important choices made to keep an organization on course by altering customers, markets, channels, competitive and collaborative advantages, alliances, skills and competencies, sources of revenue, ways to organize, and company image. Such decisions have ambiguity, uncertainty, and conflict. Ambiguity about the action to take prompts decision makers to stake out different claims about what to do and to use fuzzy arguments to support their views. It is not clear why RCA undertook and then dropped the DVD project. Did top management see a sexy new product that they wanted, or were there hidden motivations that made the move into videodisk players seem desirable? Uncertainty arises when projections lack precision. Decision makers can make things worse by ignoring the uncertainty. The risk in a product decision is hidden when a product's sales or its cost are estimated using the midpoint of a forecast. RCA's top managers treated their projections of DVD player sales in this way when the limited inventory of digital disks available to be played at the time of product launch made sales difficult to forecast with any precision. Disagreements and misunderstandings among key people about the concerns provoking action, what to do to respond, and the forecasts can lead to conflict. A tough decision can turn into a debacle when ambiguity and uncertainty go unmanaged or conflict erupts.

Decision making involves more than choosing among available courses of action. To avoid the blunders and the traps that can lead to a debacle, decision makers must work their way through a process that stages crucial activities. (Chapter 3 discusses processes that work and those that do not.) A tough decision involves several choices that lead to a pivotal decision. The pivotal decision always has a "go/no-go" character, such as deciding whether to act on an idea, follow a commitment, or make a change in how the organization does business. Locating EuroDisney in France, BeechNut's mislabeling of baby food, the Ford Pinto recall, Nestle's marketing of infant formula, and Denver's new International Airport (DIA) illustrate tough decisions that became debacles. The choices prompted by actions and events that preceded the pivotal decision in each of these debacles and the actions that followed it are shown in Table 1.1. Let's see how the blunders arose in each of these decisions.

## The EuroDisney Location Decision

Walt Disney's fascination with all things European began with early Disney stories rooted in European folklore, giving a commitment to some kind of Disney presence in Europe a very long history. The idea of a theme park in France emerged in 1976 and percolated until French dignitaries took Disney executives on tours of possible sites in northern and eastern France in 1982. Soon after, Tokyo Disneyland opened and became an instant success, shattering previous attendance records. A European park seemed the

*Table 1.1*
## FLOW OF ACTIONS IN EACH DEBACLE

| Choices | BeechNut's Apple Juice Contents | Ford Pinto Recall | Constructing the DIA | Nestle's Infant Formula Marketing | EuroDisney Location |
|---|---|---|---|---|---|
| Actions before | Purchase concentrate at 25% below market from Universal Juice<br><br>Fail to follow up on U.J. visit suspicions<br><br>Ignore LiCari's warnings<br><br>Fired LiCari for bringing concerns to CEO | Disregard disclosures about gas tank safety<br><br>Ignore NHTSA's investigation<br><br>Stifle concerns by Ford employees | Legal problems arise in Stapelton's expansion plan<br><br>City and county politicians endorse new airport<br><br>Pena elected on new airport platform | Market infant formula aggressively to developing countries<br><br>Respond to "Baby Killer" report | Realize Walt's Dream<br><br>Tokyo Disneyland success creates cash needing reinvestment<br><br>Commitments to land, hotel space, and royalties sought |
| Pivotal decision | Decide not to join PAI lawsuit against Universal Juice | Decide not to recall cars to fix gas tanks | Build a new airport | Continue third world marketing | Locate in France |
| Actions after | Disposal of $3.5 million tainted inventory<br><br>Hide tainted inventory discovered by the FDA<br><br>Agree to stop selling tainted juice.<br><br>Sell remaining inventory to developing countries | Defend position with cost-benefit data in lawsuit filed by families of people killed in Pintos<br><br>Recall the vehicles | Continental and Untied stop paying for planning<br><br>DIA site annexed by county<br><br>Critics call for a vote<br><br>Election supports DIA<br><br>Five opening delays due to design problems | Nestle sues activist groups that translated "Baby Killer" report claiming Nestle responsibility<br><br>Continue with defensive posture to counter boycott by activist groups<br><br>Chose to fight the boycott behind scenes | Cut ticket prices<br><br>Allow alcohol<br><br>Permit picnicking |

ticket to fuel the Michael Eisner legend one more time, and he authorized a search for a European site. Two hundred sites were considered, but the list was quickly narrowed to locations in Spain and France. France won out because of its central location, offering easy access to most other European countries, and because the French provided considerable financial bait. These positives were thought to be enough to offset negatives in the weather in France and the sour national disposition of the French.

When Eisner called a press conference to announce that EuroDisney shares were being offered on the Paris Stock Exchange, he was pelted with Brie cheese. Not exactly the reception he expected. But why the surprise? French intellectuals had been calling the project "Euro-Dismal," among other things, for some time.

Disney officials were determined to correct errors made in their other park projects. Investors had snapped up the undeveloped land surrounding Disneyland in Anaheim, limiting the park's expansion. The Orlando Park site had plenty of land, but Disney underestimated the demand for hotels and lost an opportunity to make huge amounts of money on hotel space. In Tokyo, Disney failed to get an equity position in the park and failed to secure royalties for the use of the Disney characters. Disney executives were determined to avoid these fiascoes. To sweeten the deal, French officials sold Disney 4,800 acres—about one-fifth the area of Paris—at early 1970s prices. With cheap land and low property taxes, Disney thought it would make a killing in real estate. Land prices had increased by 20 percent a year in Anaheim and 30 percent in Orlando. The French loaned Disney $800 million for twenty years at 7.85 percent interest, a very favorable rate in 1987. Disney took the cash and invested $700 million to form the EuroDisney Company in which Disney has 49 percent equity. Disney negotiated a management fee of 3 percent of revenues and earns an additional 5 to 10 percent of revenues from other fees. Disney was also given 17.5 percent of a private partnership that was created to own the land. Industry observers found the deal to be cleverly crafted and predicted ecstatic Disney shareholders. Still, the decision to build a park and to locate it near Paris lacked a clear picture of expected results. Was it Walt's Dream, more profit, or what?

Like other decisions with an early commitment to a solution, analysis was carried out to bolster the decision. Cost was estimated in 1988 at

$2.5 billion. The actual cost was $4.4 billion. Flush with the success of Tokyo Disneyland, attendance projections were set at 11 million. Ticket prices were set at $51 for adults and $34 for children, compared to $40 and $26, respectively in Orlando, thinking that a Disney product would sell regardless of price. Disney managers contracted for the construction of 5,200 hotel rooms priced from $97 to $395 per night. The assumed occupancy of 76 percent depended on overnight stays by park visitors. Restaurant sales projections were based on the assumption that park visitors would want lavish sit-down meals. No alcohol was to be served, in keeping with Disney "family values" practices. Disney estimated that each visitor would spend $28 per day on food and merchandise. Because of harsh French winters, much of the park was to be built inside in the hopes of maintaining a year-round flow of visitors.

None of this took into account the desires and values of the projected park visitor. EuroDisney revenues fell far below expectations. Park visitors did reach the 11 million projected, but only after steep discounts in the ticket price. Hotel occupancy at 37 percent is light years from the expected 76 percent. Disney had $960 million in losses in the first year of operation, although some stemmed from a $600 million one-time write-off. Considering operating revenue, losses piled up at a rate of $1 million per day. By 1994 losses had reached nearly $400 million. The damage to Disney's image grew as observers such as *Time* magazine featured company problems and second-guessed company decisions.

What can be said about the location decision? The European and French cultures should have been taken into consideration by Disney officials. The decision not to sell alcohol prompted a confrontation with French and European lifestyles. In much of Europe, children are given watered-down wine with meals. Europeans have a tradition of bringing food to parks, and Disney did not allow for picnics. Lavish spending for sit-down dinners was overly optimistic and inconsistent with customer expectations. An American park in the United States made "Americana" accessible to Europeans. Seeing the same thing in Europe is less appealing. Also, exchange rates were not favorable when the park opened. It cost less for many Europeans to travel to Orlando than to EuroDisney— and the weather in Orlando is better. The decision to increase ticket prices by 30 percent over American park standards ignored an ongoing European recession. Lower prices would have increased park attendance and perhaps food and merchandise sales as well. EuroDisney is within 70 miles of Paris—one of the most popular tourist attractions anywhere— and this location made EuroDisney a one-day stop on the way to somewhere else. Hardly anyone needed or wanted to stay overnight at the park. The superiority of public transportation in France compared to the United States makes it easy for people to make day trips and to avoid pricey hotels. Disney failed to visualize the park as a new experience for Europeans. Instead, they applied old formulas filled with questionable cultural assumptions. Disney officials limited their cost risk, but they failed to adapt to European culture to muster the revenues to cover their costs.

Proponents of the French location ignored warning signs, clearly expressed at the press conference, and used dubious evaluations to justify what they wanted to do. Estimates of park and hotel use were overly optimistic and suppressed the project's risk. Whenever reservations were expressed, Walt's Dream was trotted out, making desired results ambiguous. What was the aim? Make money? Have a presence in Europe? Lacking a direction, the project stumbled along without an aim to focus questions at key points in the decision-making effort. As critics became more vocal, people were targeted for blame. Scapegoating seems mandatory in a debacle, even though blame is useless.

Disney executives continue to worry about past park problems and fail to think about the next one. Disney officials recently subjected the corporation to severe criticisms when a theme park was proposed for a civil war battle site in Virginia. Nearby wealthy homeowners used a "hallowed ground" argument to express righteous indignation and to protect their property values. Here Disney officials were too focused on economics and ignored ethical and political issues.

The EuroDisney debacle marked the end of Eisner's long run as a miracle worker in which he routinely delivered 20 percent growth for the company. Company earnings have fallen by 36 percent in the past two years, and its stock price has fallen by more than 10 percent as Disney's key competitors, Viacom and Time-Warner, have leaped 10 percent to 60 percent.

## Ford Pinto's Exploding Gas Tanks

Ford's recall blunders have a long history. Consider the Pinto, which began production in 1970. The Pinto's design located the gas tank at the back of the car 6 inches from a flimsy rear bumper. Bolts were placed just 3 inches from the tank. In a rear-end crash, the bumper would push the bolts into the tank. Other sharp metal edges surrounded the gas tank. The filler pipe extended only 2.6 inches into the tank, making it apt to pull free in low-speed crashes. The design problems could have been overcome by locating the spare tire to cushion the gas tank, by locating the fuel tank further away from the rear bumper, or by using body rails that attach to the rear of the car to absorb a rear-end impact. None of this happened because Lee Iacocca, Ford's CEO at the time, wanted a "2,000 pound car for $2,000." This implicit objective for the vehicle made a recall difficult.

*Mother Jones* magazine first exposed the dangers of the Pinto's gas tank, prompting the National Highway Traffic Safety Administration (NHTSA) to launch an investigation. In 1977 NHTSA uncovered twenty-eight rear-end crashes that had gas leakage and fires, in which twenty-seven occupants had died and twenty-four suffered burns. Feeling some pressure to fix the tank, Ford officials came up with a polyethylene shield to prevent the tank from being punctured by the bolts, at a cost of $2.35 per vehicle. A flak suit to cushion the tank from impact, at a cost $6 to $10 per vehicle, was also considered. These and still other options were rejected. Ford officials conducted a cost-benefit study at this point, which put the cost of repair at $137 million (12.5 million vehicles at about $11 each). Using NHTSA data, Ford officials set a price tag on human life at $200,000, each serious injury at $67,000, and each burned car at $700. Using an estimated 180 deaths and an equal number of seriously burned victims, "benefits" were projected to be $49.5 million. Benefits were less than costs so Ford decided not to fix the cars.

Three girls experienced car trouble and parked their Pinto on the berm of a freeway. The girls were struck from behind in a low-speed crash and burned to death. That same year, Ford had decided to recall the Pinto—scheduled to start one month after the fatal accident. Ford's recall notice was received by one of the victims' families six months after the accident. A $120 million lawsuit ensued. A technicality saved Ford. The jury was asked if Ford did everything in its power to recall the defective vehicles, not whether Ford had knowingly produced a defective product. Ford won the lawsuit but suffered a huge dent in its reputation. The media had a field day, and observers viewed this incident as the beginning of the long decline for U.S. automakers.

Court records suggest that Ford's top decision makers were aware that the Pinto was unsafe and concluded it would be cheaper to incur the losses from lawsuits than to fix the cars. Ford's production staff also knew of the risk, but was never given the opportunity to tell top management about it. Ford's "profit drives principle" philosophy of the time blocked voicing the risk. Ford's approach to the Pinto recall tainted relationships with outsiders, such as the NHTSA. To this day, Ford is suspected of withholding data and misrepresenting information when making vehicle recall decisions. This contentious relationship prompted industry observers to question Ford's role in the Firestone tire recall, the recent ignition recall that affects 22 million cars built since 1984, and others.

## BeechNut and Its Bogus Apple Juice

BeechNut was founded in 1891 as a meat packing company. As the company diversified, food products, including baby food, were added. After several acquisitions and spin-offs, the company chose to concentrate on baby food. An image of "natural" foods was promoted. By 1980, Nestle had acquired the company, and top management at BeechNut were put "under the gun" to improve profitability. After some intense effort, Beech-Nut reached the parent company's goal, and top management felt considerable pressure to maintain this newfound profitability. As part of this effort, BeechNut sought a less expensive supplier of apple juice concentrate. Universal Juice offered concentrate at 25 percent below prevailing market prices and was selected as the new supplier, enabling BeechNut to cut costs by $250,000 per year.

The cost of the apple juice led people to speculate about its source. BeechNut visited Universal Juice a year later to inspect the facility, finding 55-gallon tanks but no mixing vats. BeechNut's research and development director, Jerome LiCari, became concerned and sent samples of the concentrate supplied by Universal Juice to an outside laboratory. The test results were reported to John Lavery, vice president of operations, and revealed that the concentrate was "not natural" and may have had corn syrup additives. At this point, Lavery had Universal Juice sign a "hold harmless agreement" indemnifying BeechNut against damages. Not satisfied with this, LiCari sent samples to two other labs the following year. Results were inconclusive but suggested that a switch to beet sugar from corn syrup may have been made. The lab told LiCari that beet sugar was harder to detect, offering a reason for the switch.

BeechNut's financial position worsened during this period, and conflict between Lavery and LiCari escalated. Lavery told LiCari that he had to have proof that the apple juice was adulterated before he would switch suppliers. The tension between the men grew over the next two years. At one point, Lavery told LiCari to put the problem concentrate into mixed juices where it would be harder to detect. This prompted LiCari to send a memo to the CEO citing his concerns and describing the evidence he had collected about color and acidity. Lavery responded by threatening to fire LiCari. After an unsatisfactory performance review from Lavery the next year, LiCari resigned.

As the events at BeechNut were unfolding, the Processed Apples Institute (PAI), a cooperative representing apple growers, hired a private investigator to look into rumors that adulterated apple juice concentrate was being sold. The investigator found that Universal Juice buys no apples and that BeechNut was its biggest customer. A PAI representative followed a shipment from Universal Juice to BeechNut, and the PAI representative then met with Lavery and two others and asked them to join a lawsuit against Universal Juice. They refused.

Top management was in a quandary. They could hardly claim that they had no suspicions or that they had been hoodwinked by Universal Juice. Also, they had $3.5 million in inventory. BeechNut did not recall the product. Instead, they stalled the investigation to unload the inventory, simultaneously concealing their contract with Universal Juice. Within a few months all but 250,000 cases of the 725,000 in inventory had been sold.

The FDA did not have the authority to stop BeechNut from selling apple juice. And BeechNut's management refused to recall the apple juice on the ground that it posed no health hazard. Bogus information about the location of the tainted inventory was provided. The FDA found only 242 cases, which BeechNut destroyed before the FDA was able to get authorization to seize them. During this time, BeechNut promotions offered six free cans of apple juice when twelve jars of its baby food were purchased. Beech-Nut sold 20,000 cases to developing countries despite knowing that it's illegal to sell products abroad that are not acceptable in U.S. markets. With most of the inventory now sold, BeechNut's management agreed to a voluntary recall but continued to sell the adulterated juice for six more months.

Later that year LiCari was at a cocktail party for the National Food Producers Association and overheard BeechNut executives crowing about how they had dodged a bullet by selling the adulterated inventory. He called the FDA and blew the whistle, providing details of BeechNut's actions. This prompted FDA officials, who were considering a civil action against BeechNut, to press criminal charges. BeechNut's CEO, Niles Hoyvald, Levary, and Universal Juice's top management were indicted. Beech-Nut admitted guilt five years later, three days before the trial was to begin. The company paid fines of more than $10 million. BeechNut executives were fined $100,000, sentenced to a prison term of a year and a day, and ordered to pay court costs. The total cost to BeechNut was in excess of $25 million.

BeechNut executives tried to suppress conflict. When this failed, they eliminated the most apparent source of conflict: LiCari. This sent a message: Do not speak out or raise ethical questions. The company's top executives assumed the posture of a victim and stonewalled the FDA. They ignored the risks of hiding the tainted concentrate from the FDA and of selling a tainted product to developing countries in violation of federal law.

## Nestle's Infant Formula Marketing

Infant formula was developed in the 1920s as an alternative to breast-feeding. Nestle and other companies realized a sharp increase in formula sales during the mid-1940s that peaked in the 1950s. After 1950 the U.S. birthrate declined, and Nestle and others in the business experienced a sharp drop in sales. Selling infant formula in third world countries seemed just the ticket to replace these lost sales. Using aggressive marketing, Nestle soon had $300 million in third world sales.

A group that focused on third world countries and their problems published a report called "The Baby Killer." The report chastised the infant food industry for its marketing practices, claiming that these practices led to infant deaths. Because of its leading position in this market, Nestle was singled out and accused of using misleading ads that suggested their formula was better than breast milk. The report also condemned Nestle's marketing practices in which uniformed Nestle people handed out free samples of infant formula in hospitals to encourage new mothers to bottle-feed. The report called for a ban on advertising in poor countries and a ban on promotions in hospitals.

In the eyes of Nestle managers, problems with infant formula arose solely from consumers' misuse of the product. Deaths were attributed to diluting the formula or mixing it with contaminated water. Nestle had fact books for each of their products, developed for each country in which the products were sold, but these books did not discuss problems of dilution or contamination. Critics said that Nestle's unaffordable prices forced mothers to stretch their supply by diluting it more than was recommended, pointing out that the cost of infant formula approaches 50 percent of a family's total weekly wages in a third world country. Company officials claimed their advertising could only assume responsibility for rooting out false statements and that they were not responsible for the poverty and illiteracy that might lead to the misuse of their product. Nestle people also pointed out that in developing countries nursing mothers unable to produce sufficient breast milk supplemented it with animal milk and water mixed with mashed root mixtures. Formula was far superior to these widely used remedies.

At this point, Nestle's managing director began a decision-making effort to rethink the situation. After a lengthy study, the company made minor changes in its marketing but continued to aggressively sell infant formula in third world countries. Company officials said they were content that, on balance, they were doing more good than harm.

Nestle was totally unprepared for the reaction to their decision. Several activist groups were galvanized by Nestle's refusal to terminate its third world marketing. Third World Action Group (TWAG) translated the "baby killer" report into German with a new title, "Nestle Kills Babies." The new version maintained that Nestle was responsible for the death and permanent injury of thousands of children because of its unethical advertising in third world countries. TWAG sued to stop Nestle's third world advertising. The judge in the TWAG lawsuit said that the accusations of immoral and unethical conduct stemmed from the company's advertising practices. The message was ignored by company leaders.

Company leaders were shaken by the vehemence of their critics and the court's decision but refused to change any aspect of their product marketing. Instead, Nestle officials chose to strike back. They sued all those involved with the TWAG publication for libel. The suit gave TWAG just what an activist group is after—a platform from which to promote its claims. Nestle eventually won the court battle, but it lost big in the international court of opinion. Buoyed by its "win," Nestle continued to maintain a defensive posture. This prompted an activist group called INFACT (Infant Formula Action Committee) to mount a boycott of all Nestle products in the United States. Senate hearings on the matter, chaired by Edward Kennedy, concluded that Nestle was responsible for how its products were used and brought in the World Health Organization (WHO) to monitor the situation. INFACT and WHO brought respected experts into the fight, which prompted yet another round of criticism that accused Nestle of making profits by their "traffic in death."

Nestle hired a new marketing vice president at this point and charged him with determining whether the company should back away from its third world marketing practices. The options considered were fight the boycott, ignore it, or alter marketing practices. Company officials chose to continue their third world marketing and to ignore the boycott, which prompted seven more years of product boycotts by activist groups. Industry analysts believe the seven years of controversy that followed suppressed sales and damaged the reputation of a company with a long tradition of being a socially conscious firm. Later, Nestle's chairman, Liotard-Vogt, agreed. He acknowledged that his company's culture fostered intense loyalty, which made it difficult for anyone to question a long-standing company position. He also acknowledged that the effects of the boycott had been covered up. Several attempts were made to neutralize these effects, including a trip to the Vatican by the CEO. At this point, the company had fifteen people working on this issue, as well as a public relations firm. Nestle went to considerable lengths behind the scenes and spent lots of money to fight the boycott but refused to spend anything to revamp its controversial marketing practices.

Nestle's infant formula marketing created so much controversy that an industry association concluded that they had been deficient in policing their members' practices. The association developed a voluntary code for the ethical advertising of infant products. The code called for sales people to discard uniforms suggesting that they were medical representatives when working in hospitals and to terminate sales subsidies to hospital employees. Nestle ignored this development and never fully adopted the code.

## The Denver International Airport

The inadequacies of Stapelton, Denver's sixty-five-year-old international airport, were well known. Stapelton was the sixth busiest airport in the United States in 1993, but its runways were too close to allow simultaneous landings during bad weather, creating delays that disrupted the entire U.S. air traffic system. Projections of future use made it clear that traffic problems would worsen. Something had to be done. Denver's Mayor Federico Pena championed a new airport, touting it as the answer to Stapelton's problems as well as a way to counter weaknesses in the local economy. The Denver International Airport, or DIA, was promoted as a way to create jobs, increase local business revenues, and make Denver a major city. A major city must have an international airport. Controversy followed. The DIA's benefits may seem dubious but its costs weren't. The airport came in at $4.9 billion, far above estimates. DIA has fewer runways than Stapelton, although expansion is possible. The cost per passenger is $16, compared to $6 at Stapelton. Passengers complain about poor service and, recalling the near-by Stapelton airport, grouse about the expensive and long commute to and from downtown Denver to the new airport.

The chain of events began when Pena was elected mayor in 1983 and canned a proposal to expand Stapelton. By 1985, Pena had persuaded the city and the county to construct a new airport, and he was reelected in 1987 using a new airport as a campaign promise. Critics were skeptical of his plans. Continental and United, with 80 percent of the flights into Stapelton, objected. Both airlines preferred making improvements to Stapelton and stopped paying for airport planning. Critics called for a vote on the airport and threatened a petition drive to force a referendum. Colorado Governor Roy Romer had no way to crush a referendum. Controversy continued to swirl until a vote to approve the sale of bonds to underwrite airport costs was passed by a 2 to 1 margin.

Airport development followed a classic benchmarking approach. More than one hundred airports were visited before a design was selected. Planning included the disposal of Stapelton's 4,700 acre site. A redevelopment foundation created to dispose of the land and the structures proposed a mixture of uses. These included a major housing project compatible with existing development that surrounded three sides of Stapelton and light industrial uses, such as training bases for United and Continental airlines. Proceeds from sales and leases were earmarked for the retirement of DIA bonds.

No one can claim that the DIA designers aimed too low. Given the opportunity to create the first new airport in the United States since Dallas-Fort Worth in 1974, a dramatic mix of technology and architecture was proposed. The DIA terminal rises out of the high plains like an extraterrestrial circus top. Its advanced infrastructure includes a $100 million communications system with video security and an eighty-channel TV network. Advanced lighting and a $20 million automatic traffic management system keep the DIA's runways open during the worst snowstorms. An $85 million subway zips passengers through two 6,000 foot long tunnels at speeds of 30 miles per hour, with automated software to run the trains. The baggage system moves passengers' luggage point to point in less than ten minutes. The airport has five parallel 12,000 foot runways, with expansion possibilities of up to 123 runways. The city annexed 53 square miles (more area than the D-FW and Chicago airports combined) for the airport, making such expansion possible. The airport was to accommodate 1,750 takeoffs and landings in a day and be the first airport to regularly land three planes at the same time on its parallel runways.

DIA proponents found it easier to make impressive plans than to realize them. The DIA's opening was delayed five times. When the airport finally opened in 1995, it did so amid a chorus of complaints. The baggage handling system and other technology had bugs that created delays and lost bags. The cost and time to reach Denver infuriated passengers. The airport's bonds came in with ratings so low they approached a junk bond, dramatically driving up interest costs. The final price tag swelled until airport revenues could not cover costs and public subsidies were required to make up the difference. The predicted volume of 26 million annual passengers proved to be 160 percent above the actual volume of 16 million. Airline carriers refused to pay the hefty gate rental fees. United claimed that its costs doubled, compared with Stapelton where the airline had just built a $60 million concourse. Arguments arose over who should pay the $71 million for the interim baggage system. BAE automated systems, the original contractor for the baggage system, balked, laying blame on last minute design changes. BAE expressed concerns that the city was behind in paying $40 million to the company. Like so many overhyped projects of this type, such as light rail for public transportation and sports arenas, projections of benefits were overestimated and costs were doctored to make the project seem feasible and desirable.

## ▼ Key Points

- ▼ Half of the decisions made in organizations fail, making failure far more prevalent than previously thought.
- ▼ Blunders that lead to failure stem from using failure-prone practices, making premature commitments, and spending time and money on the wrong things.
- ▼ Failure can be directly linked to the actions of decision makers. Forces beyond the decision maker's control, such as changes in customer tastes, budget cuts, and the like, can also prompt failure, but the practices followed to make a decision are the most important determinants of success.
- ▼ The situation being faced by a decision maker has less influence on which decision-making practices to use than previously thought. Best practice can be followed regardless of the decision to be made or the circumstances surrounding it.

# Traps That Catch Decision Makers

CHAPTER TWO

Debacles follow a chain of events that unfold as blunders create traps and traps bring about failure. The blunders of using poor decision-making practices, rushing to judgment, or misusing available resources, discussed in the previous chapter, point unsuspecting managers toward seven traps that can ensnare them (Table 2.1). Traps are set when decision makers fail to reconcile claims, overlook people's interests and commitments, leave directions vague, limit their search for remedies, misuse evaluations, ignore ethical questions, or fail to reflect on decisions to learn what works and what does not. When caught in any of these traps, managers are apt to make a bad call that can become a debacle. In this chapter, we will examine the seven traps to see how each arises and its impact, offering a preview of how to navigate around the traps. EuroDisney, Ford, BeechNut, Nestle, and the DIA decisions provide illustrations.

## The Traps

### 1. Failure to Reconcile Claims

Table 2.2 profiles the actions taken that trapped decision makers and Table 2.3 shows how to dodge the trap.

Imagine that a board member is alarmed by a loss in market share, because it matches the amount that a competitor's share has grown in the same time period, and responds by issuing a call for action, such as improving the quality of the firm's products. The call for improved product

*Table 2.1*

**HOW BLUNDERS PROMPT TRAPS**

| Traps | Failure-Prone Practice Blunder | Premature Commitment Blunder | Misuse of Resources Blunder |
|---|---|---|---|
| Failing to take charge by reconciling claims | Support for claims and its arena of action assumed by the decision maker | First claim (or claimant) that seems important is accepted | Failure to look for hidden concerns or considerations and the more pressing claims that they suggest |
| Ignoring barriers to action | Power and persuasion used to implement decisions | Action taken before social and political forces are understood | Interests and commitments of stakeholders go unexplored |
| Providing ambiguous direction | Direction assumed and never clarified | Unwilling to acknowledge a concern without offering a remedy | Little time spent to identify desired results |
| Limiting search | A quick fix or what others are doing is adopted | Pressure for answers makes the conspicuous solution seem timely and pragmatic | Little spent on a search for ideas or for innovation |
| Misusing evaluation | Evaluation used to measure costs, ignoring benefits | Defensive evaluation used to justify the conspicuous solution | Money spent defending ideas and not in exploring their risk |
| Overlooking ethical questions | Values behind ethical questions are overlooked | All decisions are seen as ethically neutral | No time or money spent uncovering values |
| Failing to learn | Fail to see how perverse incentives operate to cover up outcomes | Expectations demand good outcomes | Few resources used to learn or to do so without removing perverse incentives |

quality becomes the "claim" (Toulmin, 1979) and points to an "arena of action," product quality. Decision makers get trapped when they buy into such a claim without looking further. A trap is set when a decision maker appears to cave in to influential people or when the corrective action in a claim, better product quality, omits what prompted it—the share loss assumed by the board member to have been taken by a competitor. The relationship of the falling market share concern to the claim's arena of action, product quality, is suspect. Should dubious concerns such as this be ferreted out, the arena of action would be discredited. Often the concerns or considerations prompting a claim are not spelled out and people must speculate about what they may be.

In the debacles, decision makers selected among the claims being offered according to their proponents' leverage and then forged ahead with this claim and its implied arena of action. This was done without checking to see if stakeholders agreed with the claim being made. Decision makers assumed that their motivation to act was understood and agreed to by others. What considerations lay behind the claims for a new airport for Denver or a new park for Disney? Pena and Eisner assumed that the key people—those whose support was needed to make their decisions a reality—understood the considerations prompting them to build a new park and a new airport as they understood them. Reactions to these decisions suggest otherwise.

When decision makers are silent about their concerns and considerations, people make judgments about the importance of acting and what a decision is really about. These judgments often elude the decision maker. By not recognizing the views of concerned insiders, skeptics, and people who have something to lose, each is handed a platform to raise objections. To discredit the decision and the decision maker, opponents call attention to what seem to be errors, faulty logic, or misrepresentations. When opponents question the legitimacy of a claim and its arena of action, a decision maker is forced to scale these barriers to be successful. When costs escalated, opponents of the DIA used a "ballooning costs" argument to discredit Pena and his new airport. Decision makers often react to such criticism with a cold stare to convey that they will have no more patience with questions and interpret the silence that follows as signaling agreement. Top management at Ford and Nestle inadvertently stifled dissent and by doing so shut off access to valuable questions that were being posed by credible insiders. Likewise, people in top management at Disney, and many others, went along to get along. When questions about the park idea stopped, Eisner took this as a sign of support for EuroDisney and the Paris location.

The debacles also had hidden concerns, suggesting very different claims than the ones pushed by decision makers. BeechNut's leaders pushed

*Table 2.2*
## PROFILING THE DECISION DEBACLES

| Flow of Events | Denver International Airport (DIA) | Ford Pinto Recall | BeechNut's Apple Juice | Nestle's Infant Formula | EuroDisney Location |
|---|---|---|---|---|---|
| Claims | New airport | Vehicle has acceptable level of safety | We are blameless | Infant deaths not caused by marketing practices | Walt's Dream for park in Europe |
| Core concerns or considerations (a) Uncovered | Safety hazards at Stapelton Airport | Cost to repair vehicles | Cut costs | Deaths due to misuse of product | Past park fiascoes (land in Anaheim, hotels in Orlando, and equity position and character royalties in Japan) |
| (b) Hidden | Airport's link to economic recovery | Magnitude of reputation losses | Questions about the concentrate | Deaths caused by formula or unsafe practices | Better way to use funds |
| Directions | Economic benefits of airport for the city | Make a 2,000-pound car for $2,000<br><br>Safety doesn't sell | Minimize cost prior to disclosure | Protect market share | Best location |
| Options considered | Remodel Stapelton or build a new airport | Fix vehicle versus pay lawsuits | Joint lawsuit or dump tainted juice | Fight boycott, ignore boycott, or change marketing | Locations in France |

*Table 2.2 (continued)*

| Flow of Events | Denver International Airport (DIA) | Ford Pinto Recall | BeechNut's Apple Juice | Nestle's Infant Formula | EuroDisney Location |
|---|---|---|---|---|---|
| Extent of search and innovation | Benchmarked existing airports | One idea to fix vehicles (flak suit) uncovered | Clever tactics to avoid FDA investigation | Only conspicuous alternatives considered (e.g., pricing options ignored) | Solution (park) displaced any problem analysis |
| Use of evaluation | Demonstrate feasibility with use and cost estimates | Economic benefits of avoiding a vehicle recall | Determine magnitude of losses | Determine profit in third world sales | Insure past fiascoes not repeated |
| Impact of evaluation | New airport made to seem desirable | Ford looked silly when benefits compared to costs | Displaced to short-term losses | Continued with marketing (status quo option) | Ignored new situational constraints (French culture) |
| Barriers to action | When misrepresentations came to light, opposition was likely | Dissent stifled and people disempowered<br><br>No communication about risk | Threat to top management team<br><br>Short-term losses | Fear of lost sales<br><br>People unwilling to question higher ups | No one would argue with Walt's Dream; caught up in events |
| Ethical questions | Corporate welfare | Profit drives principle | Look like a victim or like a villain | Locus of responsibility for product use | Values implicit at Disney (e.g., no alcohol) accepted |
| Barriers to learning | Decision makers gone, blame management | Ford had twenty-one lawsuits pending when accident occurred | Caught up in top management's ethical failings | Rightness of cause kept TMT from seeing controversy | Always one park behind |

*Table 2.3*

**PRACTICES THAT AVOID THE TRAPS**

| Traps to Be Avoided | Best Practice | Steps Required | Where Considered |
|---|---|---|---|
| Failing to take charge by reconciling claims | Network with stakeholders | Involve stakeholders to uncover and reconcile concerns or considerations to formulate the claim | Chapter 4 |
| Ignoring barriers to action | Intervention or participation | Demonstrate the need to act and ways to consider the interests and commitment of stakeholders | Chapter 5 |
| Allowing ambiguous directions | Set objectives | Create clear picture of expected results | Chapter 6 |
| Limiting search | Innovation or search | Increase the number of options considered and those with potential first mover advantages | Chapter 7 |
| Misusing evaluation | Explore risk and compare the benefits of the options | Expose options with unacceptable risk and validate the choice | Chapter 8 |
| Overlooking ethical questions | Look for important values and offer mediation | Uncover and confront the ethical questions of internal and external stakeholders | Chapter 9 |
| Failing to learn from the decision-making experience | Create win–win situations for all stakeholders | Look for and remove perverse incentives and encourage honest appraisal of company actions | Chapter 10 |

aside concerns expressed by insiders about product quality and company image. No one asked about LiCari's motives or how Nestle, the parent company, would react to BeechNut doing business with a dishonest supplier. The answers to such inquires could have steered top management away from the disastrous option of dumping tainted apple juice on unsuspecting customers. By dismissing concerns about its marketing practices, Nestle's top management shut off any internal debate about how product advertising could be refocused. No one called attention to the dangerous breast milk substitutes being used by low-income third world mothers. New claims, calling for marketing plans designed to change these unsafe practices could have headed off the Nestle marketing debacle. At Ford officials were surprised to learn that many insiders were troubled by the company's failure to recall the Pinto and fix its hazardous gas tank. Company leaders also said they were unaware of the public's very negative reaction to Ford's stonewalling the recall. The pelting of cheese stunned Eisner. At this point he could no longer dismiss the concerns about the park that had been set aside in his quest to realize Walt's Dream.

Finding a claim that stakeholders can support helps a decision maker avoid this trap. In each of the debacles, little time or money was spent rethinking the claim that specified the arena of action. To avoid this trap, decision makers must uncover and reconcile the concerns and considerations of people whose support they need to be successful. Table 2.3 summarizes practices that will help you dodge this trap and the others. Decision makers take charge when they uncover the claims of stakeholders and the concerns or considerations that motivate them. Insight into people's concerns and considerations broaden our view of what needs fixing and suggest arenas of action people can support. Showing that you are aware of people's views gives your decision-making effort legitimacy. Stakeholders are more apt to support you if they understand your motivations and see how they point to an arena of action that accounts for things that are important. When the claim is seen as valid, the word spreads to others, creating momentum. Taking charge by uncovering the concerns and considerations of stakeholders and offering claims that identify a defensible arena of action is discussed in Chapter 4.

## 2. Failure to Manage Forces Stirred up by a Decision

Decision makers in the debacles used either edict or persuasion to implement their preferred course of action. Using an edict to implement, as in the BeechNut and DIA decisions, is high risk and prone to failure. People who have no interest in the decision resist it because they do not like being forced and because they worry about the precedent that yielding to force sets. When using an edict, the best one can hope for is indifference—people do not care enough to resist you. If the edict fails, decision makers resort to persuasion, now trying to explain why an action is needed. This move is fouled by the previous power play. Using persuasion from the outset, as in the DIA and EuroDisney cases, is somewhat more effective. Selling an idea with persuasion can work if stakeholders are indifferent to what you want to do. Persuasion has little effect on people with something to lose.

Edicts and persuasion fail because neither manages the social and political forces stirred up by a decision. Top management had no idea what was motivating the BeechNut whistle-blower. Had BeechNut officials taken the time to identify these motives, the risk in selling tainted inventory would have been apparent. Pena assumed that the motives of his opponents were self-serving. He had no idea what had enflamed his critics, and he ignored the interests of the two carriers, United and Continental, that had just made large investments in Stapelton.

When interests and commitments are ignored, people's worries fester and grow. Ford's unwillingness to recall the Pinto troubled insiders, and its top-down management style limited access to such information. Involving knowledgeable people in a discussion of the recall decision would have brought to light many of the risks in stonewalling a vehicle recall. Because of the company's secretive "just do as I say" approach to management in that era, Ford became known as a "bad place to work." In such a culture it is futile to say much about top management's decisions as they are being made. There are better ways to get your decisions adopted.

Decision makers in the debacles spent little time exploring the interests and commitments of people that could be disrupted by a decision. Being forthcoming about reasons and motives helps to neutralize opposition. Involving potential critics in the decision-making process clarifies their views, and involvement may shift the critic from a position of opposition to one of support. Had Nestle and Disney officials done this, the views of their critics could have been understood and addressed. Uncovering these interests and commitments and managing them pays dividends.

Successful decision makers pushed implementation to the front of their decision-making efforts to uncover and manage people's interests and commitments. If power must be shared, teams are created and involved in making the decision. People are more apt to disclose their interests in such an arrangement. Even when disclosure is limited, the act of negotiating a solution promotes ownership in the agreed-upon plan and increases the prospect of success. Even when not forced to do so, savvy decision makers use participation because it improves the chance of a successful implementation.

Another useful approach, called "intervention," extends the networking approach in claim identification to demonstrate the necessity of acting. Current performance is documented and credible performance norms are identified to show key people the importance of a decision. People are more likely to be supportive when they are aware of the performance shortfalls and the level of performance thought to be possible that motivates the decision. Implementation practices that avoid the trap set by unmanaged social and political forces are discussed in Chapter 5.

## 3. Ambiguous Directions

Direction indicates a decision's expected results. In the debacles, directions were either misleading, assumed but never agreed to, or unknown. Using economic benefits to justify the DIA is both misleading and dangerous. Pena's critics asked if there was a better way to spend $5 billion to produce economic gains for the greater Denver area. Misrepresenting expected benefits gave his critics the means to attack the decision. Being clear about what is to be gained by having a new airport puts a "best face" on such projects. Many major infrastructure projects, such as mass transit systems, are put in jeopardy when champions trumpet "economic benefits" as the expected outcome. More logical and defensible mass transit benefits would be to reduce urban congestion and enhance environmental protection. Debacles often have bloated or unrealistic expectations. Bogus benefits make decisions failure prone.

Difficulties also arise when directions that are assumed by the decision maker are not made clear to key players. Realizing "Walt's Dream" appeared to be Eisner's aim for EuroDisney and was an implicit direction behind key choices, but this was never codified or explained. This prompted people to make their own assumptions, and it is easy to see how people could come up with a different direction. What about the best use of company profits? Had a profit direction been guiding the EuroDisney decision, insiders would have been apt to see Eisner's park and location choices as wrong-headed. A profit direction would draw insiders toward ways to enhance the bottom line. A direction that codified realizing Walt's Dream would make the rationale behind the Eisner choices clearer but would also steer insiders away from looking for profit-enhancing ideas. Had profit been used as a direction, it is doubtful that Eisner would have built a theme park in Europe, or perhaps anywhere, at that time. Such a direction would have put Walt's Dream on notice that a profit result was expected.

Unknown directions prompted still other debacles. Decision makers at Ford had no idea what was directing people's efforts. Ford insiders exported a direction taken from the Pinto's original aims—make a 2,000-pound car to sell for $2,000—and from a "safety doesn't sell" mind-set. Both were rooted in the distant past and failed to address contemporary issues. Safety had become an issue in the Pinto era, and price was less of an issue with consumers. BeechNut's top management failed to make their "cost control" direction clear to others. Key insiders had no idea what motivated the choices of company officials. This denied decision makers at BeechNut access to ideas that could offer ways to escape the morass prompted by cost pressure from the parent company. Clarifying your direction eliminates these misunderstandings and opens up the search for answers. Quality and its impact on revenue as a direction for the BeechNut recall decision would have opened the door to questions about dumping the concentrate.

Being clear about expected results is set aside in the rush to find a remedy, also sidetracks direction setting. Fearing criticism, decision makers act as if they must have a way to deal with a claim as soon as one is acknowledged. The need to disarm the real or imagined critic makes it hard to admit doubt. Doubt can be a powerful force pushing you to think more deeply about what is needed.

Decision makers who feel compelled to begin with an answer fail to offer a clear picture of expected results. The idea and its assumed benefits displace the need to think about the results that you hope to produce. People will see these benefits differently and form different impressions about what is wanted. Without clarity about your reasons for taking action, disputes arise as people find courses of action that deal with their idiosyncratic notions of expected results. Such disputes are a prime cause of conflict in decision making: the recommended action is discussed but not

the hoped for results that prompted it. People who argue about their preferred course of action often fail to tell others what results they are trying
to realize. Being clear about what is wanted by setting an objective clears
away ambiguity and conflict and helps the decision maker find an appropriate course of action. Direction setting is presented in Chapter 6.

## 4. Limited Search and No Innovation

In each debacle, decision makers embraced a quick fix. The first seemingly workable idea that was discovered got adopted. Having an "answer"
eliminates ambiguity about what to do but stops others from looking for
ideas that could be better. Ford's top management opposed a recall. This
made the search for ways to fix the gas tanks a fool's errand. BeechNut's top
management thought only about selling the tainted apple juice, making
cooperation with the FDA and related options untenable. Disney's commitment to a park in France made it impossible to consider other types of
projects, or other locations. If we must have a park, why not locate it where
the weather and the people are sunnier? A quick fix mentality made it difficult for these decision makers to search for innovative options, or even an
additional option, although innovation and multiple options are univer-
sally recommended.

Decision makers who avoid pressures for a quick fix are confronted
with a new challenge: the allure of current business practices. It is difficult to move away from the tangible to the unknown. In the debacles,
many of the proposed actions are variations on current practices. In the
EuroDisney debacle, fixing problems that arose in past park decisions dis-
placed finding what would make a new park appeal to its expected customers. BeechNut officials were committed to discarding the tainted
inventory. This narrowed the search for solutions to ways to sell the inventory. Company executives never considered how a "come clean" posture
could improve the company's financial health. When the CEO of Johnson
and Johnson found that Tylenol might have been tampered with, the product was quickly recalled and disposed of, not once, but on two occasions.
These actions prompted sales for Johnson and Johnson that more than
covered the cost of product recall. The possibility that a recall might stimulate sales, and help BeechNut financially, never occurred to company
leaders. Calling for an innovative (new to the organization) or radically

innovative (new to the industry) idea is difficult, if not impossible, under such conditions.

To reduce time and cost when making a decision, company leaders go on a site visit to find out what respected organizations are doing. The business practices of the visited company, such as what is thought to be the latest application of a CAD-CAM system, are then copied. Managers believe that the equivalent of a field test has been conducted by the other organization so the practice must have value, providing a workable if not ideal solution. This can work out when the other company's circumstances are much like your own. When the companies lack compatibility, however, a retrofit is needed and costs quickly escalate. These costs are almost always underestimated, as is the time to do the required tailoring. Decision makers drawn to seeing "how others do it" are also pulled away from innovation and search.

The search for ideas, and for an innovative one that provides "first mover" advantage, is often waylaid by the desire for a quick fix and the lure of current business practices. Getting caught in a limited search trap increases the risk of failure. The traps of limited search and no innovation and how to avoid them are discussed in Chapter 7.

## 5. Misuse of Evaluation

Once a quick fix is discovered, decision makers take a defensive posture and collect information to justify its adoption. After all is said and done, more time and money is spent doing this type of evaluation than all the other decision-making activities combined. Pena spent huge sums on evaluations of his new airport. It is no surprise that each evaluation spoke glowingly of the idea. Disney spent considerable time and money evaluating the deal with the French and comparatively little time asking hard questions about other ways to make money. Ford focused its efforts on how much it would cost to fix the Pinto's tank compared to the cost of litigation. Little was spent to find cheaper ways to fix the tank until a vehicle recall was forced on them. The money spent on defensive evaluations to justify a preferred course of action would be better spent to uncover a more effective action.

Evaluation has little value unless expected results dictate the data to be collected. Major infrastructure projects, like the DIA, stress expenditures and use evaluation to estimate costs, ignoring hoped-for benefits. Cost was stressed and the likely consequences of a decision disregarded in the BeechNut and Ford recall debacles as well. In the EuroDisney location decision, the preoccupation with evaluating the French deal drew decision makers away from questions about risk. Nestle's management focused their evaluations on estimating sales and profits in third world countries and ignored making projections of the threatened boycott's economic impact. Such evaluations find what the idea champion expects to find, offering shallow and predictable results.

Evaluations that explore risk and compare options to one another or to performance norms can be insightful. Expected results must be clear before such evaluations can provide useful information. If management had adopted a profit direction for the EuroDisney decision, the analysis of best and worst case assumptions about hotel occupancy and ticket sales to determine the project's profit-making risk would be thrust on the table. Such an analysis would expose Disney officials to factors that limit overnight stays (the park is a day trip from Paris) and ticket sales (it was less costly at the time for many Europeans to go to Orlando). Both reduce revenue projections and the likelihood of turning a profit. Such an evaluation uncovers uncertainty in the park location decision and thereby strips away ambiguity and conflict over what to do. Factors that drive revenues and the like upward and downward were ignored in the debacles so the risk in each of these decisions was hidden. Ways to avoid the traps in defensive evaluations and tools that identify the amount of risk in a decision and compare options are offered in Chapter 8.

## 6. Ignoring Ethical Questions

Tough decisions pose ethical dilemmas. Ignoring these dilemmas sets a trap that ensnared decision makers in the debacles. DIA decision makers ignored questions about who pays, who benefits, and who decides. This is typical of large-scale infrastructure projects such as sports arenas, rapid transit systems, and arts centers. The Sydney Opera House's many cost overruns were subsidized with public funds. The tax-paying public in Australia, a country committed to populism, paid for an elitist idea decided upon by a liberal politician, a dangerous if not an ethical dilemma for the politician. Businesses that require their employees to travel are well represented on the boards and councils that decide on airport expansions.

Business representatives maneuver government into underwriting bonds that finance such projects or endorse referendums to pay for them with tax dollars. Airports can be seen as corporate welfare decided upon by business interests, funded by the public, and offered for the convenience of business travelers.

Most would agree that it is ethically questionable to push a self-serving idea, oppose a good idea because it presents a personal threat, or engage in conflicts of interest. Questions about ethics also arise during testimony to a legislative body or to higher management, in which budget needs are not exactly misrepresented but are not accurately represented either. Ethical issues crop up a bit more subtly through alternatives that are never presented and criteria to judge an alternative that are selected because they favor a preferred course of action. Views of what is ethical depend on who is being deceived. Deception is tolerated and even encouraged when directed toward an "outsider."

Values lurk behind an ethical position. These values were never understood in the debacles. Was Disney's no alcohol policy merely a ploy to attract parents with small children or was it a commitment to a moral position? When park attendance lagged at the park, Disney dropped its no alcohol policy to stimulate ticket sales. No value-driven position here. At Ford "profit drives principle" was believed by insiders to be a company value. This made the unwillingness of company officials to recall the Pinto understandable. BeechNut poses an even more severe test. Company leaders postured to look like the victim. The prospect of looking like a villain, if the facts were to come out, was not recognized until it was too late. Law breaking was justified in the name of trying to appease the Nestle parent by strict adherence to the parent's cost reduction expectations. Selling tainted inventory to developing countries would have been unthinkable had ethics been sewn into the fabric of company culture. Nestle's executives saw their marketing efforts as pragmatic. Others saw them as unethical. When the actions of decision makers appear to go beyond what is thought to be ethical behavior, it can prompt whistle-blowing by insiders (as in the BeechNut decision) or boycotts by outsiders (as in the Nestle decision). Even when these extreme reactions are avoided, decision makers plant the seeds of distrust when their behavior appears to be unethical to insiders or to outsiders, as in the Ford and DIA decisions.

To avoid distrust, whistle-blowing, and boycotts, ethical issues must be confronted. Organizational leaders view concerned individuals who pose ethical concerns as decisions are being made as raising questions to protect the company. These same questions posed after a choice has been made are usually seen as grousing by a malcontent. This suggests that people should be encouraged to speak out and pose ethical questions during decision-making deliberations. Astute managers create forums for ethical concerns to be voiced and offer mediation to those who disagree. The forum enables a decision maker to look for values behind the positions of people who raise questions. The decision maker can often affirm these values and make a minor modification in a preferred course of action to carry on much as before. Had Nestle affirmed the values of the groups that opposed them by addressing the questions of safe use of their product in their marketing, they would have cut the ground from under the arguments of their opposition, and any attempted boycott. BeechNut could have spent more time exploring what the PAI sought to gain by their lawsuit before deciding whether or not to join. If these tactics fail, offer mediation. Ford and the DIA decision makers could have held hearings and conferences to find out what their critics were saying and to defuse unwarranted criticisms and misunderstandings. At best, new insights are discovered. If not, the company leaders have taken steps that show they considered the views of their critics—a position that boosts the legitimacy of a proposed action. Companies with mediation win lawsuits involving whistle-blowing. Companies without it lose them. Ethics is discussed in Chapter 9.

## 7. Failure to Learn

Decision makers are apt to stumble down the same failure-prone path over and over again without learning. Learning is thwarted when leaders show no tolerance for mistakes and errors or for a failed decision. In such an environment, people conceal bad outcomes. To make things worse, chance events make outcomes muddy. It is often difficult to separate good decisions with bad outcomes from bad decisions with good outcomes. Good decision-making practices cannot guarantee good outcomes because of chance events. Bad luck, such as when product demand falls below expectations because of unexpected bad weather, can be mistaken for bad decision-making practices. Good luck, such as windfall profits due to a favorable turn on interest rates or consumer interest in a product, can cover up failure-prone decision-making practices.

Some organizational leaders expect good results and ignore the chance events that make a good decision outcome unlikely, or even impossible. In such an organization those that get caught up in a failed decision will reveal outcomes in carefully measured doses, if at all. People at Disney expressed surprise when EuroDisney revenues were far below projections—or so they claimed. Ford officials seemed startled by the litigation that followed a fatal crash with a Pinto. BeechNut covered up one bad choice after another until the situation became unmanageable. DIA decision makers made design changes to hide the airport's ballooning cost. Nestle's management saw their cause differently from their critics and ignored the many warning signs of eroding public support for the company's position.

People accountable for a failed decision find themselves caught in a no-win situation: some failure is inevitable, but their superiors do not tolerate failure. Individuals in such a bind have but two options: own up or cover up. Choosing to own up makes the day of atonement today; choosing a cover-up makes it tomorrow or perhaps never. Put in this bind, people seldom own up to failures and delay the day of atonement as long as possible. This creates even more trouble. Several actions of deception are necessary to put things off. Offsetting bad news with good news deflects potentially threatening questions. The cover-up is two tiered: the distorted good news and the blatant act of creating misleading information. These games of deception become "undiscussable" because to reveal them would also reveal the lose-lose position created for the organization. There must be a cover-up of the cover-up to cover one's tracks. This makes the decision and its outcome undiscussable, keeping information that is required to learn from higher ups.

The real culprit here is the perverse incentive that keeps people from owning up to what has taken place. A perverse incentive always has this effect, making it difficult for people to come forward with their insights about what happened and why. Insiders at Ford quickly learned not to question higher ups. LiCari at BeechNut had considerable reason to hold back after his inquires were forcibly rebuffed. Disney staffers were aware of the tendency to focus upon the past park problems, but staffers thought it futile to argue against Walt's Dream or Eisner's seeming wish for a French location. Pena made it clear he would tolerate no opposition to his pet project. In each of these decisions, perverse incentives created barriers to learning why these decisions went wrong and how to avoid similar failures in the future. Learning demands a culture in which decisions can be discussed without this blame-finding mentality.

To root out a perverse incentive, you must show that it no longer applies. This is both time-consuming and difficult. When Peterson took over as the CEO of Ford, he went to great lengths to consult with his top management team to get their ideas. It took years to show them that this was sincere and that the "do as I say" practices of the past no longer applied. Only after Peterson had rooted out these old perceptions could he deal with the distrust that had been fostered by them and embark on new product designs that led to the highly successful Sable and Taurus.

To show that quality mattered at Harley-Davidson, a new CEO had to demonstrate that he wanted things to change. The cost-based incentives inherent in fast-running production lines had been drummed into the workforce over many years. To root them out, top management called on Harley's workers to stop the production line if they spotted a quality problem. It took six months before someone stopped the line to fix a quality problem. Management had to wait until this happened to recognize it by awarding a bonus, which set in motion a new understanding about what counts. After perverse incentives have been rooted out, managers can set learning in place by creating win-win situations in which everyone benefits. Steps to create a learning environment with a win-win mentality that avoids the traps prompted by perverse incentives are considered in Chapter 10.

## ▼ Key Points

- ▼ Decision makers are prone to using tactics with poor track records, applying them in two-thirds of their decisions. Success will increase by as much as 50 percent if better tactics are used.
- ▼ The prospect of success improves when managers probe to uncover hidden concerns, take steps to manage the social and political forces that can block them, identify the results they want, search widely and

encourage innovation, and estimate benefits linked to expected results along with the risk in realizing them.

▼ Ethical dilemmas often go undetected as decisions are made and crop up later, causing responsible people considerable embarrassment. This can be avoided if decision makers encourage ethical questions be voiced as the decision-making effort unfolds.

▼ Perverse incentives get people to adopt a defensive posture that blocks learning how to improve decision making. Perverse incentives must be rooted out and a win-win environment created before learning can occur.

# Decision-Making Processes Prone to Success and Failure

## CHAPTER 3

To carry out a decision-making process, one engages in a series of activities to collect information that reveals possibilities. Process spells out the order or staging of these activities. In this chapter, two of many possible processes are considered. One illustrates a frequently used process that leads to failure. The other demonstrates best practice. First, the stages will be described to show what is done in each. Then ways to sequence these stages are presented, illustrating best and worst process practices using the debacles described in Chapter 1.

## Decision-Making Stages

An extensive literature review was conducted to discover what thoughtful writers find to be required stages and the best ordering of stages for decision making. This led me to prescriptions made by people who have studied the best way to do research, design, social change, and problem solving. Also, studies by Schon (1987) and others, which document how expert architects, urban planners, social and behavioral scientists, engineers, system theorists, and the like go about their work, elaborate on these recommendations and suggest others. Five decision-making stages emerged from a comparison of these prescriptions and findings: collect information to understand the claims calling for action, establish a direction that indicates the desired result, mount a systematic search for ideas, evaluate these ideas with the direction in mind, and manage social and political barriers that can block the preferred course of action during implementation.

## Understand Claims

Claims identify the "arena of action" or topic the decision maker expects to address, and by their exclusion other topics that will be ruled out. A claim is derived from a need or opportunity stakeholders believe to be important. A claim takes shape when stakeholders note a need-based concern or an opportunity-based consideration and draw a conclusion about what must be done. Managers are bombarded by claims from informed insiders, users or customers, judicial renderings, new industry practices, regulations and regulators, and suppliers. Their own views, as well as the views of important people outside of the company, also come into play. For example, the Environmental Protection Agency may contend that a firm is engaging in environmentally dangerous dumping of waste materials. The union, management, the board, and others interpret this contention and offer claims about what the company should do. Subsequently, a trade journal may disclose a novel product, suggesting a new initiative by a competitor. Stakeholders identify a consideration abstracted from the opportunity and offer it as a way to beat the competitor by moving into a previously overlooked market and making a claim about the actions required to pull this off. Claimants may have different takes on what is important. These different takes prompt different views of what should be done, which can lead to very different claims. The concerns or considerations that prompt a claim are seldom disclosed with the claim and can be deliberately hidden.

Decision makers choose among the claims according to the power of the claimant or the claim's substance (Cyert and March, 1963). Does the competitor's new product really pose a threat? Do the claimant's connections demand that his or her views be accepted? Claims can be self-serving or symptomatic when dictated by the claimant's power, sweeping aside other claims based on important concerns and considerations. Faulty claims and self-serving ones pull the decision maker away from pressing issues.

In the claim stage, overlooked concerns and considerations of stake-holders are sought. By taking into account such concerns and considerations, a claim can be fashioned that points people toward an arena of action with sufficient support to mobilize and sustain the effort.

Decision makers take one of two paths to identify an area in which to take action. They can choose among claims and claimants, or they can explore claims to increase their understanding of the concerns and considerations of stakeholders and prioritize these concerns and considerations. The decision maker who elects to choose among claims and claimants moves into an idea-imposition process. Decision makers who take steps to expand the pool of claims before selecting one begin a discovery process.

## Set a Direction

Directions are derived from the claim motivating action. How the direction is set provides decision makers with two additional procedural options. A direction can be opportunistic and latch onto a ready-made idea found in the claim, or it can identify a need embedded in the claim and offer a problem or an objective. To articulate a need-based direction, the decision maker examines the reasons for action and decides what results are required. This is done by identifying a problem to be overcome or by setting an objective to be met. A problem identifies what is wrong that needs fixing, such as exploring why utilization is declining. An objective indicates the desired result, such as increased revenues. Decision makers who are opportunity driven offer a ready-made solution as a substitute for setting a direction.

## Uncover Ideas

Decision makers who adopt a "need-type" direction search for remedies to overcome the problem or meet the objective. People who study decision making recommend that you uncover multiple options and innovative ideas. Multiple options increase the number of ideas considered and improve your chance of finding a superior solution. Innovation requires a new idea, one that has not been recognized previously. Some call for "radical innovation," ideas that are new to an industry. Radical innovation is credited with giving many organizations a decisive advantage in the marketplace. Michelin dramatically increased its market share by introducing the radial tire, a complete break with the bias tire design then in use throughout the tire industry. Xerox with its Xerography dry copy product ran over companies making carbon paper. Decision makers seeking innovation use consultants or staff specialists to search for custom-made ideas. Decision makers who wish to keep secret possible actions search alone.

## Evaluate Ideas

Evaluation assesses the ideas uncovered in a search. Information such as costs, benefits, and acceptance is often collected to judge the merits of an idea. Evaluation is also used to assess the amount of risk in each option being considered. Risk measures the chance that the hoped-for results will be realized. Evaluation information provides a basis to select among ideas or to rule out ideas that have unacceptable risk.

## Implement the Preferred Idea

Implementation puts the decision to use. This can be done in several ways. The acceptance of stakeholders can be promoted by involving them, or their representatives, in the decision-making effort and by canvassing them early in the process. Involvement entices stakeholders to go along with the decision, making participation an integral part of each process stage. Another approach, called networking, guides stakeholders one at a time through steps that alter their objectives, social ties, and self-esteem and reinforces the positive aspects of an evolving decision. Edict and persuasion can also be used. In persuasion the decision maker marshals arguments to sell the decision to others by dramatizing its alleged benefits. An edict prescribes the behavior necessary to realize the decision. Implementation can be initiated early in the decision-making effort by using participation or networking to tailor ideas to make them acceptable. Using persuasion and edicts pushes implementation to the end of the process.

The decision maker selects among tactics that can be used in each stage to fashion a process. These choices create processes that are more or less successful. Let's turn our attention to two process types, one notable for its success and the other for failure.

# Notable Process Types

A decision-making process lays out the sequence of activities to be followed. The process stages identify what decision makers worry about as a decision is being made. Different people emphasize different things. Some stress finding a workable idea and deemphasize direction setting. Others emphasize implementation, and still others consider all of the process stages and give them equal weight.

A tactic indicates how managers go about uncovering the things that are called for in a given stage, such as setting directions with an objective or coping with what others do. Decision makers select tactics that push them through the decision-making process in different ways. Some select among claims or their claimants. Others explore claims by uncovering concerns and considerations. Directions can take shape as a need or as an opportunity. If you choose to be need-directed, multiple options and/or innovation can be sought. Implementation can be proactive and pushed to the front of the process with networking or participation tactics. Or you can be reactive and take steps at the end of the process to install a preferred course of action with edict or persuasion tactics.

Two of these paths are of particular interest. One produces a *discovery process* offering a "think first" approach that increases the chance of being successful. The other, called an *idea-imposition process*, is linked to failed decisions and decision debacles. Let's consider each of these processes separately and trace the actions taken and those skipped, and their sequence, illustrating each with the decision debacles presented in Chapter 1. This extends the notion of best practice to process.

## The Discovery Process

A trend or an event alerts a stakeholder by calling into question current business practices. The alert points to something inside an organization, such as an inefficient operation or a loss of legitimacy, or outside it, such as an innovation by a competitor or a loss of customers. Claims are made to reflect the question and information gathering follows. This can be done by staff who examine industry reports, such as Dun's or Value Line, to clarify performance questions and make comparisons to the performance of others. Or decision makers may collect information by talking with stakeholders or trusted associates to verify what claimants are saying. *Concerns* draw attention to an unsatisfactory condition and *considerations* identify an opportunity. A claimant's concerns or considerations are interpreted to suggest an arena of action, what the decision is about.

Decision makers who use a discovery process work their way through a process that stresses claim validation, implementation, and direction setting. These three stages are considered early on because they have the greatest impact on success. A premium is placed on learning through the discovery of decision topics, barriers to taking action, and desired results. The discovery process is outlined in Figure 3.1, with the crucial stages highlighted.

**Claims Identify the Arena of Action.** The successful decision maker looks beyond the initial claim. Claims made by a cross section of informed people are uncovered to reveal concerns and considerations that are hidden or have yet to be disclosed. Claims about changes in customer taste

*Figure 3.1*
**THE DISCOVERY PROCESS**

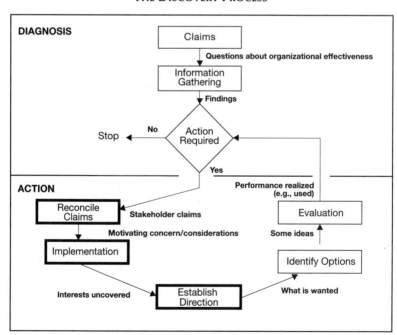

Highlighted stages (boxes) identify crucial stages

and customer expectations are investigated by talking with customers, salespeople, suppliers, alliance partners, and others who may have insights. An amalgamation of claims from several sources suggests a plausible range of claims. The concerns and considerations behind these claims paint a picture of what the decision is about. EuroDisney and DIA critics could have been polled to uncover the considerations motivating their claims. Informed insiders at Ford and Nestle could have been asked to voice their claims to seek out the concerns motivating them. Consulting with informed BeechNut employees could have given better understanding of LiCari's motives.

The concerns and considerations uncovered provide you with new ways to think about the arena of action. Was the EuroDisney decision about best location or whether to invest in a park? Should Ford shift the arena from stonewalling a recall to investigating ways to carry out a cost-efficient recall? Nestle's arena of action was limited to defending their marketing practices and did not consider how to use the company's marketing approach to discourage unsafe infant feeding practices in third world countries. DIA decision makers limited their arena of action to selecting among new airport plans, ignoring the question of whether a new airport was a wise investment for the many airport stakeholders.

*Implementation to Manage the Forces Blocking Action.* When decision makers ask "Who can block action?" they bring social and political issues to the forefront. If a new airport is needed, how can others be convinced that the need is real and the plan a reasonable one? Ford could have taken steps to get the NHTSA and other critics to see its side of the recall question. Participation can be used when interested parties are more localized, such as asking Disney insiders for a park location recommendation or BeechNut asking insiders for ways to cope with the increased cost that would be incurred by actually putting apples in their "apple juice" products.

*Direction Setting to Indicate Desired Results.* Directions guide the search for ideas by indicating what is wanted as an outcome. Walt's Dream was interpreted to imply a French location. What about a location that maximizes attendance at the park or one that increases the exposure of Disney-Americana to Europeans? This suggests attendance or exposure as the desired result. Was the DIA about safety or increased business activity for the Denver area? Safety as the expected result would have put a different light on the need for a new airport. Did Ford have a cost or a sales objective? Should BeechNut and Nestle make their implicit cost and sales directions explicit? Direction setting clears up these questions by identifying an agreed-upon outcome to guide the search for ideas.

**Uncover Ideas.** If claim, implementation, and direction have been attended to, the remaining stages are easier to carry out and less controversial. Had Pena neutralized critics with a clear-cut safety direction, he would have had a clear path to pursue his passion and search for novel airport plans and innovative ideas in its design. Had Disney executives opened up the location question, they would have found it easier to uncover location options by starting a competition among cities, as VW and Honda do to locate manufacturing plants in the United States. Ford could have mobilized its staff to find a cost-effective tank fix, and Nestle could have asked its staff to develop a marketing plan that stressed safe infant feeding practices. BeechNut could have initiated an effort to find cost-cutting actions that could have offset the expected increase in the cost of their "apple juice."

**Evaluate Options.** Evaluation is straightforward in a development process. The direction specifies what is wanted, such as lower cost. This makes cost an appropriate and reasonable way to measure benefits. The political overtones of using evaluation to defend a course of action are taken away and replaced with documenting and verifying benefits. Identifying the Disney location with the least risk—one with the largest expected park attendance and hotel occupancy—is less controversial than collecting data to make the French location look good. Comparing the safety of air travel through Stapelton with that of the proposed new airport is more apt to be accepted than trying to show how a new airport can stimulate business in the greater Denver area. If cost-effective solutions had been accepted as a direction, an evaluation of the cost effectiveness of fix options for the Pinto gas tank and marketing plans for Nestle would have lacked controversy.

## The Idea-Imposition Process

Trends and events and the claims they provoke are handled much differently in an idea-imposition process. Studies by staff, examination of industry reports, and talks with stakeholders or trusted peers are carried out as before. In the idea-imposition process, a claim is selected after a review of the information gathered. Concerns and considerations behind the agreed-upon claim, such as coping with changes in customer taste or new computer technologies, are ignored to focus on the most visible or widely supported claim. When such a claim and its documentation draw attention to an unsatisfactory situation, action follows.

Decision makers who use an idea-imposition process skip some stages and change the order of others, as shown in Figure 3.2. An orderly path is seldom followed because decision makers jump to conclusions and then try to implement the solution they stumbled upon. This bias for action causes them to limit their search, consider very few ideas, and pay too little attention to people who are affected, despite the fact that decisions fail for just these reasons.

Decision makers following an idea-imposition process uncover an idea early on, which limits search and in most cases terminates it. No one looks for any other ideas. Implementation is attempted after the solution is uncovered and evaluated. Because managers latch onto an idea early on and use most of their resources to test its merits, learning is limited. The

*Figure 3.2*
**THE IDEA-IMPOSITION PROCESS**

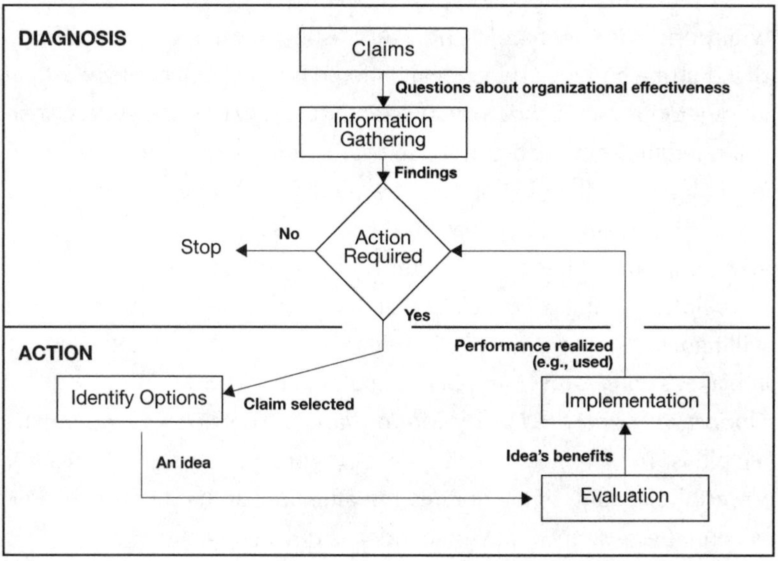

more effective discovery process establishes directions and identifies options as separate activities. Options are developed in response to the directions established. In an idea-imposition process, several stages that play an important role in the discovery process are skipped and important activities are deferred.

*Claims and the Arena of Action.* Decision makers prone to failure select among competing claims according to the power of the claimant. The danger in ignoring a claimant is believed to be more important than the claim's message. The motives of a decision maker following such a quest can be quite transparent to observers who then ignore, obstruct, or give only token efforts. The decision maker must scale the barriers set up by stakeholders who become offended by or skeptical of the motives behind taking action. If the claimant is inconsequential and has little power, the choice can be made by the seeming logic in what is being proposed. The claim with the most compelling logic can be supported. This can also provoke opposition when there are other claimants who have as yet unheard concerns and considerations. At this point, alienated stakeholders who were not given a chance to offer their views erect barriers.

The arena of action in a debacle seldom changed from that found in the claim bought into by the decision maker. Decision makers in the debacles persevered even though critics disputed their claim and offered counterarguments. Pena had to power over his opponents to hold onto a new airport as the arena of action. At Disney, Eisner was fixated on a park in Europe and the "sweet deal" offered by the French, never asking what other cities in Europe would offer. No one would question Eisner. This limited the arena of action to an evaluation of the French deal. Ford stonewalled a recall and Nestle stonewalled a marketing change, and by doing so they maintained arenas that were set out early on in these decision-making efforts. Because these brash commitments were never challenged, little learning occurred. A fatal flaw in all of the debacles was the unwillingness to think about any information unless it supported the decision maker's claim and its implied arena of action.

*Opportunity and the Ready-Made Plan.* The debacles all had ready-made plans. The claim and its implied opportunity suggested an idea. Or a powerful claimant, who captures the attention of the decision maker, offers one. Because the ready-made idea is quickly identified, it provides instant relief for a beleaguered decision maker. In each of the debacles, the core idea that made up the decision was available early on and seldom changed. The idea of a park in France near Paris surfaced years before Disney acted on it. There was little if any debate about an old versus a new airport in the DIA decision. BeechNut's top management was committed to dumping the tainted inventory, which made them unwilling to hear about anything else. Ford and Nestle refused to alter their early commitments to resist a recall and to change the marketing plan. It took years of activism and bad press to force them to reconsider.

This commitment becomes a trap in which "new ideas" are always variations on old ones. No one dares to challenge the status quo, fearing that key players have too many vested interests to back away from these interests. This perception of sunk cost, the fear of failure, and the reluctance people have to starting over keeps the decision maker focused on making things work. This coaxes them to carry on even when their cause is doomed as in the BeechNut case. Decision makers pushing opportunities are confronted with skeptics who see the decision makers as pushing an idea because they have something to gain. Even when this is not the case, time and money must be devoted to defending the idea—money that could be better spent on finding new ideas. Many fear the unknown, not knowing what they want until they see a concrete possibility. As Wildavsky (1979) observes, decision makers don't know want they want till they can see what they can get. Having such an answer eliminates ambiguity but limits the search for new ideas that could be better.

***Evaluating the Opportunity.*** Once an "opportunity" is found, evaluation soon follows. Each decision maker in the debacles slipped into a defensive posture, attempting to justify the opportunity and defend the reasons used to support it. A "defensive evaluation" runs up the bill for analysis, often into the millions. Such an evaluation seldom turns up anything of value. The DIA proponents pulled in outside consultants and paid them handsomely to do cost and feasibility studies. In this case, the consultants knew what they were expected to find. Such evaluations offer little beyond shallow and predictable observations. Disney spent far more on the analysis of the French deal than it did on anything else. BeechNut determined the value of the tainted inventory but did nothing to estimate the potential costs of dumping it. Ford and Nestle projected their expected losses but spent little on exploring the costs and benefits of other options. In each case, the evaluation offers little beyond a defense. The uncertainty in the opportunity was never considered in the debacles, so the risk in these decisions was unknown.

Little money is spent comparing options because four of five decisions consider only one idea. When there is but one idea, evaluation can still be useful if the idea is assessed against expectations. Such an evaluation can uncover the wisdom of installing the idea, but it will be controversial without a direction indicating desired results that point out which benefits count.

***Installing the Plan.*** Decision makers in the debacles spent little of their time or money on implementation until near the end of the process. The tactics available at this point are failure prone. Decision makers can apply power, persuasion, or some combination to get people to comply. A memo is written or someone is hired to tell people what to do. If this fails, decision makers resort to persuasion, trying to explain to stakeholders why the decision is essential. Sometimes this is done in reverse with an application of power following a failed demonstration. Both are doomed to failure if the interests of important stakeholders are threatened by the decision. Eisner and Pena had little hope of getting their critics off their backs with arguments about potential consumers' interest in a European park or the airport's economic benefits.

People who see themselves as disadvantaged and lacking the power to openly resist resort to tokenism and withdraw. Ford and Nestle got insiders on board but, in doing so, lost their ideas about what to do to fix things as these decisions spun out of control. Compliance has a price. After a power play, people will only tell you what they think you want to hear and will no longer tell you what they believe to be true.

## Shifts to the Idea-Imposition Process

The discovery process has an excellent track record, but to realize this degree of success the discovery process must be continued through all of its stages. As pressures mount to be pragmatic and to move things along, you will find it difficult to carry out each and every process stage. The dual pressures of pragmatism and timeliness can intensify to the point that they can persuade you to switch tactics. A shift in tactics can occur in any process stage and lure an unsuspecting decision maker into the idea-imposition process, as shown in Figure 3.3 on the following page. Let's trace the pressures that can cause you to shift your tactics and the consequences of such a shift.

Any departure from the staging of activity in the discovery process reduces the prospects of success. Changes in approach are prompted by the three blunders discussed in Chapter 1. This takes place in two ways. One motivation arises when a quick fix pops up and seems to be a useful, if not ideal, way to proceed. If the idea is adopted, there is a shift to an "idea tactic" that abandons best practice. The emergent idea that allows for a quick fix makes learning from a careful search for ideas seem superfluous. A contention that time or money is being misused can push you to alter how things are being done. Decision makers respond to a call to cut costs or to speed things up by dropping one or more of the tactics called for in the discovery process and substituting one that seems to be cheaper and faster. My studies show that they are neither cheaper nor faster. The temptation to do one or the other, or both, will arise repeatedly as you work your way through the process stages. Once the move to the idea-imposition process is made, no one in my studies was able to get back to the tactics called for by the discovery process, making this move one way. There is some good news. Moving to an idea-imposition process is less damaging if it occurs further along in the discovery process. Let's see how the three blunders enticed decision makers to adopt tactics that moved them from a discovery to an idea-imposition process, beginning with the first stage in the discovery process.

## Claim Reconciliation

The discovery process begins with the decision maker polling a diverse group of stakeholders to uncover their concerns and considerations. Polling sets in motion what can appear to be a long and costly effort. Because some insiders and outsiders will be pushing to get on with it, the polling may have only grudging acceptance, giving it a tenuous base of support. Should an idea emerge that seems to fit the bill, such individuals will call for its adoption. Shifting from a polling tactic to an idea tactic moves the process to an idea-imposition type. Once such a move is made, decision

*Figure 3.3*
### SHIFTS BETWEEN THE TWO DECISION-MAKING PROCESSES

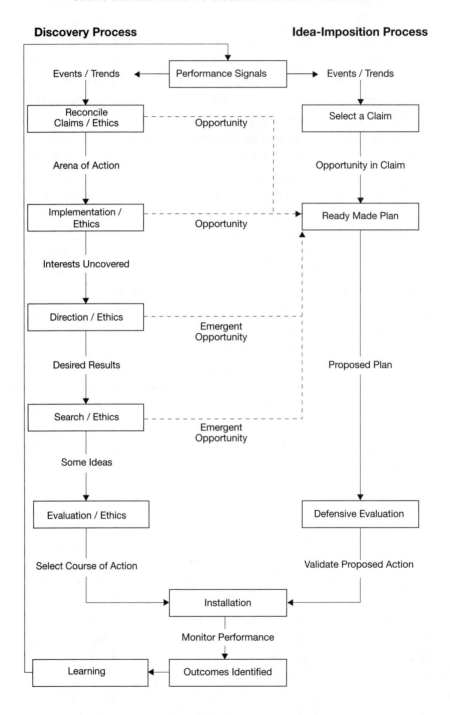

makers are unable to return to a discovery process and a learning mode. Effort shifts to defending the emergent idea and demonstrating its value.

The arguments for such a shift in tactics are hard to deflect because of the pragmatism of having something that works, or seems to work. Both time and cost appear to be saved by such a move, but this frequently proves to be illusory (see Chapter 4). The cost and time required to do the needed retrofits are always underestimated. The quick fix is pragmatic and timely in less than one of five decisions.

## Attending to Social and Political Issues

If you get through the claim reconciliation stage, you will have polled stakeholders and amassed information about possible decision topics and whether the expected effort warrants the organization's time and resources. These insights make it easier to deal with quick fix proponents. The idea must now pass a test offered by an enhanced understanding of concerns, which indicate needs, or considerations that suggest opportunities. Also, commitments made to stakeholders about their concerns and considerations must be met. Proponents of a quick fix must hurdle these barriers to show how their ideas can serve the needs or offer the features called for by an opportunity. This puts quick fix proponents on the defensive, and few of their ideas will survive such a test. To scale hurdles created in claim reconciliation, the force of the idea in a quick fix must seem compelling and appear to fit the deeper understanding of what is needed or the opportunities available. Sometimes such a case can be made. If so, the networking or the participation tactic called for in stage two of the discovery process is abandoned. This does happen, but it occurs less often than in the claim stage.

A strident call for increased frugality or rapid action accompanied by a workable idea can set aside an effort to build understanding and support by networking or by involving others to get their ideas. People can derail early implementation by contending that effort being expended to muster support and understanding is overly patronizing, or just not required. Networking and participation are stopped if successfully branded as too time-consuming and overly costly or as overkill. As you will see in Chapter 5, it is the appearance not the reality of things that often carries the day. Networking and participation are more efficient and effective than people realize.

Dropping either the networking or the participation tactic delays implementation by pushing it to the end of the process. This limits you to tactics of persuasion or an edict, which have less chance of success than networking or participation. This delays implementation until a preferred course of action has been carefully evaluated and defenses gathered, which limits you to using either persuasion or edict tactics.

### Setting Directions

Slipping into an idea-imposition process during direction setting is prompted by many of the same impulses noted previously. Higher-ups with a short time horizon or a low tolerance for ambiguity may pressure you to produce results. They create a clamor that proponents of a discovery process and its "think first" approach may find difficult to keep at bay. Even a small effort devoted to setting objectives or uncovering problems can appear tiresome and little more than an academic exercise to individuals with such urges.

A discovery process that unfolds through the first two stages gathers considerable information about possibilities. There are concerns, considerations, and an agreed-upon claim as well as an informed network of people who understand what the decision is about and why it seems wise to act. This creates a sterner test than at the previous stage when logic but not political support could be used to argue against what may be an ill-conceived quick fix. Even so, some ideas may seem convincing and be adopted over the opposition of others who want to mount an objective-driven search to find a really good idea. Adopting the quick fix shifts to an idea-imposition process and makes further direction-setting efforts impossible. The damage is still considerable. No one will know what is wanted as a result if such a shift occurs. This complicates evaluations because there are no clear expectations to measure against. Capricious arguments that support the quick fix are possible because of this, and they are difficult to counter. Proponents employ such arguments in their political maneuvering, creating conflict.

### Searching for Ideas

You have claims, a network of support, and a clear statement of the desired result when you reach this point in the discovery process. Armed with all this information, you have considerable ammunition to block an ill-conceived idea being sold as a quick fix. Idea proponents can be asked how the idea fits with the arena of action, whether people's concerns and considerations are attended to, and if the idea will produce the agreed-upon results. When an idea emerges that can pass each of these tests, it will have some merit. Adopting it may not give the best result, but there is much less chance of a debacle.

When an idea emerges outside the search effort that meets all these tests, the question shifts to whether further search can be profitable. To answer this question, a decision maker looks at the results to date and estimates what a further search can provide. The decision maker must also identify baggage that the quick fix will bring. Continuing a search typically pays off, and the idea in the quick fix can be tossed into the kitty and considered along with others. Terminating a search under such conditions can be seen as stopping on the verge of success, even if there is much left to do. Staying with a search maintains the support that has been carefully built over the previous two stages of effort. Switching to the idea-imposition process, even if the idea is defensible, can squander some of this support. People with little tolerance for the wait or people feeling pressure to act will be drawn to a quick fix, even though it has this baggage. When tolerance is low and pressures strong, a quick fix can prompt the switch away from the search tactic to the idea tactic. This limits you to assessing the emergent idea and using the evaluation results to argue for its adoption. This will have little effect on the disgruntled former participant, but others who see the idea as meeting if not exceeding expectations may find it acceptable. Some of the motivations and consequences of terminating a search are discussed in Chapter 6.

## Evaluation

When you reach this point in the discovery process, you have almost reached the end of the effort. There is an arena of action, a cadre of supporters, clear expectations, and some ideas with potential. This gives you several commitments and understandings, but a change in tactics can still upset things. An ill-chosen evaluation approach that creates an image of manipulating things to serve a selfish interest can prompt failure.

Best practice calls for a comparison of competing ideas to select the one that comes closest to providing the hoped-for results. Decision makers do this less often than you may think. Decision makers may feel pressure to act quickly. Or they may see something that is in their interest or the interests of those they must cater to and believe they must call for adoption of this idea. This calls for a subjective assessment and a personal interpretation of benefits. Decision makers feeling the heat from higher-ups may just announce that "this is the thing to do," merging implementation with an implicit evaluation by resorting to an edict. When decision makers resort to subjective or implicit evaluations, they abandon best practice evaluation tactics and move into the idea-imposition process. Evaluation and implementation become intertwined, making it impossible to get back to the preferred discovery process.

Risk can be misunderstood as well. This can be intentional, setting aside risk to make someone's idea seem acceptable. Ideas with high risk can appear to have little or no risk merely by ignoring questions about risk. To push a pet idea, risk is swept under the carpet. Or risk may be overstated and paralyze the decision maker. Here an option with no risk or the appearance of no risk may be sought. Decision makers gravitate to ideas that seem risk free and reject those with modest risk and high potential payoffs. Evaluation is rendered useless by overmanagement or undermanagement of risk. Both move from the discovery process to an idea-imposition process and commit decision makers to using tactics of persuasion and its well-reasoned justification to carry the day or edict to get their way. Sloppy arguments or a show of force at this point reduce the chance of success. The follies of using bad evaluation tactics to certify someone's preferred course of action and misrepresenting risk are considered in Chapter 8.

## Some Process Learnings

All of the debacles presented in the book followed the path shown in Figure 3.2. Concerns about Stapelton's inadequacies were interpreted as a claim that called for a new airport. The new airport "opportunity" persisted as defensive evaluations were undertaken to answer critics and provide information for Pena to use in his attempt to persuade people to support his quest. Top managers at Ford bought into the claim that the Pinto had an acceptable level of safety. This made it easy to stonewall a recall. Analyses of the fix option and its seemingly high cost provided more support. Ford's top management powered over concerned insiders and ignored others to pursue their no-fix decision. BeechNut's top management thought they could posture as the victim if caught and dispose of the tainted inventory as the PAI ruminated about its planned lawsuit. Power was applied to critics, such as LiCari, slamming the door on any internal debate about the wisdom of selling a tainted product in developing countries. Nestle ignored the claim that it was selling "infant death." Power was applied to maintain the option of continuing its marketing plan through years of organized opposition. Walt's Dream was interpreted as a park in France, preferably near Paris. The idea prompted an evaluation of the French deal. Eisner used his position of power to make EuroDisney a reality by locating it near Paris.

All debacles follow such a process. A claim suggested by a powerful claimant is adopted. The arena of action implied by the claim is never questioned, and the idea called for by the claim or offered by a powerful claimant is identified, evaluated, and installed. Following the discovery process in Figure 3.1 would have opened people up to new ideas and possibilities that could have avoided some of these debacles.

## ▼ Key Points

- ▼ Process depicts how decision makers stage the activities thought to be crucial in decision making.
- ▼ Both the stages of activity and the order of these stages are important.
- ▼ A discovery process puts the more important stages of reconciling claims, implementation, and direction setting early in the effort and is more apt to be successful. Innovation is feasible and evaluation meaningful in a discovery process.
- ▼ All of the debacles used an idea-imposition process in which the decision maker selected among claims and imposed a ready-made idea. Failure is four times more likely when this process is used.

# Traps in Failing to Lead the Effort with Agreed-Upon Claims

Claims identify the "arena of action"—what the decision is about. When a claim makes sense to key people, it mobilizes support and points the decision-making effort in a useful direction. When it does not, the decision heads off in an unproductive direction and the support needed to sustain it may not develop. Here we consider the dual themes of taking charge by uncovering concerns and considerations to fashion claims and the consequences of failing to do so. A failure to fashion a claim that captures the concerns and considerations of stakeholders sets the first trap. Let's begin by demonstrating how a decision-making effort can be thwarted when a claim fails to capture concerns and considerations and coaxes stakeholders to give lip service to the effort or to oppose it.

## The Call to Action

Decision making begins when a stakeholder notes a trend or event with sufficient importance to prompt a "consideration" or create a "concern." A consideration suggests an opportunity. A stakeholder sees or hears about something that appears to be useful, such as a new I-business idea that connects information platforms or an approach to customer service that has startling qualities. The claim points to the opportunity. The message is usually clear cut—let's put the opportunity to use. To make this argument, a proponent must be clear about how the opportunity would work and its expected benefits. The difficulty here is to recognize relevant considerations. A decision maker who listens selectively to claimants, based solely on their influence, can miss good ideas. Ways to uncover these ideas are offered later in this chapter.

A claim that stems from a consideration appears much like a claim prompted by a concern. Both call for action with an idea. A consideration-based claim hides little, but a concern-based claim often does, which can trap the unsuspecting decision maker. The claim–concern link is often murky because concerns stem from a need. A stakeholder who sees a trend or event as posing a personal or organizational concern folds in a host of unspoken beliefs and aspirations to make a judgment about the need for action. The conclusion drawn becomes the claim (Toulmin, 1979). Unlike the consideration–claim link, the connection between the claim and its roots in a motivating concern can be visceral. A claimant may not understand the connection. For example, a sales manager loses patience with a series of fouled up orders that have delayed delivery (the concerns) and calls attention to logistical failures in distribution (the claim). The claim says nothing about the fouled up orders, so little is revealed about motivations. Decision makers who act on such claims have little insight into what needs fixing.

If you buy into a claim without understanding its motivating concerns, you can misdirect effort. The situation gets worse when the claim has no connection to the concerns of the other stakeholders or lacks the support of these stakeholders. In the logistical example noted previously, insiders may question the sales department's ordering practices (conflicting concerns) and customers may regard product quality (hidden concern) as more important than delivery time. When leaders rally people to act on a claim that overlooks important concerns, the resulting decision can become a debacle. To see how this can happen, let's explore two decision debacles, one with hidden concerns and another with conflicting concerns. Shell's disposal of the Brent Spar oil platform illustrates hidden concerns. The decision to launch the siege at Waco illustrates conflicting concerns. Tables 4.1 and 4.2 offer profiles of these two decisions.

|  | *Table 4.1* | |
|  | **FLOW OF EVENTS IN THE DEBACLES** | |
| Choices | Shell's Disposal of the Brent Spar | The Waco Siege |
|---|---|---|
| Actions before | Regulate spar to backup use<br><br>Ruptured tanks not repaired; sealed and filled with seawater<br><br>Refurbishing found to be uneconomical<br><br>Uncover disposal options | ATF bungles attempts to serve warrant for firearms violation (4 ATF officers and 2 Davidians killed)<br><br>FBI takes over and surrounds compound<br><br>Turn off power to compound, use noise<br><br>Negotiations<br><br>Negotiation and pressure<br><br>Plans for assault rejected by Reno |
| Pivotal decision | Deepwater disposal | Armed assault approved by Reno |
| Actions after | Defend position by attacking Greenpeace's claims<br><br>Capitulate<br><br>Dismantle Brent Spar in port | Seventy-six killed by fire and gunshots<br><br>Investigation to fix blame<br><br>Reno takes responsibility, offers resignation<br><br>ATF chief fired, bureau downgraded<br><br>Engagement tactics revised |

Source: Adapted from Nutt and Backoff (1992).

# Shell's Disposal of the Brent Spar

The Brent Spar is a floating oil storage facility and loading buoy 137 meters high, weighing 14,500 tons, and costing more than a billion dollars. The spar served as a tanker and loading facility for the entire Brent oilfield in the North Sea near Scotland. Completion of the Brent system pipeline

Table 4.2

THE DECISION DEBACLES

| Choices | Shell's Disposal of the Brent Spar | The Waco Siege |
|---|---|---|
| Claims | Deep-sea disposal of an oil platform is legal | ATF shootings demand prosecution |
| Core concerns/ considerations (a) Recognized | Ways to dispose of obsolete oil rigs | How to force a surrender |
| (b) Hidden | Potential opposition | Motives of key people |
| | Public Image | |
| Directions | Keep disposal costs "reasonable" | Arrest those responsible for law breaking |
| Options considered | Deep-sea disposal | Wait |
| | Dismantle on site in harbor | Attack |
| | Refurbish | Leave |
| Extent of search and innovation | Limited: variations of sink, refurbish options | Limited: ways to use force |
| Use of evaluation | Estimate disposal cost, employee injury rate | Minimal: loss of life estimates |
| Impact of evaluation | Made favored option seem desirable | None |
| | Stress technical criteria | |
| Barriers to action | Mobilization of opposition by Greenpeace | Police call for justice for their people |
| | | Public reaction to violence |
| Ethical concerns | Some problems of deep-sea disposal kept confidential | Apprehend lawbreakers or safety for innocents |
| | Overly optimistic environmental impact estimates | Self righteousness |
| | Inaccurate inventory of toxic waste | Downplay risks to Attorney General |
| | Improper environmental impact study (speed of structure deterioration) | Use bogus information |
| Barriers to learning | Commercial expediency | Punishment mentality |
| | Assume a license to operate | |
| | Seeing other oil company actions as unrelated | |
| | Precedent for future disposal | |

diminished the Brent Spar's importance, and discovery of ruptures in two of the spar's tanks called into question its structural integrity. The tanks were made watertight and filled with seawater, giving Shell time to look at the costs of refurbishing the spar. Company staff found that it would take $150 million and two to three years to do repairs. The time and cost figures persuaded Shell officials to decommission the spar.

Shell now faced a predicament: How to dispose of an obsolete oil rig. Company officials decided to take advantage of an international law that allowed deep-sea disposal. Crude oil was removed from the storage tanks and internal pipe work, and each was flushed with seawater. The contaminated seawater was pumped into a tanker and carted away for disposal. Buoyancy tanks were rigged to prevent flooding in preparation for dumping at a deep-sea site in the North Sea. Shell told government officials in the United Kingdom and Norway of their plans and the analysis that supported it and asked for approval. Approval was granted, and Shell made a public announcement indicating their intentions.

Company officials were shocked at the response. Just before disposal was to begin, Greenpeace activists began a high-profile publicity campaign. The activists flew to the spar by helicopter and boarded it, prompting a media feeding frenzy. From the deck of the spar, with worldwide media courage, Greenpeace spokespersons argued that the planned deep-sea dumping was environmentally irresponsible. The media trumpeted Greenpeace's accusations and support for the Greenpeace position was roused around the globe. Shell was forced to find another way to dispose of the Brent Spar.

What led Shell to this debacle? The company spent three years and millions of dollars to evaluate disposal options. Directions for the disposal were implicit but pointed toward keeping costs "reasonable." This led Shell officials away from questions about potential opposition and toward the technical problems of disposal. Three options were examined: onshore dismantling, in-field disposal near its current location, and a deepwater disposal. Options of refurbishing or minimal maintenance to continue the spar's use, rejected earlier on economic grounds, were revisited. The rehab option called for refitting and towing the spar to a new location. This was dismissed. No one would have any use for an obsolete, refitted oil platform. Little time or money was spent asking what the company hoped to achieve. Had the officials set a direction for the disposal, such as finding an environmentally responsible option acceptable to its stakeholders, they would have pushed a very different set of options into view.

Like so many debacles, evaluations soaked up most of the time and money. Technical questions dominated. There were concerns about vertical or horizontal dismantling: whether to drag the spar horizontally to a sheltered site to cut it up or to do so vertically at the current site. Some options were more difficult to carry out, making the loss of contaminants and accidental sinking near shore more likely. Technical difficulties, the risk to Shell's workforce, and the environmental impact of the options were measured. All were expressed in cost terms so cost became the primary consideration. An in-field disposal option, near the spar's current location, proved to be the least expensive but would lead to local environmental damage and fishing restrictions. Company officials found this unacceptable, and this option was discarded. This narrowed the choices to deep-water disposal and onshore dismantling. Onshore disposal called for nineteen marine and land operations, including repairing tanks at sea, rotating the spar to the horizontal, towing, loading parts onto a cargo vessel, off loading, and disposing of waste material—all of which posed considerable danger of worker fatalities. The onshore option also seemed to increase the environmental hazard because mishaps were more likely. Lawsuits, fines, and environmental cleanup costs would make any mishap very costly to the company. Deep-sea disposal was selected because it posed less environmental risk, had less expense, and would be easier to plan for than onshore dismantling.

Company officials saw themselves as environmentally responsible. After all, they had rejected the least costly option of in-field disposal because of its environmental impact and had considered environmental concerns before settling on a deep-sea disposal. Plans called for the spar to be sunk in 2,000 meters of water, 240 kilometers from shore, at a location with little marine life on the seabed. Contaminants such as radioactive salts in the sludge would be diluted, limiting their impact to a few hundred meters from the spar's resting place.

Others saw it differently. Greenpeace's high-profile publicity campaign called Shell's plans "environmentally irresponsible." Some of the Greenpeace concerns were valid: Shell had suppressed some of the results of analyses; the toxicity of the contaminants had been understated; the spar's inventory was inaccurate; and the environmental impact study was faulty. When company officials made their case in response to the Greenpeace claims, it became apparent that some of Shell's claims supporting the deep-sea option were overly optimistic.

Greenpeace was more concerned with precedent than company analyses. To them the spar symbolized the way an industrialized society goes about disposing of the waste it produces. Global headlines labeled Shell an "environmentally irresponsible company." Governments that had approved the plan backpedaled. Consumer boycotts, some actively encouraged by politicians, most notably in Germany, began. There were outbreaks of violence and threats to Shell employees. Shell ignored the public outcry, sought and received a reaffirmation of support from the British government, and proceeded with their plan. Consumer boycotts ensued, and the loss of goodwill began to damage Shell's brand names. With the exception of Britain and Norway, all EU governments now backed Greenpeace's position. Opposition persisted even after Greenpeace's claims about toxicity and structural integrity of the Brent Spar were shown by Shell to be grossly inaccurate. The press noted that Shell had overstated its position as well, contending there would be 30 tons of sludge when it was actually 75 tons. The press called the Greenpeace inaccuracies justified because they created "balance."

The public outcry caught Shell by surprise. Although there has been plenty of bad press for big oil, company officials failed to connect the outrage over the Exxon *Valdez* and other oil spills to their actions. Both sides of the controversy worried about precedent. Future disposal costs and restrictions worried Shell officials. The public worried that deep-sea dumping by Shell would prompt others to follow this practice, with long-term damage to the deep-sea ecosystem. The principles behind this position slowly emerged on the "screens" of Shell officials. A few days before Shell was to sink the spar, Shell officials realized that their plan was no longer tenable. If they went ahead and exercised their legal right to sink the spar, the company's "license to operate" would be called into question, if not revoked, by the public. Shall had lost people's trust and had to regain it.

How did Shell get so far off track? Company records show that officials paid little attention to what they wanted to realize as an outcome. This caused them to attack symptoms, how to dispose of the rig and the disposal cost, and to ignore deeper questions about the deep-sea environment. Had Shell framed things as an environmental issue, different options would have emerged. Shell had some environmental awareness, but it remained a secondary consideration.

There were ethical dilemmas. Data were fudged. Reports suppressed. And Shell's motivation to keep the disposal affordable was not revealed. Failing to see how oil companies' actions had become interdependent delayed learning. The public had become outraged by big oil's indifference to the environment and its failure to make amends when disasters occur. These concerns had mounted until people were ready to pounce on any offender, particularly when something could be headed off. Had Shell seen this, officials might have probed beyond the obvious and asked deeper questions about the results they wanted and were apt to get if commercialism was the only consideration.

Shell officials formed a distorted view of the debacle. Heinz Rothermond, a managing director, saw the outrage as "unprecedented" and merely "symbolic." Thinking about the public's reaction to oil disasters would change this, as would a longer term outlook that considered future disposals and their cumulative impact. Shell's emphasis on disposal economics swept away concerns about reputation, long-term ecological dangers of deep-sea dumping, and the prospect of stricter regulations should their actions appear irresponsible. Had Shell looked at their stakeholders broadly and at worst case scenarios, such concerns would have emerged. Shell did allow environmental protection to win out, but the public saw this outcome as being forced on Shell rather than being prompted by social responsibility. Shell did learn by seeing how public opinion can affect their bottom line, and today Shell takes a broader view of company stakeholders. Not all companies are this open to introspection. Covering up errors, such as the toxic waste estimates, could have kept people in a defensive posture. Shell's ability to get beyond this is a valuable lesson in learning.

## The Waco Siege

The Waco debacle led to eighty-two deaths: four law enforcement officers and seventy-eight Branch Davidians. Collateral damage included a sharp drop of confidence in the FBI and other law enforcement agencies. Many believe law enforcement agencies are ill equipped to deal with confrontations and are prone to vengeance and that law enforcement officials tolerate ineptness and encourage overly aggressive behavior.

The Branch Davidians, a Mount Carmel community established by a disaffected Seventh Day Adventist, sparked the confrontation. Davidian history suggests motives. After the death of their founder, the Davidians experienced a long decline. Membership dropped from ten thousand to thirty-five by the late 1970s. David Koresh took over leadership of the Davidians in 1983 and prompted a modest revival by stressing fundamental Bible teachings, fellowship, and cohesiveness. According to observers (Voss, 1997), Koresh solidified his position with a prediction that the book of Revelation would be realized by an attack on the community. Observers claimed Koresh saw himself as the seventh and final messenger of God who would restore things before the Second Coming of Christ. He taught his followers that they had been chosen to fight the final battle of Armageddon. After several reports and loads of independent analyses, observers continue to debate whether Koresh was delusional or just another con man. There was little doubt that Koresh used religion to deceive people or that his followers were highly communal and susceptible to his authoritarian leadership. The survivalist mentality fostered led to stockpiling weapons and food at Mt. Carmel. Koresh allegedly told cult members to stay in the compound until all were killed to prompt "God's judgment" and the beginning of a "new age" (Voss, 1997).

In early 1993 rumors surfaced that an arsenal was being built at Mt. Carmel that included automatic weapons and other weaponry prohibited by law. This prompted the Bureau of Alcohol, Tobacco, and Firearms (ATF) to get a search warrant. The ATF gathered in front of the compound and practiced for days. The parading about suggested a confrontation when a simple knock on the front door may have been all that was needed to serve the warrant. When the ATF agents finally descended on the compound to serve the warrant, a shootout ensued in which four agents and two Davidians were killed and twenty agents were wounded. The bungled attempt by the ATF to serve the warrant prompted U.S. Attorney General Janet Reno to call in the FBI. An expert team of FBI negotiators and behavioral experts initiated talks with the Davidians as SWAT teams and the FBI's elite

Hostage Rescue Team (HRT) took up positions around the perimeter of the compound. Reports show that the FBI believed the compound contained more than a hundred armed men, women and children, and a year's supply of food.

People in law enforcement roles, and their supporters, demanded that the Davidians who had killed law enforcement officers be arrested and prosecuted. The rage being expressed can be summed up by the views of R. J. Craig, leader of the HRT team, who said, "a crime has been committed and I'm talking about murder . . . and (we) must do something about it" (*Frontline*, 1995). As pressure grew, the FBI's tactics changed from conciliatory negotiation, to tactical pressure with negotiation, to pressure alone.

The change in tactics was unfortunate. Early negotiations had met with some success. Within four days, twenty-one children left the compound and Koresh agreed to surrender. When Koresh recanted, claiming "God told him to wait," the FBI Ground Commander Jeff James and HRT leader Craig, over the objections of the negotiating team and the FBI's behavioral experts, began to crank up the pressure. First, the FBI turned off electrical power to the compound. This was followed by blasting recordings of dying animals and the chants of Tibetan monks over loudspeakers and shining high-intensity lights into the compound throughout the night. The FBI hoped this would raise questions about Koresh's control of the situation and stress the others, prompting more to leave the compound. It had the opposite effect.

Observers report conflicts between the negotiators and the tactical (SWAT and HRT) units and little coordination (Stone, 1993). FBI behaviorists recommended against direct confrontation. Tactical units ignored this and paraded Bradley armored vehicles in front of the compound as negotiations were being carried out. Pressure being employed by the tactical units suggested that negotiators had little influence and were not trustworthy. Even so, fourteen adults left the compound in the next sixteen days, and more might have come out had negotiations been seen as more credible. There were uncertainties. Should negotiators treat Koresh as if he was the Messiah or stress his self-interests? There were concerns of mass suicide. This risk seemed quite real given the behavior of other cults, such as the Jonestown mass suicide. Koresh was confronted with this and, according to eyewitnesses, said: "I'm not going to commit suicide. If I did I'd be lost eternally." The children who left the compound, according to the psychiatrist who interviewed them, reported talk of suicide among the adults, creating more ambiguity. This led to an FBI memo that concluded Koresh had taught people that if he dies they are to "follow him," even if this means killing themselves (Dennis, 1993). The FBI interpreted an order by Koresh for mass suicide as the ultimate in control over a group, and Koresh appeared to seek such control in all his actions.

The stalemate dragged on, prompting a meeting between the on-site team leaders, which resulted in a briefing of Reno. The tactical team leaders told her the remaining Davidians would not leave voluntarily and recommended tear gas to force them out of the compound. Reno stalled, asking for an assessment of the medical dangers and military soundness of the plan. The FBI assured Reno the tear gas was not flammable and pressured her to act on their plan. The press escalated the pressure by pushing for a rapid resolution of the confrontation. *Frontline* said, "You can't just let these people sit." Still Reno waited for further information. At this point a report surfaced that Koresh had molested children, and this sealed the Davidians' fate. Later Reno could not recall who had made this claim, could not find the report, and offered no evidence of molestation or abuse.

On April 17, fifty-one days after the standoff began, Reno approved the plan and advised President Clinton of her action. The FBI used the tear gas the next day. A fire broke out that swept the compound, and seventy-six bodies were found in the debris, including seventeen children. Thirteen adults and three children died of gunshot wounds. It appeared the fire had been set deliberately. Evidence was found that flammable oil had been spread throughout the compound. Survivors contend that tear gas and gunfire were responsible for the fire.

The Waco debacle can be traced to a lack of direction and poor intelligence. Arresting people who wounded and killed ATF agents was the implicit purpose and was never challenged by anyone in authority. This direction made it easy to dismiss the "wait" and "leave" options and to stress the "attack" option. To wait, the FBI had to commit to a prolonged siege of the compound that would delay bringing the Davidians to justice. A political blood bath seemed likely, reminiscent of the hostage fiasco in Iran during the Carter years. If food supplies could last a year, waiting seemed unthinkable. If the FBI left, some of the guilty might escape. Both the leave and the wait options had the risk of a mass suicide and putting children in harm's way. The implicit aim of punishing Davidian killers drew the FBI toward an attack option.

Intelligence was faulty. According to experts, the FBI failed to recognize that they were dealing with a violent sect. The FBI made no effort to understand Koresh's religious convictions, overlooking ways to reach him and his followers through the sect's beliefs. Had the situation been treated as dealing with a violent sect, waiting and negotiation, used in prison riots with hostages, would have had more credibility. Safety for hostages in such situations is always paramount. Better intelligence would have tipped the direction toward safety and away from revenge. Embracing an inappropriate direction prompts people to seek the wrong result.

Waco brought out the blame mongers, as do all debacles. Committees were empanelled to investigate, the press called for scapegoats, zealots used the situation to push their causes, and opportunists wrote books. The Treasury Department, home of the ATF, issued a long report. The Justice Department did the same, focusing on the FBI's role. Congress investigated and issued a partisan response. The party out of power claimed a whitewash, in which "politics were being danced on the graves of federal law enforcement officers." The party in power called the report "political chest beating." Zealots exploited the situation to further their causes. NRA supporters claimed the Clinton administration set up the situation to muster support for a total gun ban. ACLU supporters wanted to rein in out-of-control law enforcement officers prone to using deadly force and physical abuse, to stop entrapment, and to put limits on the rules of engagement. Others called for suspending constitutional protections to disband paramilitary groups.

Defensive behavior from those who could be held accountable grew with the blame mongering. An FBI spokesman claimed that agents were under orders, making actions taken at Waco beyond their control. Larry Potts, a senior FBI officer who was later demoted, scoffed at the notion of missed opportunities. Jack Zimmerman, a lawyer, testified that he had worked out a surrender plan with Koresh. People on the scene said that the FBI was unwilling to wait "10 more days." The ATF report claimed they were not equipped to handle operations like Waco. Ignoring this, the ATF director was sacked and five others suspended. The director's successor, John Magaw, refused congressional requests for personnel records of all those involved with the Waco fiasco, arguing that data was being sought indiscriminately, which was likely.

Some years later, new revelations show that the FBI used flammable tear gas canisters, involved the Delta Force in the operation against federal law, and may have shot at Davidians from helicopters. This prompted a new investigation. New questions arose. Did the FBI lie to Reno? The FBI appears to have hidden a videotape that shows the signature of a flammable tear gas grenade. After the siege, the Texas Rangers spotted such a canister and asked an FBI agent about it. The agent replied, "We'll get back to you on that," but never did. The canister disappeared. Was the Delta Force, a military unit, used in a domestic operation in violation of federal law? Did FBI personnel fire at the Davidians? These are grave questions, but they may have no bearing on the outcome. Films show flammable canisters harmlessly bouncing off buildings. These at least fell nowhere near where the fires started.

Ethical dilemmas arose. There seems to have been a snowballing of self-righteousness about the loss of life. The longer law enforcement agents were involved in the standoff, the greater their frustration. This frustration grew until their desire to arrest people overrode their concerns for the children's safety.

In sharp contrast to all this blame mongering and scapegoating, Reno offered to resign, accepting full responsibility despite being given misinformation. This standup performance may have saved her job. It also led to moving away from blame to making corrections based on the learning about the experience. New rules of engagement were developed, which led to a peaceful end for the eighty-one-day standoff by the Montana Freeman in 1996.

## Distorted Claims

A claim and the arena of action it suggests will mislead you if the concerns of stakeholders are not fully understood. The Shell and Waco debacles show how hidden or conflicting concerns distort the claim and trap the decision maker.

### Hidden Concerns

Shell sought a disposal option for an obsolete oil rig. The company wanted a solution that was cost-effective. This led them to make disposal cost a bigger concern than environmental protection. Deep-sea dumping was legal, so Shell's management fashioned a claim that introduced their favored action. Company officials believed they were acting responsibly because the costs and dangers of dismantling the Brent Spar and dumping at different locations had been considered.

Shell's officials believed they had been candid. They had consulted with the governments of Norway and the U.K. to get approval for their deep-sea dumping plans and shared most, if not all, of the analysis that supported it. Shell officials defined their stakeholders much more broadly than did decision makers in the EuroDisney, Pinto, BeechNut, and Nestle debacles and still failed. Company officials were stunned at the public outcry provoked by Greenpeace's activism.

Shell officials paid little attention to public unrest about oil company irresponsibility building on the crests of periodic price gouging, oil spills, and stonewalling with legal action to slow environmental cleanups. Shell's officials saw past actions of their company as different from the pack and believed the public would accept their claim and trust them to make a responsible decision. Shell could not imagine being lumped with Exxon and their ilk. These beliefs blinded Shell officials. The notion of a public stakeholder and the public's concerns about deep-sea dumping were overlooked. The prospect of companies around the globe being allowed to dump anything they wished into the deep-sea environment galvanized new concerns about big oil. Greenpeace gave these concerns a voice. This invalidated Shell's claim, rendering their analysis and careful negotiations useless. The immediate company concern of finding an inexpensive disposal site created a trap that kept the company officials from looking for deeper concerns about the environment and the prospect of stricter and more oppressive regulations if their actions appeared to be irresponsible.

### Conflicting Concerns

The Waco siege was prompted by a concern that weapons were being stockpiled at the Branch Davidian compound. This concern led to a claim that called for a search of the compound. The outcome of the botched attempt to serve a search warrant prompted new concerns and new claims. All along this unfortunate path, unresolved disagreements created one trap after another that ensnared Reno and her agents. Misconceptions mounted until serving a simple warrant had morphed into a claim of forcing surrender. The motives of the key players and their concerns were never challenged and others were never understood. Let's review a few. Police and police supporters wanted revenge for the loss of life of "their people." The agents on the scene were spoiling for a fight so they could exact revenge, calling it "justice." Koresh's motives were never clear. There was evidence that he was delusional, thinking a confrontation would bring on Armageddon in which he and his people could be saved. There was also evidence that he was a con artist whose sole motivation was to control and exploit people. Claims about Koresh take shape quite differently depending on the motive one assumes. The negotiation team was concerned about the safety of the children and others who might have been trapped by the extremists and made claims about the need to ensure their safety. Reno became trapped by these conflicting claims. Rather than trying to reconcile them, she chose to pick the one that seemed the most compelling.

## Blunders Prompting the Claim Trap

Blunders of premature commitments, misused resources, and poor practice can lead you to accept faulty claims. Let's see how this took place in the Shell and Waco debacles.

### Premature Commitments

Shell officials had no need to rush in making a disposal decision. The Brent Spar was secure at its old site and could have been left there as a debate about disposal was played out in a public arena. There was no timetable to serve a warrant on the Davidians. With the compound surrounded, where could they go? Concerns about how the Davidians would respond called for caution, not rapid action.

In both debacles there was mounting pressure to "get on with it." Artificial pressure to act makes it difficult to seek out hidden concerns and reconcile conflicting ones. Managers who make claims in the face of such pressure are not likely to pause and look further. This makes it difficult to appreciate the concerns of others and the competing claims each would prompt. Pressure goads you into selecting among competing claims instead of finding concerns suggesting a claim all could agree to.

## Misused Resources

Little time or money was spent exploring claims to find the concerns behind them. Decision makers at Shell invested in analysis to find the best disposal option. Had a claim been put in environmental terms, environmentally friendly options as well as low-cost ones could have emerged. The ATF and FBI invested in a show of force to make the Davidians capitulate. Both the ATF and the FBI resisted allocating time or money to negotiations to discover what was motivating the Davidians' actions. Claims about the Davidians and what they would do were little more than guesses based on the speculations of uninformed observers, such as the media.

## Poor Practices

Claims are often dictated by caprice in a debacle. The claimant with the loudest voice and the most clout captures the attention of a decision maker (Cyert and March, 1963). Little or no intelligence about the claim is collected, although such intelligence is always recommended (e.g., Simon, 1977). The claims made by the most vocal and powerful get acknowledged; others are ignored. Little in the way of claim analysis or uncovering competing claims occurs.

The FBI made loud and persistent claims about the need to apprehend wrongdoers. Claims about safety and Davidian motivations were swept aside by the FBI's strident position. No attempt was made to verify or explore the FBI's claims or to identify the claims of others to uncover and consider the concerns prompting them. Shell's management wanted to be rid of a troublesome disposal problem. Claims about cost swept aside hidden concerns about long-term environmental impact and precedent. Gathering intelligence about such concerns could have headed off both of these debacles.

Debacles have little in the way of decision-making practice to critique. Claims emerge from the vocal and the powerful. Defensible arguments are accepted without any analysis or attempts to find other views. Some stakeholders' claims are overlooked and conflicting claims are never resolved. When conflicting and hidden concerns emerge in such situations, the claim used to mobilize action will seem wrong-headed. This brings critics into the fray who debate the claim but not the concerns behind it. The ensuing conflict can doom a decision.

## Origins of Faulty Claims

Decision makers, like all human beings, have difficulty extracting diagnostic information from the signs and signals attracting their attention. Errors or misunderstandings arise from availability and vividness biases (Hogarth, 1980; Nisbitt and Ross, 1989). Let's look at the effects these biases have.

### Availability Biases

Decision makers are prone to using information that is readily available, overlooking information that may be more diagnostic. This is often done spontaneously and, to a large extent, indiscriminately without any rules to guide what is and is not accepted as fact. For instance, the astute subordinate reminds his or her boss of "successes" just before raises are given. A mediocre but politically astute subordinate can dupe the boss in this way by offering information that is timely, but not diagnostic. Decision makers are drawn to available information because of anchoring, personal experience, and selective perception.

People become anchored by the first information they observe and give it more weight than information that arrives later on. For instance, Disney management continued to fret about past park problems, Shell worried about regulation because several governments had threatened a "windfall" profit tax during the OPEC embargo, and Nestle refused to let go of its belief that third world sales were essential for company success.

People treat a personal experience as if it represented a random sample that can be generalized. If your first trip to Las Vegas results in a big loss, you are apt to agree with the old adage: "There are two kinds of people that leave Las Vegas—losers and liars." People who stand in an unemployment line overestimate the unemployment rate. Like the Las Vegas losers and the unemployed, decision makers focus their powers of observation when confronted with a claim. The context in which to judge urgency and importance is missing, making the claim seem more urgent and important than analysis would reveal. Your feet do not hurt unless you stand in the line. The threat of retribution was very real for Reno, as were the quandaries of an obsolete oil rig disposal to Shell. Decision makers focus their attention on events that have meaning for them. This can lead you to buy into claims that misrepresent what is at issue.

People are drawn to things that have personal significance. The testimony of a graduate of your educational institution at the White Water hearings during the Clinton administration is more memorable than the testimony of someone you have never met. Have you read a letter to the editor in *Time* magazine from someone from your hometown—even though you had never met the writer and have no interest in the topic? The successes and failures of people we know can be riveting, that of others less so. Decision makers are drawn to claims when they share a sense of identity, kinship, or prior association with the claimant or the claim. We see things *selectively*. We are confronted with much more information than we can process in a meaningful manner. Being continually assaulted with information forces us to be selective. Rules are applied that let us see only what we are willing to see. This leads you to recognize some claims and dismiss others. Experience, anticipation, and causality biases filter claims in unfortunate ways.

Experience is a "great teacher," but it tends to focus a decision maker on claims that can be understood. Claims that are inconsistent with that experience are dismissed. Those in marketing are apt to view claims in marketing terms, accountants in financial terms, strategists in new product ideas, and so on. The decision maker with a marketing background is more apt to accept claims that express concerns about changes in consumer taste and market share. Those with a financial background would be drawn to claims based on cash flow or profitability concerns. A claim is salient if it corresponds to your experience. Claims that do not are more apt to be dismissed or discounted. The FBI agents saw things in punishment terms; the hostage negotiation team saw them in safety terms.

Decision makers anticipate what will make a claim salient, and by then looking for this information they create a self-fulfilling prophecy. A critic who publicly opposed an acquisition is apt to look for information that documents postacquisition problems, such as culture clashes and the inability to exploit market channels. Industry observers now contend that the merger of Chrysler and Daimler-Benz combined incompatible cultures and that the synergy in their product lines was more apparent than real. Shell officials looked for data that confirmed their preferred deep-sea disposal option and discounted information that raised questions about it. Reno wanted to avoid a drawn out siege and the media feeding frenzy it was sure to bring. This gave information supporting rapid action more salience for her.

You are drawn to claims that agree with your notions of causality. This can be demonstrated by an interviewer who looks for information that confirms his or her first impression. Information that refutes this position is discounted by putting it in a "special case" category. If an opponent discovers that the favored candidate for a vice president position had been fired from a previous job, proponents would call the firing a "local personality conflict." Characterizing it as "local" provides a basis for disregarding the information. Ford, Disney, and Nestle officials dismissed the arguments of critics in this way, believing that they had the company's best interest at heart and that the critic did not.

## Vividness Biases

Decision makers are overly impressed by vivid information. TV ads for Volvos that begin with pictures of beautifully restored MGBs and Thunderbirds capture the attention of the car-conscious consumer because of their vividness. To be vivid, information must be emotionally appealing, concrete, image provoking, and personal, like the restored MGBs and Thunderbirds. As G. B. Shaw observed, "the death of a single person is a tragedy, the death of millions is a mere statistic."

Experiences with a powerful impact evoke images that influence how we see ourselves and others. Well-reasoned arguments are swept away by the vivid concern. Decision makers in the BeechNut, Nestle, DIA, EuroDisney, and Waco debacles had vivid images of their concerns. BeechNut's top management had been put on notice that their jobs were on the line unless they maintained the company's recent increase in profitability, which in their mind demanded a low-cost supplier. Threatening one's job is pretty vivid. Officials at Ford were seduced by the original hype of a

2,000-pound car for $2,000. A recall would put the Pinto's success in jeopardy. Nestle officials were obsessed by the loss of market share in their infant formula product line, Disney by Walt's Dream, Pena by the allure of a new airport, and Reno by a drawn out siege and the frenzied media attention it would create. These powerful images swept aside other claims and the concerns behind them that would challenge the claim.

Emotional appeal stems from personal attachments. The plight of someone you know has more salience than the plight of a stranger. People can recall specific events that surround a family member's death such as time of day, weather, location, and so on. Decision makers faced with a claim that appears to have serious consequences for themselves and their friends find it more important than a pallid claim that involves people they do not know.

Detail and specificity create vividness. Indicating who is effected, what decisions failed, and how things can turn into a debacle makes a claim *concrete* and thereby more vivid. These concrete images seem to demand attention, making it difficult to learn about negative instances and missing information for which concreteness is lacking. Managers swept away by a claim about the virtues of a new information system are not apt to ask about downtime and software adaptability. Information about the virtues of the system is more available and more apt to be accepted as supporting the claim. BeechNut was pulled toward information depicting the consequences of a cost increase in their apple juice and away from the consequences, to them and the company, of a disclosure of inventory dumping.

A claim's proximity or closeness in terms of its time, location, and familiar surroundings also creates vividness. A claim that calls attention to last week's cost overrun that was experienced in your plant is more vivid than a cost overrun a year ago in a colleague's plant. First-hand experience creates vividness. Eyewitnesses to crimes call for stiffer sentences than do people who just hear about crimes. Smart defense lawyers use this in jury selection. Managers often note, "I was there." Go see for yourself. Personally observed information is given more weight than other kinds of information. This makes decision makers skeptical of computer printouts, statistical analyses, and even conclusions in respected journals until they have witnessed the claim being made. These motivations favor claims that are provincial and explain the reluctance of managers to accept innovations.

## Taking Charge

A triggering claim motivated by concerns or considerations filled with availability and vividness biases can be misleading or even wrong headed, but the forces at work to act on it are powerful and difficult to set aside. When confronted with such a claim, you can expand your horizons by opening up to stakeholders that have yet to be heard. This requires an investment in intelligence gathering.

Taking charge calls for increasing the pool of intelligence used to make a claim. Crafty decision makers defer claim making until concerns and considerations are better understood. To do this, focus groups, much like those used in marketing, are employed to identify the views of important stakeholders. Several such groups are often needed to uncover the scope of concerns and considerations held by stakeholders. Investing a few hours to do this will pay big dividends. Next we will consider the makeup of these groups, how they are formed, the procedures to follow, and ways to use the results.

### Participants

Stakeholders include technical experts, internal people with relevant experiences, suppliers, stockholders, creditors, customers, alliance partners, supportive sister organizations, competitors, the communities in which the company operates, environmental groups, the general public, and still others. Polling each as a constituency to uncover their views opens up the landscape to important cues that indicate what a decision is about (Freeman, 1984). Looking for both positive and negative effects on each constituency enhances your credibility as a decision maker by showing that a wide variety of views of claims and supporting concerns and considerations have been sought out and carefully considered. This helps you to mobilize support and makes it easier to defend an action that may disadvantage some stakeholders.

Not all constituencies will have an interest in the decision. Shell's disposal decision had a larger impact on people outside the organization than inside it. Had Shell involved people who represented views about dumping in the locations thought to be feasible, groups with environmental concerns would have been heard. This would have given top management at Shell a heads-up on how the company was viewed and the nature of emerging objections to the planned deep-sea dumping. Reno had lots of insider information from law enforcement agencies but was shut off from concerns in the nearby Waco community, experts with knowledge of hostage negotiations, and public concerns about militant groups and police abuses of power. Companies are often insular. By turning inward, officials overlook the image created by their actions that can turn off potential customers and future business, as in the EuroDisney, Nestle, and Ford debacles.

## Which Stakeholders?

The positions and interests of stakeholders, and the centers of power they represent, suggest people to involve in focus groups. This can be done systematically by having knowledgeable insiders, such as members of a top management team (TMT), uncover and then rank stakeholders. To do this ranking, stakeholders are rated in terms of their prospects of supporting or opposing the decision and then ranked according to their importance. A 1-to-5 rating captures the intensity of the expected opposition or support position, and a 1-to-10 ranking can be used to specify importance. The rankings are tallied for the raters and arrayed on a grid to classify stakeholders, as shown in Figure 4.1 (see Nutt and Backoff, 1992, for additional details on the ranking procedures). The number and nature of the stakeholders in each of the grid categories suggests the amount of effort required. Large numbers of stakeholders in the antagonistic category suggests opposition can be expected and whom to target in an attempt to win them over. Stakeholders in the antagonistic group are prime candidates for a focus group. Those seen as advocates can be mobilized to help in handling those in the antagonistic group. Problematic stakeholders are targeted for attention in the next stage of the process dealing with implementation.

## Why a Focus Group?

When well managed, a focus group provides several benefits that more than justify the time and cost. Such a group offers a summation of views, which can highlight key concerns and considerations. A group will screen out erroneous and unfounded concerns. Suggestions and ideas from the best informed sway others. A group heightens interest in a task, making it seem important to all and enhancing the prospect that people will disclose their concerns and considerations. A large pool of information is created, bringing to light previously unknown difficulties and predicaments that people have.

Figure 4.1
**STAKEHOLDER ASSESSMENTS**

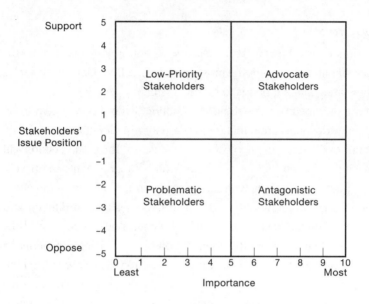

Source: Adapted from Nutt and Backhoff (1992).

## Managing Focus Groups Made Up of Stakeholders

Complex interpersonal dealings among the members of a group develop as they engage in stressful tasks, such as identifying concerns and seeking agreement about those that have the greatest importance (Collins and Guetzkow, 1964). Obstacles may be erected in these interpersonal dealings that keep a group from running efficiently and effectively. Interpersonal obstacles arise from beliefs about other members. An inferior member depresses the team's efforts and damages its results. Groups are more effective if members see one another as competent. Careful selection and demonstrations of competence, citing member experience and accomplishments, help to overcome this. The results of a group can be damaged by status distinctions. Those who see themselves as "high power" talk to those thought to have "low power" until their status is clear and then restrict their communication to the other high power members. This alienates individuals seen as having low power and limits their contribution or provokes them to disrupt the group's work. To overcome the difficulties stemming from power differences, involve people with about the same status and form groups made up of people representing the same stakeholder constituency.

## Group Process

Interpersonal and structural obstacles arise as a group uncovers concerns and considerations and finds the most crucial ones. Both kinds of obstacles must be managed if a group is to be successful.

Some group members withhold information, even if it is known to be important. Individuals are reluctant to share information that can damage their status or the status of people they must cater to. The group's efforts will improve if these contributions are teased out. Nonparticipants can have a chilling effect, as do people without a clear-cut role. To improve the effectiveness of a group, draw out people who find speaking up difficult and clarify roles. The facilitator should describe each person's role and how the group can benefit from this kind of contribution. People experience "participation penalties" if their ideas are not readily accepted, which encourages a fight or flight response. Neither is helpful. If people can voice their ideas without sanctions or criticism, the group's results will improve. People are drawn to power and try to exercise it by controlling the conversation in a group. "Rhetoric leaders" have a point of view that is either off-putting, because it runs counter to what others in the group believe, or egotistical, because they dominate the discussion and drive out the contributions of others. The rhetoric leader will task those interested in resolving the questions put to a group and create conflict. Limits on the influence of people who exhibit this behavior are needed.

A silent reflection group process (SRGP) provides a way around these difficulties. An SRGP encourages disclosure, ensures participation, eliminates participation penalties, enables everyone to have an equal voice, and nullifies the power-hungry member (Delbecq et al., 1986). The SRGP has four steps. First, a facilitator explains what is wanted, what the decision appears to be about, and the need to understand all relevant considerations and concerns. The group is then told that their purpose is to advise the company about their views. To do so, the company wants to understand the considerations and concerns of each group member.

Information is collected by having group members silently list both the claims they believe are warranted and the concerns and considerations that prompt them. Some concerns may yield several conclusions stated as claims. Members list their claims and the supporting concerns or considerations without discussion until all views are fully documented. Next, the claims and concerns or considerations are recorded on three separate sheets to de-couple them. Each member is asked to offer one claim and one supporting concern or consideration on each pass. The facilitator lists them by going around the group one person at a time until all are recorded. Next, discussion is used to elaborate, explore, and explain. At this point, the facilitator allows questions for clarification. Group members, in the last step, vote to select the most important claims and the concerns and considerations that support them.

## Using the Results

The decision maker compares the claims and their motivating concerns and considerations across the stakeholder groups. The claims are plotted on a grid (see Figure 4.1) to see where the arenas of action overlap and which of the stakeholder groups agree and which disagree, and the importance of each. The decision maker looks for a set of claims that identifies an arena of action that can be accepted by most stakeholders, the most influential, those the company must cater to, and so on. Several arenas of action may be suggested by this analysis, and the decision maker uses acceptance, influence, or dependence criteria to select an arena. Knowing stakeholder objections provides insights, and steps can be taken to reassure or to offer a palliative to those constituencies whose considerations or concerns are not acted upon.

Some antagonist stakeholder groups may refuse to participate. To deal with such stakeholders, begin by heading off potential coalitions. Neutralize connections between low-priority and problematic stakeholders. Nestle could drive a wedge between groups that opposed them and take steps to prevent these groups from uniting with the World Health Organization. Use supporters to try to win over the problematic and then mount campaigns to manage antagonists, such as when Shell asked friendly government spokespersons to meet with representatives of those opposing the company. Work through the antagonistic stakeholder groups beginning with those that are least opposed before dealing with others. Continue to use information and support gathered in previous negotiations. The current negotiation can draw counterarguments from what was learned and what worked to pacify another antagonistic stakeholder group. Find ways to appease if support is still being withheld. Nestle could offer its marketing plans and ask people to identify objectionable practices, then fashion a marketing plan that eliminates these practices and ask for support. Determine whether any stakeholders in the antagonistic category must be surprised or kept in the dark until others have been consulted. Handle these groups after all the others have been consulted. If support is not possible, bargain to seek neutrality. To do this, ask for an arena of action that the antagonistic stakeholder can support. Look for an arena with a win–win in which all parties can agree that something should be done. Or find an arena that the strongly opposed do not care about so they will drop out. Use those in the advocate group to sell to the indifferent and the problematic, and then to bargain with an antagonistic stakeholder group, showing the extent of support. Target moderates in the problematic and low-priority categories for education attempts in the next stage (Chapter 5).

People who are consulted in this way are shown that you have gone to great lengths to uncover concerns and considerations. The show of good faith in broadly seeking out people's views demonstrates the importance of the decision and your commitment to getting to the bottom of things. Stakeholders are more apt to buy in if there has been broad consultation. This helps to spread the word to others, making the momentum essential to the decision-making effort easier to sustain.

## ▼ Key Points

- ▼ Seek out stakeholders with different points of view and ask each to provide a list of their claims and the concerns and considerations that prompt them before selecting the arena of action.
- ▼ Reconcile contradictions in the claims being offered by exploring the concerns and considerations supporting each. Refashion a claim that embraces the crucial concerns and important considerations.
- ▼ Find common themes in conflicting claims to make a diagnosis.

# The Traps in Unmanaged Social and Political Forces

$S$uccessful implementation calls for the understanding and careful management of people's "interests." If these interests can be uncovered and understood, the social and political forces that the interests stir up are usually manageable. In each of the debacles, implementation follows evaluation. When implementation is delayed until evaluation is complete, the social and political forces stirred up by the decision have been at work for some time. This chapter considers traps set when decision makers fail to head off the social and political forces by delaying implementation. We will look at ways to head off these forces with an appropriate implementation tactic.

## Forces That Block Decisions

Interests arise in perceptions about one's turf and the needs for achievement, self-esteem, recognition, security, social relationships, valued practices, and the like. People become aroused when such interests are put in jeopardy. The reasons for opposing a decision are not widely shared, so they are lost on the decision maker. An employee with a health problem, for example, may not share his or her reasons for opposing a decision that alters early retirement rules. Opposition takes shape in subtle ways through delay, token compliance, and attempts at negotiation to hold up a decision

or limit its use. Or, if opponents are powerful enough and sufficiently provoked, there may be a pitched battle to block a decision. More often resistance is tacit. The savvy decision maker heads off both types of resistance
by shaping the decision so practices, resources, and relationships valued
by people are retained.

Social and political forces were stirred up in the debacles when people's
worries were left to fester. Implementation in the debacles was treated as a
"mop-up" exercise in which the decision maker either sold a preferred
course of action or issued the equivalent of a decree calling for its adoption.
This places implementation at the end of the decision-making process and
increases the chance of failure threefold. To see how this takes place, let's
explore debacles using the failure-prone persuasion and edict implementation tactics. The acquisition of Snapple by Quaker shows how edicts are
used. The arena tax support decision shows the futility of persuasion. Tables
5.1 and 5.2 profile these decisions and the steps taken to make them.

*Table 5.1*
**FLOW OF EVENTS IN THE DEBACLES**

| Choices | Snapple Purchase by Quaker | Tax Support for Sports Arena |
|---|---|---|
| Actions before | Gatorade purchase<br><br>Board delegates broad authority to Smithburg<br><br>Rumors of Quaker takeover | Four failed attempts to increase taxes for the con-struction of an arena<br><br>Form loose confederation of city and company interests to get NHL expansion team |
| Pivotal decision | Purchase Snapple | Seek tax support |
| Actions after | Attempt to fix synergy problems<br><br>Attempt to revamp advertising<br><br>Labeling and packaging changes<br><br>Try to buy out independent bottlers to break contracts<br><br>Sell Snapple | Form consortium without Hunt<br><br>Build NHL arena with private money, donated land<br><br>Hunt builds privately financed soccer stadium with private money on public land |

## Quaker's Purchase of Snapple

Quaker is a highly diversified company with a one hundred year history. Products include premium ice teas, single-serve juice drinks and lemonades, hot cereals, pancake mixes, grain-based snacks, corn meal, hominy grits, value-added rice products, and sports beverages. Quaker's brands hold the number one or two spot for 85 percent of its product categories. Quaker has pursued an aggressive growth strategy, acquiring Stokely-Van Camp (makers of Gatorade), Continental Coffee, Adoria Pasta, and Snapple during this period.

William Smithburg, Quaker's CEO, masterminded these acquisitions, most notably the Gatorade purchase. His success was rooted in luck rather than in good decision-making practices. According to industry reports, Smithburg made his acquisition decisions impulsively. He based the acquisition of Gatorade on little more than his taste buds—he tried the product and liked it (Burns, 1996). Industry analysts were highly critical of the Gatorade purchase, but Smithburg proved them wrong by using innovative advertising to grow a $220 million purchase into one worth $3 billion. In the wake of this success, Quaker's board of directors gave Smithburg complete freedom in making future acquisitions. Smithburg's luck didn't hold, and his decision to acquire Snapple created a debacle that seriously damaged Quaker and ultimately cost Smithburg his job as well.

Smithburg's addiction to extreme sports is reflected in his business decisions. The thirst for thrills and success at beating the odds led him to target and acquire Snapple, another flashy brand he planned to promote following the formula used with Gatorade. Quaker's highly successful pet food and bean divisions were sold to raise $110 million of the $1.8 billion price tag. No effort was made to look at the possibility of borrowing or issuing stock to raise this sum. Due to complacency and fear of retaliation, no one challenged the Snapple purchase or any of the moves to finance it.

Concerns about growth prompted the Snapple decision. Gatorade had recently lost some market share, and Quaker had become a takeover target as its product lines matured. Smithburg set out to use new growth, and its debt, to head off a possible takeover. To reposition Quaker, Smithburg reverted to what had worked in the past—acquire a moribund product that

| | | |
|---|---|---|
| | *Table 5.2* | |
| | **THE DECISION DEBACLES** | |
| **Choices** | **Snapple Purchase by Quaker** | **Tax Support for Sports Arena** |
| Claims | Need flashy product to continue growth | A sports team enhances a city's economy and social life |
| Core concerns/ considerations (a) Recognized | Takeover target<br><br>Gatorade market share slipping | Fund constructed<br><br>Sell tickets |
| (b) Hidden | Threat to CEO in takeover | Extent of public support |
| Directions | Thwart a takeover | Make arena a reality |
| Options considered | Snapple, a splashy turnaround situation | Tax support<br><br>Private funding<br><br>Combination, without voter approval |
| Extent of search and innovation | None | Past deals and current practices |
| Use of evaluation | None (due diligence missing) | Minimal (cost estimates) |
| Impact of evaluation | None | None |
| Barriers to action | Performance accountability | Extent of public support |
| Ethical concerns | Personal interests over organizational ones<br><br>Scapegoats | Who pays, who benefits, who decides<br><br>Trade public schools for a sports team |
| Barriers to learning | Luck treated as good practice<br><br>Correction limited by original faulty direction | Misrepresent plans<br><br>Blame mentality<br><br>Fail to see image of bad faith |

he could market into a star. To do this, he skipped direction setting and search. Directions for the Snapple decision were not made public, and perhaps never codified. The company's long-standing but implicit strategic aim of growth seemed to dictate events without asking if growth remained the best objective for Quaker. Did the company need to take steps to thwart a possible takeover? In fact, what's wrong with a takeover? Takeovers are usually good news for shareholders as an average of 36 percent above market value is paid to purchase a company. But Smithburg had a lot to lose in such an event, and this hidden concern dictated his actions. His "golden boy" image would have little value after a takeover, particularly a hostile one. The Quaker board respected and deferred to Smithburg, enabling him to indulge his need to take risks. He was apt to have a more restricted role after a takeover or perhaps no role at all. This goaded Smithburg into making Quaker an unattractive takeover target through defensive restructuring. The Snapple deal appeared to have the desired result. Takeover talk was scotched on Wall Street and Quaker's stock fell by 10 percent. Without a board of directors to look out for stockholders' interests, these interests are apt to be subordinated to those of insiders. Would the Snapple purchase have been made if shareholder wealth was the strategic aim? A direction to increase shareholder wealth would have raised questions and opened the door to other ideas.

Smithburg's approach was novel, and eccentric. Tasting products to measure value does leave a few questions unanswered. Smithburg's tactics relied on past practice and the conspicuous solution. Benchmarking what others do can work, if the idea fits in its new locale. But Smithburg benchmarked his past successes without being clear about why he had been successful. Several important assumptions were made without testing any of them. Synergies were assumed. Unfortunately, Snapple had neither manufacturing nor distribution synergies with Gatorade. Snapple distributors would have to give up their lucrative supermarkets to carry Gatorade to its smaller outlets. Distributors needed the economies of scale in servicing large stores so there was little margin in Gatorade for them. Independent bottlers had long-term contracts to produce Snapple. Gatorade was centrally manufactured, thwarting manufacturing synergy. Smithburg assumed he could duplicate his success by advertising Snapple as he had Gatorade, but cutting-edge advertising is risky. Smithburg failed to discover that Snapple was carrying over $20 million in obsolete material because of poor inventory management.

Was the Snapple acquisition made to protect Smithburg's job and ego or to create shareholder wealth? His fiduciary duty to company shareholders seemed to be overlooked, posing one of several ethical dilemmas in this decision. Personal image also got in the way. Smithburg thrived on excitement, and industry observers claimed he was bored with the mundane but profitable core businesses at Quaker. He had received accolades for outsmarting Wall Street in the Gatorade deal and wanted to re-create this excitement with another acquisition. Pet food is boring, but a failing company that can be rescued—quite another matter! Self-righteousness posed yet another ethical trap. Blame was focused on others as Smithburg attempted to revive Snapple, firing executives who were unable to fix the synergy problems he created. Smithburg denied fault, avoided responsibility, and found others to shoulder blame; he then had to cover these tracks in a futile attempt to save his job.

With each missed performance target, Smithburg put more money into corrective efforts such as packaging, labeling, and advertising. As sales for Snapple continued to plummet, Quaker tried to renegotiate contracts and buy out Snapple's independent bottlers. This made corrections based on the original, faulty direction and ignored looking for a better direction to guide corrective action, such as creating shareholder wealth. Smithburg persisted in his quest by terminating managers who were unable to carry out his error-correction plans. He fabricated deficiencies to cover up his Snapple purchase oversights (Burns, 1996), even forcing out his heir apparent who had been groomed at Quaker for twenty-three years. Repeated failures of his corrective moves prompted Smithburg to tighten his control. His restless energy once lavished on highly visible public roles turned inward as he ditched most of his management team and delegated less than ever. The noose tightened with each corrective action that ignored the larger question of corporate well-being. Smithburg felt compelled to misrepresent the situation, conjuring up "spins" to offset the huge losses. Snapple was called an "exciting new beverage market" that has "domestic and international market expansion (with) the potential for double-digit sales and profit growth for years to come (and) an annual earning growth of at least 10%" (Quaker Annual Report, 1995). A move to dump Snapple and cut company losses was not discussible. This was abundantly clear to all, so no one proposed it.

Smithburg's success with Gatorade prevented learning. A windfall outcome after a faulty decision process reinforces bad tactics and creates overconfidence. It is difficult to learn when bad tactics are applied to a decision that has a good outcome. Smithburg covered up his true motives and his lack of due diligence in the Snapple acquisition. Substantial information was available about Snapple that would have dimmed the light of Snapple's apparent glow. Neither Smithburg nor his board, who must also bear responsibility for the debacle, did anything to explore competition in the beverage industry, the extent of synergy, signs of worry in bloated inventories, or marketing difficulties.

The huge losses incurred in the Snapple acquisition almost brought Quaker down. Things got so bad Quaker tried to package its entire beverage business, including Gatorade, just to dump Snapple. Two years after the Snapple acquisition Smithburg announced its sale to Triarc Corporation for $300 million, far below the $1.8 billion purchase price, and his intention to step down. Analysts at Sanford C. Bernstein noted that it would have been hard for Smithburg to keep his position considering the black mark left by the Snapple acquisition. He remains unemployed. The company was able to recoup $250 million in previously paid capital gains to soften the blow. Still, Quaker took a $1.4 billion loss in the first quarter of 1997, as well as operating losses of $85 million in 1996 alone.

## Tax Support for Nationwide's Sports Arena

For many years local visionaries in Columbus, Ohio, the fifteenth largest city in the United States, have lamented the city's cow-town image. Among the missing pieces was the repeated failure to attract a major league professional sports team. Recent events gave local visionaries new hope. Fat-cat major league sports team owners are pushing to improve their playing facilities to counter falling or negative margins. Luxury boxes provide a way to pump up the revenue stream, providing the funds to sign better players and remain competitive. Of course, it is these same owners and the outrageous contracts they have given players that create a need for new revenues. Nevertheless, owners threaten to relocate their teams unless taxpayers spring them from long-term stadium and arena leases, signed in good faith, and foot the bill to build new arenas or stadiums. Some cities with sports teams balk at being held hostage by what they see as greedy owners who created the very revenue shortfall the taxpayers are expected to remedy. Columbus visionaries saw all this as a chance to attract a disgruntled owner to their city.

Deals vary by city and owner. In Detroit, the Tiger baseball team ownership agreed to put up all the funds to build a new stadium if the city provided land and infrastructure improvements. Jack Kent Cook, the Washington Redskins owner, asked for a 50:50 deal. In Cincinnati, a relatively new multipurpose stadium on the Ohio riverfront, which housed both the Reds and the Bengals, was deemed unfit for rehabilitation by both teams. Both wanted new riverfront land and tax support to build a new stadium, and the taxpayers of Hamilton County agreed to a new tax to fund both stadiums. Demands are offered as non-negotiable, and teams threaten to move unless their demands are met. Cities bidding for teams are told that they must have an arena/stadium built and ready for use before the professional sports league, controlled by team owners, would even consider them for a team. Season ticket sales of two-thirds of an arena or stadium's seating capacity are also expected.

Teamless cities get involved in a one-sided courtship. City leaders are drawn into a no-win bidding war, much like Honda and Volkswagen prying funds from cities bidding for one of their factories. Negotiations must be handled with care. Owners of an existing team can get miffed and pull up a moving van. Leases are left for lawyers to work out. Loyal fans and decades of community support are dismissed without a second thought. Team owners on the move con communities to "up the ante," asking for more with each negotiation, and back out of commitments when a sweeter deal is offered.

Columbus leaders, frustrated by four previous failed attempts to attract a major league sports team, were prepared to jump at any chance to secure a team—despite the company they would be keeping. When the National Hockey League included Columbus as a potential site for an expansion team, it galvanized yet another effort. The lure of a team was irresistible, even though Columbus is hardly a hockey town. Local companies such as Nationwide, Bank One, and Worthington Industries offered to donate money and formed a "leadership team" with the mayor. Lamar Hunt, the Dallas-based owner of the local professional soccer team, the Crew, saw a chance to get an arena for his team that had been playing in Ohio Stadium, home of the OSU Buckeyes, and jumped into the fray. The Dispatch Printing Company, publishers of the only local newspaper, agreed to help. Local developers also jumped on board. The leadership team forged ahead by calling for a .5 percent sales tax to build two facilities, a hockey arena and an open-air soccer stadium, with taxpayer money on public land. The tax would cost each Columbus area taxpayer about $20 per year. The leadership team put up the money for the NHL's $100,000 application fee and forged ahead with the plans to put the tax proposal on the ballot in the next election as Issue 1.

The plan called for a three-year sales tax increase to raise $203.5 million, with the rest of the $300 million for the project coming from state grants, private funds, and interest. Money was to be raised in other ways as well, such as seat licenses and naming rights. Bank One offered to pay $35 million over eighteen years for naming rights. The package included a 21,000-seat arena for hockey costing $110 million, a 35,000-seat soccer stadium at $72.5 million, and $102.4 million for land and site improvements. The city and county were to donate the land, make road improvements, and clean up the proposed site—the old Ohio State Penitentiary, a long-standing Columbus eyesore. Tax abatement was also requested, with Columbus City Schools to get a lump sum payment and some money from a small hockey ticket surcharge. The leadership team claimed there was no "plan B." The NHL made it clear that an expansion franchise was contingent upon having an arena seating about 20,000 and 12,000 in advance season ticket sales.

Community response was less than supportive. As one of the leaders of the opposition said: "This guy (Hunt) has his resources, why does he need to reach into our pockets for some $200 million?" Another said, "What makes a city great, a hockey team? If that were the case we'd be vacationing in Buffalo" (The Other Paper, May 7, 1999). Others noted that St. Petersburg and others had bought into the "build it and they will come" hype and still awaited a team. The mood of the public could be summed up as "let's call their bluff. If it's good business, private money will be found."

Local community groups were aghast at the plan. Columbus public school officials contended that the local school system was being cut out of millions in tax support. If existing practices of property valuation were followed, tax on a $300 million project would be $65 million. The leadership team estimated this at less than $10 million. Nationwide's contributions seemed self-serving. The company's offer to donate a parking structure, adjacent to the old penitentiary site, was a bit hollow, the garage was a "white elephant" due to its low use. There were objections to land giveaways, the projected price of tickets, parking costs, and land use as well.

Polls showed that Issue 1 was in trouble. The tax had some support from the more affluent suburbs and younger voters, but nowhere near enough to pass it. The leadership team pushed ahead anyway and opposition became more vocal. Issue 1 was soundly defeated in the spring election.

Within twenty-four hours, the nonexistent "plan B" surfaced. The new plan dumped Hunt and the soccer stadium, proposing that a $125 million, 18,500-seat hockey arena (20,000 for concerts) be built with private money. Nationwide picked up 90 percent of the costs, and the Dispatch Printing Company paid the remaining 10 percent. The owners were given a 99-year lease on the old Ohio penitentiary site. For this, the city was to receive 20 percent of Nationwide's parking collections. Also, the city agreed to provide infrastructure improvements for access roads and to clean up the old penitentiary site. The bill for these improvements came in at $32.8 million, and the structure at $150 million. Franklin County estimated the land value to be $11.7 million. The mayor was able to circumvent the voters and put public money into the project this way. The tax abatement remained, with the schools to get $10 million instead of the $32.4 million they would have received had the arena been taxed following past practice. Bank One Corporation left for Chicago, leaving local commitments in the wake, and Nationwide claimed naming rights instead of offering them for resale.

The soccer stadium was built with private funds as well. After yet another failed attempt to obtain tax support, this time in a wealthy Columbus suburb, Hunt acquired access to property on the Ohio State Fairgrounds. The Crew will pay $50,000 annually for the site over a twenty-five-year lease, and Hunt built a 22,500-seat open-air stadium for $28.5 million, financing it through the Hunt Sports Group. This figure is less than half that asked for in the first proposal. The Hunt Sports Group can get 50 percent of its investment back through stadium construction credits. The credits allow Hunt to retain ticket revenue otherwise to be shared with major league soccer, providing an annual $1.45 million holdback. The stadium seats

30,000 for concerts, providing another revenue source. Parking is plentiful and the site is located adjacent to I-71, with easy access. An agreement with the Ohio Expositions Commission, which operates the Ohio State Fair, allows Hunt to make money from parking.

Columbus has a major league team and the Crew has a permanent stadium that makes their crowds look big. (Crew officials could never accept the look of 15,000 people in Ohio Stadium, which seats 100,000.) Columbus will also have a major league sports team, but people will have to pay dearly to see them play. A family of four will have to spend $200 to see a hockey game.

Key players in this decision seemed willing to dip into the taxpayers' pockets to support a project that was sure to make them money. Nationwide put an unused parking lot to use and got parking revenues at the same time. The city played with tax appraisals to subsidize the arena with funds that the Columbus public schools needed, and were entitled to. Key participants manipulated appraisals to favor the arena and to disadvantage the public schools. Ethics seemed to be suspended whenever the arena was threatened, and bogus claims of economic benefit were used to sell the arena. Putting a positive spin on things got out of control as proponents made wild claims about the taxes to be generated from the business activity prompted by the hockey team. Had the original leadership team looked at the numbers, it would have been clear tax money was not needed to build the arena (see Chapter 8).

The emergence of plan B after Issue 1 failed raises suspicions of duplicity. Claiming plan B had no prior discussion is hardly credible, and lingering ill-will could hamper future infrastructure investments needed to improve downtown Columbus. Nationwide missed opportunities to build community support for its team and could lose its investment if locals do not flock to see hockey games. Local observers claim there is a three-year window; fickle local fans will demand a winner by then or ticket sales will go south. There were rumblings of this when, amid considerable local fanfare, the hockey team was named the Blue Jackets, a cross between an obscure bee and an equally obscure reference to the Civil War. Critics had a field day. Signaling their disdain for the entire effort, they wondered if fans would chant "go blue" and called for renaming the team the "mad cows."

## Implementation Tactics in the Debacles

The Quaker acquisition and the arena tax support decisions illustrate "persuasion" and "edict" implementation tactics often found in debacles and failed decisions. Persuasion tries to sell a preferred course of action, and an edict applies power to install it.

### Persuasion

Persuasion calls on a decision maker to collect arguments that support a preferred course of action and to garner the endorsements of experts, and then combine them with salesmanship. The arena's leadership team commissioned studies to demonstrate how Columbus could benefit from a sports arena. The spokesman for the leadership team, a local developer, used these arguments to urge passage of Issue 1. When the sales approach fails, decision makers often resort to demonstrations that dramatize what can be gained. Opposition to the arena prompted proponents to create diversions. Scale models of the proposed site development were produced, and the *Dispatch* reported that the dilapidated penitentiary buildings would be removed and replaced by job-creating infrastructure. Persuasion is widely used by decision makers, but it has a low rate of success (see Table 5.3).

Decision makers mistakenly see persuasion as low risk, believing it is more successful than its track record indicates. If arguments can be fashioned that seem convincing to them, decision makers believe they can convince others. When the best available arguments are unable to sway people, failure is likely. Gathering documentation to support the merits of a decision is done at the expense of gaining the acceptance of key people affected by it. Unmanaged social and political concerns, such as job security and vested interests, scuttle many persuasion-based implementation attempts.

Decision makers in the arena debacle failed to detect the taxpayers' shift from smoldering resentment to organized opposition. The tax abatement scheme also galvanized people who believed the Columbus public schools were being fleeced. Dubious claims of the arena's economic benefits and job creation prospects stirred up critics and goaded them into organized opposition. Citizens who saw the arena as using public funds for

| | | | | Table 5.3 | | | |
| THE SUCCESS OF IMPLEMENTATION TACTICS | | | | | | | |

| Tactic | Frequency of Use | Adoption[1] | Perceived Benefits[2] | Installation Time[3] |
|---|---|---|---|---|
| TACTICS FOUND IN DEBACLES | | | | |
| Persuasion | 36% | 49% to 58% | Adequate to good | 26 months |
| Edict | 40% | 38% to 50% | Adequate | 17 months |
| BEST PRACTICES | | | | |
| Intervention | 6% | 90% to 100% | Good to excellent | 11 months |
| Participation | 18% | 80% to 89% | Good to excellent | 14 months |
| Comprehensive | Not observed | — | — | — |
| Complete | 6% | 90% to 100% | Good to excellent | 16 months |
| Delegated | 10% | 79% to 84% | Good | 10 months |
| Token | 2% | 67% to 70% | Adequate to good | 20 months |

(1) Adoption rates indicate the range of decisions sustained for two years to those that were fully put to use.

(2) Based on evaluation of stakeholders.

(3) Time from the end of development to adoption or rejection.

private gain united with critics in a grassroots effort to defeat Issue 1. The leadership team seemed only dimly aware of the amount of anti-Issue 1 sentiment that had sprung up in the community. Without much organization and little funding, the opposition appeared to pose little threat. In addition, the leadership team failed to anticipate the opposition of parents and public school officials to tax abatement proposals. This gave critics yet another platform to raise objections. As opposition grew, arena backers dredged up still more arguments supporting the arena, but such arguments have little effect on people who see themselves as losers. The DIA, EuroDisney, and Shell decisions also show how persuasion is dependent upon the indifference of stakeholders and has little success when people have something to lose.

## Edicts

An edict issues a directive: a memorandum is written, job training is conducted, or someone is hired to make the decision a reality. This is done without consulting with people who have a stake in the changes the decision would bring. A memorandum sent to all hospital employees and members of the medical staff announcing a new pricing policy for emergency room services, explaining the new policy and when it would go into effect, is one example of the use of an edict. Edicts are the most frequently used tactic for implementing a decision, and the least successful.

Decision makers understand that they must draw on their position power to issue an edict. This seems justifiable and workable because of decision makers' prerogatives and the need for timely action. Decision makers seem oblivious to the high failure rate of an edict. Failure can be traced to overestimating one's power and to people who resist being forced. To use an edict, you must draw on "social credit," the store of good-will you built up by honest dealings and positive accomplishments, and trade it for rapid action. Repeated use of an edict exhausts the store of social credit. When social credit is used up, resistance to an edict takes a variety of forms such as sabotage, token compliance, delays, and outright refusals to comply (Bardach, 1977). The decision is withdrawn when the uproar that results appears to outweigh its benefits. Even when one uses an edict successfully, the turmoil that results delays things so timely action is seldom realized.

Decision makers who routinely use edicts develop a reputation for being heavy-handed, putting their decisions in jeopardy as Smithburg did in the Snapple acquisition. Attention is directed away from the merits of the decision and toward the way implementation is carried out. Considerable expense, time, and effort are expended trying to overcome the resistance provoked. More often than not, these efforts fail, no matter what the decision's merits. Consider a firm that tried to force people to use a management information system (MIS) developed by one of the firm's subsidiaries. The system had no external buyers, making the targeted in-house users see it as suspect. Department managers resented being forced to adopt an MIS of "questionable value" that could adversely affect their performance. When asked to participate in a pilot effort, they simply refused. The CEO of the firm entered the fray. Incentives, in the form of budget supplements, were offered if a department would agree to do a pilot test that operated the new MIS along with its current system to compare results. No one stepped forward so the CEO issued a decree that dictated a department for the pilot. The department selected to work with the subsidiary sabotaged the effort by continuing to rely on its old information system and by providing erroneous information to the new system, causing it to malfunction. Disgruntled people in the department bandied the malfunctions about to show that the MIS was faulty. When the pilot failed, the subsidiary's MIS system was abandoned.

In the Snapple acquisition, Smithburg implemented with an edict. Past successes had built his social credit with the board. These accomplishments created so much goodwill that the board gave him a license to do whatever he wanted. Subordinates were well aware of this and deferred to this power. Even with his track record, the repeated use of edicts finally did Smithburg in. People who use their power to issue edicts on a regular basis gradually drain their social credit and set themselves up for a fall.

Decision makers in the Waco, BeechNut, Ford Pinto, and Nestle debacles also used edicts to implement their decisions, believing this was justifiable in their attempts to get things done rapidly. Using one's power to issue an edict appears to be both feasible and pragmatic, but my studies show it is neither.

## How the Blunders Fashion Implementation Traps

Premature commitments, misused resources, and poor practice create implementation traps. The arena's leadership team, Smithburg, and decision makers in the other debacles who relied on persuasion or edicts to implement their decisions were victimized by these traps. Let's take a closer look at each.

### Premature Commitment

Decision makers with a plan feel a need to put it to use, which creates an artificial sense of urgency. Decision makers in the debacles considered thus far had no need to rush an implementation, but a sense of urgency arose nonetheless. Some seemed to want a fast resolution to get things off their "screen" and move on to the next issue; others acted quickly to head off questions about a pet idea or any appearance of a lack of action on their part. Both prompt artificial time pressure. When real time pressure is present, as in the Waco debacle after the botched attempt to serve a search warrant, the need for rapid and decisive action is all but impossible to resist.

Decision makers in my studies who acted quickly, whether faced with a self-imposed or a real deadline, were drawn toward using an edict. An edict is seen as a way to get things done rapidly and to avoid delays. And rapid and decisive action is believed to head off questions from impatient higher-ups.

Persuasion can also be seductive due to its seeming pragmatism and apparent timeliness. Telling people about the merits of a course of action is a time-honored way to sell an idea, and deferring implementation until a worthy choice emerges is widely embraced. Conflict arises when stakeholders have a different take on benefits or how the preferred course of action helps the organization avoid a thorny issue. Persuasion can head off such conflict if questions about the merits of the impending decision are fully answered. Typically, some questions and ambiguity will remain. This requires still more selling to put a positive spin on things, to support the case, and to offer a negative read on the critic and what the critic has said.

### Misused Resources

Decision makers put little of their time or money into managing social and political forces stirred up by a decision. Those using persuasion make a modest investment to find evidence that supports a preferred course of action and arguments that overcome people's objections. Once the evidence and arguments have been marshaled, the decision maker uses them to argue for adoption. Decision makers are always surprised to find how long this takes. Eisner saw the EuroDisney location decision as a "no-brainer," which people would accept with minimal coaxing. As objections arose, vast amounts of time were required to explain the location and cajole people to accept it. Pena had similar experiences as he tried to sell the DIA to doubters, as did decision makers at Shell and the Nationwide arena.

An edict is viewed in the same way. A decree appears to get things moving rapidly, with a minimum investment of time and money. Decision makers who use an edict overestimate their leverage and fail to see that the repeated use of their power will make their decisions prone to failure. Timeliness evaporates as you cope with passive resistance and fix the firestorms provoked by the edict. The Pinto, Nestle, BeechNut, and Waco decisions were questioned or blocked, making the edict anything but timely. The magnitude of the time and effort needed to carry out an edict often surprise and dismay decision makers.

## Bad Practice

Edicts and persuasion fail because nothing is done to manage the political and social forces a decision stirs up. Neither is able to defuse such forces, and opponents are enflamed by these tactics. People with interests are goaded into action when persuasion or edicts are used. Taxpayers became arena opponents when an apparent boondoggle also shortchanged the public school system. As views about the expected consequences of a decision play out, expectations are formed and attempts are made by stakeholders to shape it so valued resources, business practices, and relationships can be preserved. Threatened people engage in passive-aggressive resistance and tokenism—or pitched battles if their power allows—because valued things or things in which they have an interest can be lost. These acts heighten the conflict, and still others are pushed to take sides either by jumping on the decision maker's bandwagon, engaging in delays, or joining a palace revolt. Because hollow and self-serving arguments and power plays affront them, still others enter the fray and become opponents.

Edicts and persuasion are used because they are time-honored ways of implementing one decision and because they are thought to be effective. Both assume that people will review what is being proposed and reserve judgment until they can understand and appreciate its benefits. Proclamations and coaxing have little chance of prompting this reaction when the interests of people are threatened, even if the organization appears to benefit. Both tactics assume that actions called for by a decision fall into a "zone of indifference" in which stakeholders are indifferent to, if not supportive of, the decision. Bad assumptions about power, people's attitudes toward force, and entropy trap decision makers who use these tactics.

Power is implied by persuasion and drawn on with an edict. Often the failure of one brings on the other, as in the EuroDisney and DIA debacles. Decision makers who fail to convince stakeholders to accept their ideas drift into applying ever-increasing amounts of power to salvage their plans. When persuasion fails, a demonstration can be mounted. If this also fails, you must push even harder. When an edict fails, more power must be used to neutralize the opposition: individuals are removed, structural changes are made to bring in supporters, or both can be carried out. Vast amounts of power are required as you move from a decree, to removing opposition, to making structural changes that accommodate what you want to do. The chance of success declines with each increment of power that is applied. Even CEO's operating in an autocratic environment with carte blanche from the board, such as Smithburg in the Quaker Snapple debacle, must use power with care. An overuse of power undermines the trust and confidence needed to operate day to day. This occurs even when subordinates have been conditioned to accept autocratic behavior. Decision makers seem unaware of the "paradox of power": The less one uses power the more power one has. Having power but not using it draws attention to the many prerogatives that were *not* exercised, yet many decision makers have a "use it or lose it" view of power. Such decision makers squander their power on trivial things to show who is the boss and who is in control. Every decision becomes a test of will. To meet the test, opposition is crushed.

People may rebel when power is used. Forcing or the appearance of being forced by the unilateral actions of a decision maker can create opposition in people with no stake in the decision. To such individuals, yielding to a power play sets a bad precedent. Opposing it now sets the stage for later when things count. This coaxes people to send a message by blocking you.

A decision can lose its impetus as it moves among layers in an organization. This loss is even more pronounced for decisions that must move agency to agency in government. Increased entropy, in which a decision loses its momentum, leads to incomplete adoptions or failed decisions. Shell's deep-sea disposal became more problematic as the decision moved through several agencies and forums. The same difficulty arose for the leadership team in the arena tax-support decision. The leadership team's meetings with officials representing various branches of the overlapping local governments and authorities in the Columbus area bogged them down. Misunderstandings had to be cleared up, and assertions by the *Columbus Monthly, The Other Paper,* and others outside the Dispatch's orbit had to be countered to keep things on track.

Entropy will always be present to slow things down. Positive energy that can push things along is missing unless people have an investment in the decision and its success. Edict and persuasion tactics limit the investment.

# What to Do

Intervention and participation implementation tactics have a much better track record than do edict and persuasion. Both intervention and participation push implementation to a position early in the decision-making process to identify and manage people's interests and commitments. Attention is directed toward the claim used to justify action and how the decision maker goes about making the claim that can mobilize support.

## Intervention

Decision makers often assume that the concerns or considerations motivating them to act are obvious to others. Much of the time key people are either unaware of the reasons prompting a decision-making effort or disagree about its importance. This can cause you considerable grief as you try to reassure the doubting or belligerent stakeholder, gobbling up time and delaying action. Key players often remain skeptical as justifications are belatedly offered and speculate about the decision maker's hidden agenda, even when there isn't one. The intervention tactic deals with such perceptions. Intervention is the least frequently used tactic and the most successful, with a nearly 100 percent success rate.

To carry out intervention, you must demonstrate the imperative to act to the problematic stakeholder and others with interests not yet managed (see Figure 4.1). To do this, current performance is compared to norms that discredit the performance. This new norm is justified by benchmarking the performance levels of respected organizations. For example, a norm is applied to market share or profit to show that comparable organizations produce greater market share or more profit. You then point out actions that the other organizations have taken to realize this level of performance. Considerable time is then spent networking with people with interests, explaining where the new norms came from, documenting performance, and calling attention to ideas that could work. The "performance gap" that results from comparing performance to the new norm is used to justify the claim, providing reasons for a decision-making effort and indicating what is wanted as an outcome.

After demonstrating that current performance is inadequate, illustrations of how business practices could be improved are offered. The claim that emerged from the focus group analysis in Chapter 4 can be probed to find things that may work. The benchmarked organization offers still other ideas. Committees are sometimes used as a sounding board, offering a commentary on what has been discovered and seeking ideas. After a decision has been installed, you then show how the actions overcame the performance deficiencies.

Consider a decision to add burn care in a teaching hospital. Hospital trustees are wary of offering high-cost services such as burn or coronary care because third party payers (e.g., Medicaid and HMOs) do not insure the full cost of treatment. To overcome this objection, a hospital CEO showed how the cost for burn care could be covered by a variety of sources: endowments, reimbursements, and cheap resident manpower. The CEO presented the trustees with a demonstration of financial feasibility and a description of how others had enhanced their image, and thus endowments, with this service. A candidate for the burn care director position then demonstrated to the trustees treatment procedures and staffing, showing how resident recruitment had been enhanced at other hospitals that added such a service. It was suggested that resident recruitment efforts could be harmed in the future without burn care service. The hospital CEO reported back to the trustees, providing data on image, resident recruitment, and cost after a pilot test of the unit.

## Participation

Decision makers use participation by delegating aspects of the decision to others, such as a task force. Problematic stakeholders and people with important points of view, vested interests, and knowledge become task force members. The claim uncovered by the focus groups is used to indicate what is wanted, such as reducing fringe benefit costs, consolidating operations, or retaining accreditation, and constraints and supporting resources, such as staff, are stated. For example, a university hospital redesigned its PBX system by involving staff representatives in a group and giving them the latitude to select any staffing schedule they wished as long as costs would not increase. To make participation fully effective, you and the task force leader must agree not to veto what the group wants to do.

Despite its prominence in business school course offerings, participation is used in less than one in five decisions. Although used more often than intervention and a bit less successful, participation follows the pattern noted for intervention in which a very successful tactic is seldom applied. Participation has a good success record and is even timely, requiring much less time to carry out than either the edict or the persuasion tactic.

The extent of stakeholder involvement and the role of the task force provide options. Involvement may be partial or full, and the extent of involvement in solution development may be limited in various ways. The four types of participation are shown in Figure 5.1. The success rate for each participation type is shown at the bottom of Table 5.3.

**Comprehensive Participation.** In comprehensive participation, the decision is delegated to a fully representative task force. This type of participation would seem to have the best chance of creating ownership and widespread acceptance, owing to the breadth of the role and the inclusion of all interested parties. Comprehensive participation is similar to "System 4" as described by Likert (1967). No one in my studies put comprehensive participation to use, suggesting that this amount of involvement is rarely, if ever, allowed in practice.

**Complete Participation.** Complete participation involves all of the interested parties but restricts their role. For example, an insurance agency CEO asked his agents to review plans to merge with another agency and to suggest changes in the agreement thought to be beneficial. In a decision to offer ambulatory surgery, all users (attending physicians and nurses) were involved in critiquing the proposed physical structure and suggesting operating procedures. To use complete participation, you ask the task force to

*Figure 5.1*
**TYPES OF PARTICIPATION**

**ROLE OF TASK FORCE**

|  |  | Limited | Unlimited |
|---|---|---|---|
| **EXTENT OF STAKEHOLDER INVOLVEMENT** | Partial | Token Participation | Delegated Participation |
|  | Full | Complete Participation | Comprehensive Participation |

comment on the decision rather than to specify the course of action to be followed. Participants can be asked to set directions or offer ideas, or to uncover claims as in the previous chapter. Staff specialists develop the plans in line with the directions set and ideas offered. The program planning method calls for this type of participation (Delbecq et al., 1986). One-third of the decision makers using participation selected complete participation, and most were quite successful.

**Delegated Participation.** In delegated participation, representatives of the interested parties make the decision. Task force participants have selected benefit packages for aging programs, designed laboratories, made contingency plans for strikes, carried out renovations, and planned internal operations in this way in my studies. A delegated approach is used in about half of the decisions in which participation is applied. Apparently, decision makers believe that giving representatives the prerogative to make a decision is enough to promote ownership in the recommended action. Strategic planning groups with members drawn from organizations' boards of directors and top management teams call for this type of participation. Delegated participation is found in social planning programs that develop or modify services. User representatives are involved in planning activities to lay out details. The PBX project, noted previously, used this type of participation: not all the operators were involved, but participants were allowed to dictate the terms of a new schedule. In delegated participation, participants are typically supportive of an ensuing decision, but their ability to persuade others to go along with it depends on whether the prerogatives of nonparticipants are threatened. Delegated participation is less successful than complete participation. Decision makers who use it realize fewer adoptions and a decline in benefits.

**Token Participation.** Token participation limits both participants and their role and is the least effective form of participation. For example, a task force may be asked to identify consumer concerns or considerations. These concerns and considerations may fail to be representative if the participants do not include a cross section of stakeholder views and beliefs. Task force members may be unaware of some stakeholder concerns or considerations or have a vested interest in misrepresenting them. Moreover, the members of a representative task force, although personally committed to the group's suggestions and findings, may fail to convince others. This explains why middle managers avoid token participation and top managers employ it in less than one of five of their decisions using participation. Compared to other types of participation, decision makers had the least success with token participation. Adoption rates fall, estimated benefits decline, and duration increases when token participation is used. The success record of token participation is only slightly better than that of persuasion. The involved people spread the word, which helps to increase acceptance, but not to the extent of that obtained by complete or delegated participation.

To get the most from involving people in making a decision, you must recognize that involvement is more important than the role of the participant. When feasible, giving all affected parties a voice in the decision improves your chance of success, regardless of your position power. As long as you agree to act in accordance with the task force's findings or recommendations, any reasonable role given to a task force will increase your chance of success. Task forces that are asked to identify concerns or considerations, suggest ideas, or evaluate proposals produce comparable success rates. Token participation is less successful because participants are small in number and have a limited role. Questions about the motives of the decision maker are often asked by the disadvantaged or uninvolved stakeholder.

No form of participation is as successful as intervention.

## ▼ Key Points

- ▼ Personal interests and commitments keep people from embracing ideas that seem best for the organization. Implementation prospects improve when these interests and commitments are uncovered and dealt with as decisions are being implemented.
- ▼ Demonstrate the need for and feasibility of dealing with the claim motivating action by networking. The support needed to move a decision-making effort along and increase its prospect of success is created when people agree on the need to act and see its urgency realistically.
- ▼ If time is limited, use participation to overcome the resistance people feel toward change and to promote ownership in the individuals who will be affected by the decision. The prospect of success will increase as

greater numbers of people are asked for their views. Avoid using token participation when all of the affected parties can be involved. Token participation is similar to persuasion and about as effective.

▼ Limit the use of persuasion to situations prohibiting both intervention and participation. Persuasion is more successful than an edict but nowhere near as effective as intervention or participation. Rational arguments directed at people with something to lose are seldom successful.

▼ Decision makers have a tendency to invest too little of their time and money in implementation. Participation and intervention require more decision maker involvement but are easily justified by their improved prospects of success.

▼ Avoid applying power indiscriminately and too often. Eventually, social credit disappears and every decision becomes a test of wills, morale deteriorates, and the organization sacrifices the creativity of its members for their compliance.

▼ Edicts encourage resistance. Even people who have no stake in a decision will resist an edict because they do not like to be forced and are concerned about the precedent that would be set by not resisting it.

# Traps in Misleading Directions

I n Chinese gardens sitting areas are placed across from open-air windows to direct a visitor's view toward vistas the architect believes merit attention. The windows provide a frame that directs one's view toward what the designer believes to be the best views of collections of flora and sculpture and away from the less desirable views.

Decision makers also frame things to indicate what is wanted, the results a decision seeks to provide. Like the window in the Chinese garden, the frame provides a direction that points toward certain kinds of remedies, and away from others. The savvy decision maker opens the window and stands at different locations so more can be seen. The classic Japanese garden with its raked stones and strategically placed rocks provides an illustration. No matter where you sit, the entire picture that the garden conveys cannot be taken in. The garden is designed to force visitors to change their position to take in the entire view. This change in stance is called *reframing*. The broader field of view that results allows more cues to be seen, which opens people to other possibilities.

In the debacles, the framing offered in the direction was either misleading or argumentative. Framing is argumentative when expected results are assumed, but never agreed to, or are vague. Officials at Ford were not clear about the results they wanted for the Pinto's recall decision so the missing information was filled in. A misleading frame suggests one thing while wanting another. To sell the DIA, Pena claimed economic benefits

111

when his purpose was to get the FAA off his back. Such directions provide windows that look out over landscapes with no cues about what to do. A misleading view limits the range of possibilities that can be seen. In this chapter, we turn our attention to identifying hoped-for results and how this should be presented to others to avoid misdirecting a decision-making effort. Instead of political rationality, which has been the focus of the last two chapters, logical rationality is addressed here, showing how directions that lack clarity or mislead can derail a decision-making effort.

Directions can liberate, limit, or conceal. A direction liberates when it opens up the search for solutions. It limits when boundaries are prescribed that dictate a solution or some of its features. Directions conceal when expectations are never made clear. This prompts participants to seek solutions with totally different aims in mind and to make faulty assumptions about desired results. To see how this can happen, consider the telescope consortium decision profiled in Tables 6.1 and 6.2.

## The Telescope Consortium

Viewing time is the bottom line for astronomy departments, and the limited number of telescopes worldwide makes viewing time a fully committed commodity in very short supply. Without viewing time, grant funds

| Table 6.1 FLOW OF EVENTS IN THE TELESCOPE CONSORTIUM | |
|---|---|
| **Choices** | |
| Actions before | OSU's national reputation lagging |
| | Big science initiatives to jump-start reputation |
| | Success with supercomputer, cancer hospital, and arts center |
| | Telescope consortium formed |
| | Consortium expanded, costs increase |
| Pivotal decision | Cancel project |
| Actions after | Default on University of Arizona payments |
| | Buy viewing time from University of Arizona as part of settlement |

| Table 6.2 | |
| THE TELESCOPE CONSORTIUM | |
| --- | --- |
| Claims | University reputation needs to be improved |
| Core concerns/considerations<br>  (a) Recognized | Reputation tied to telescope access |
| (b) Hidden | Source of funds<br><br>Payback<br><br>Best use of funds |
| Directions (implicit) | Higher ranking for astronomy department |
| Options considered | Build telescope |
| Extent of search and innovation | Limited: no other partnerships sought, big science |
| Use of evaluation | None |
| Impact of evaluation | None |
| Barriers to action | Raising needed money |
| Ethical concerns | Red squirrels<br><br>Aspirations of project champions |
| Barriers to learning | Trustees' concerns about prerogatives set aside when performance is good |

from the National Science Foundation (NSF) and other prestigious agencies are all but impossible to get. Lacking outside funding, university science departments are doomed to mediocrity at best. The Ohio State University's (OSU) astronomy department had no telescope access, putting them in a no-win position. This changed when the University of Arizona approached OSU to team with them to build a new telescope. The new telescope was to provide viewing time that had been denied to each of the parties due to limited supply and long-standing commitments to current users.

As these events were unfolding, OSU named a new president who was charged by the trustees with improving the reputation of the university. The new president developed a "big science" plan that called for large resource investments to vault select academic departments into national prominence. The Astronomy Department at OSU, which had brought in a meager $25,000 in grants the previous year, was one of several in need of a major overhaul. Seeing an opportunity, the department chairman unveiled the proposed telescope partnership to the new president and asked for his support. The university president connected the telescope to his big science ideas and offered the project to the board of trustees. The trustees approved an 8 meter optical telescope at a cost of $10.8 million as a way to thrust the astronomy department into national prominence. Operating costs were estimated to be $500,000 annually. (The budget of the entire department at the time was $638,000.)

The telescope was to be built in Arizona, one of the few places in the United States that allowed optical astronomers to get a clear view of the night sky. OSU astronomy faculty would have access to one of the world's largest telescopes with a computer hookup, giving faculty members the means to study astronomical phenomena from their offices. This is typical practice; astronomers seldom go to a telescope site to do their work. It is too cold. The promise of leading edge technology provided a way to attract high caliber faculty and research dollars. Faculty wrote proposals that anticipated the planned telescope. NSF funding, with just the promise of telescope access, jumped from $25,000 to $500,000. The department estimated that federal grants of $2 million to $4 million per year could be expected with an operational telescope. Because national ratings are tied to grant support, the national standing of the department was expected to leap upward.

In the next three years, the project grew from the original pairing of OSU and Arizona to include an international partner in the Italian Astronomical Community, funded by the Italian government, and the University of Chicago. To accommodate the new partners, the project became more ambitious. Now the project consisted of an 11.3 meter optical and infrared telescope, to be the world's largest, and a twin 8 meter telescope. Costs ballooned to $20 million. Problems arose. The project mushroomed into one quite different from that approved by OSU's board of trustees. The new and bigger effort skirted a review, by-passing the university's vice president for research and provost, who determines funding feasibility, and the board of trustees.

Fund-raising plans had yet to be thought out. This left the project's impact on OSU's budget and the balance of outside-inside funding unclear.

No financial payback analysis had been conducted. Because the project lacked a feasibility study, the expanded telescope project was not included on the university's financial campaign list. There were environmental concerns. Activists claimed that the project would threaten Mt. Graham's endangered red squirrel population. To protect the squirrel habitat, a lawsuit was filed to prevent cutting the trees on Mt. Graham called for by the project. Questions about negative publicity, liability, and further court action by animal rights groups prompted additional hassles. At this point the University of Chicago withdrew from the project, leaving the others with the task of finding a new partner. Discussions with the University of Toronto, the Max Planck Institute, and the University of Maryland were not fruitful. The failure to find a fourth partner put the telescope at risk. Then, amid a budget crisis, the university president and the chair of the Astronomy Department resigned, leaving the project without an influential champion.

The state legislators saw a chance to play politics and head off a "boondoggle." They stepped into the fray and questioned whether tax dollars should be used to build something in another state. "Why not build in Ohio?" they asked, knowing the answer. OSU failed to meet the University of Arizona's payment schedule. Missed and late payments caused friction between the partners. Without a telescope, NSF would cancel most of its funding. The new university president canceled the telescope, leaving OSU with payments due to its partner, the University of Arizona, and lots of planning costs.

Let's trace the events that led to this debacle. What claims prompted the telescope? The university president and department chair saw the situation differently. The chair wanted better faculty and the president wanted to improve the university's reputation. The president could reach his aim through the Astronomy Department or in other ways. Direction was never made clear. Was "national reputation" or "better astronomy facility" the aim? Many options could have enhanced the university's reputation that had more "bang for the buck." None were considered. Other departments on the verge of a reputation breakout and their needs were overlooked as funding commitments were agreed to. In big science departments, success is tied to providing expensive infrastructure. In others, hiring good people and giving them small budgets and graduate student access is all that is needed. Inventorying such opportunities would have provided more options. Note how the benefits of "improved astronomy facility" implied a direction that limited search. Had the broader "university reputation" direction been used, a different set of options would have turned up.

The numbers failed to add up (for a complete analysis see Chapter 8). Even the most optimistic revenue projections of grant funds would not offset OSU's share of the telescope's cost. OSU would have to feed the project with $3 million to $15 million a year to realize the aim of an improved astronomy faculty. This would hamper quality improvements being planned elsewhere in the university.

The telescope evolved into a complex multi-institutional project demanding ongoing coordination among the partners and support at the highest level. None was present. No project manager was ever appointed. The board of trustees felt they had been misled. The telescope lacked a major advocate, making it easy prey for budget slashing. Sunk costs were ignored, creating more problems as OSU was billed for a project they would not be able to participate in. OSU settled the dispute with their partner by trading viewing time for some of their sunk cost. These times, however, fall far below those that were planned.

The university Senate appointed an ad-hoc committee to "learn from our mistakes." The report concluded that the debacle could have been averted had review procedures been followed. Others saw it differently, arguing that big science was needed and that OSU's ponderous review procedures telegraphed needed moves and lost the university first-mover market advantage. The president had successfully courted a few well-healed donors to realize a supercomputer, a cancer hospital, a major arts center, and still other big ticket projects. Each required stealth, behind the scenes negotiations with the donor, and rapid action once a deal had been struck. Past efforts had all been successes, so repeating these tactics for the telescope seemed reasonable. So the rules were ignored. Note the perverse incentive here. The trustees pressured the president to improve the university's ratings but stressed prerogative over performance when things turned out badly.

# Direction Setting Tactics Used in the Debacles

The direction setting approaches employed in the telescope project and in the Shell, Waco, Quaker, and arena decisions illustrate idea and problem tactics that are found in failed decisions. The idea tactic imposes an answer. The problem tactic identifies a difficulty to be overcome. Both tactics are failure prone.

## The Idea Tactic

When a decision maker stumbles on an idea in the claims motivating action and fashions it into a ready-made solution, the idea tactic is put in play. The anticipated benefit of the idea becomes the direction. For example, during a recent energy crisis, the CEO of an air-conditioning manufacturer was approached with an idea for a solar heat pump. A license was offered to sell the heat pump in exchange for developing a heat wheel, a key part of the solar heat pump's design. The CEO, seeing the idea as a way to pump up lagging sales, bought the license and assigned his engineers to design the heat wheel. The engineers spent eight years in a futile attempt to devise a heat wheel that had both moisture retention and durability but failed to find a suitable material for the wheel. The CEO made no attempt in this eight-year period to move away from the design problem, to redesign the solar heat pump without a heat wheel, or to look for a better way to provide energy-efficient home heating and cooling. When the declining cost of energy took the edge off finding new sources of energy, the CEO abandoned the project.

An idea tactic muddies the purpose. Once the CEO had accepted the solar heat pump concept, the expectation of an increase in sales was never verified or even discussed with anyone in the organization as the decision process unfolded. Decision makers who become fixated on an idea fail to ask "reframing" questions, such as "How do we increase sales?" Commitment to the idea becomes a trap, which often leads to failure. Decision makers fear failure. They conjure up images of higher-ups asking if money is being spent without producing anything of value or of having to explain that it will take longer than anticipated to get results. The threat in admitting to a failure, sunk costs, and a reluctance to start over keeps decision makers from abandoning an idea and trying to find a better one.

People are drawn to the seeming pragmatism of the idea tactic. Beginning with an answer sweeps away ambiguity. At first this is comforting, but it subsequently limits your ability to see attractive options. Furthermore, beginning with a ready-made solution can be rash when you have little understanding of needs. Instead of seeking such an understanding, you are drawn to exploring the virtue of an idea and the reaction of key people to it. The more insistent you become, the more time you must spend defending the idea. Nevertheless, many decision makers are drawn to being decisive in this way. Consider the telescope decision. The university president saw an opportunity to solve two dilemmas at once: the lagging reputation of the Astronomy Department and the university's need for big science to vault it into national prominence. Others see the ready-made idea as a way to quickly manage a situation that poses a threat, such as BeechNut's top management dumping their apple juice inventory to wiggle out of a bad situation. And speedy action is always favored, even in situations that have no real time pressure such as the EuroDisney and arena decisions. The seeming pragmatism disappears when the decision maker must struggle to verify the virtues of an idea, coax support from others, and modify the idea to make it workable. Decisions are seldom successful when made in this way (Table 6.3).

| | | | | |
|---|---|---|---|---|
| *Table 6.3* <br> **THE SUCCESS OF DIRECTION SETTING TACTICS** | | | | |
| Tactic | Frequency of Use | Adoption[1] | Perceived Benefits[2] | Development Time[3] |
| TACTICS FOUND IN DEBACLES | | | | |
| **Idea** | 37% | 38% to 56% | Adequate | 9 months |
| **Problem** | 26% | 45% to 54% | Adequate | 12 months |
| BEST PRACTICE | | | | |
| **Objective** | 37% | 66% to 72% | Good | 8 months |

(1) Adoption rates indicate the range of decisions sustained for two years to those that were fully put to use.

(2) Based on evaluation of stakeholders.

(3) Time measured from point where claims were noted until a course of action had been developed.

*Problem Tactics*

Decision makers apply a problem tactic when they define a problem and then analyze its distinctive features to uncover clues that suggest a remedy. The director and his staff of the Ohio Department of Claims saw a growing backlog of Social Security benefit appeals and called for a change in handling procedures. Analysis led to a pooling idea that grouped similar claims for mass handling, but the backlog analysis failed to look for the reason for the growing number of claims. After the backlog grew to the point that claims took a year to process, the director stumbled upon a loophole in the legislation that inadvertently eased eligibility requirements. The director made the legislature aware of the oversight and the loophole was closed. In the meantime, the agency was subjected to constant criticism and legal action for its slow, error-prone claims management.

Defining a problem is a time-honored way to guide decision making. Decision makers want to find out what is wrong and fix it quickly. The all too frequent result, however, is a problem definition that proves to be misleading and misdirects people's energy. Symptoms are analyzed while important issues are ignored. Consider the Waco debacle. Reno's attention was focused on sidestepping a drawn out siege. Avoiding the problems that could be provoked by such a siege, and the ensuing media feeding frenzy, pulled Reno and her aides away from exploring the motivations of the Davidians and how to deal with them. Shell's top management focused on the problems of an obsolete oil platform's disposal, and Smithburg at Quaker the problems in a takeover. All were misled by problem eradication that pulled them away from thinking about more important issues. A problem tactic is no more successful than the idea tactic.

## Blunders That Create the Misdirection Trap

Decision makers in the debacles made premature commitments about a direction, allocated no resources to direction setting, and engaged in questionable practices to establish their intentions. These blunders drew the decision makers in each debacle toward ready-made ideas and problem solving. Both tactics create traps that make success unlikely.

### Premature Commitments

Novel, complex, and contradictory decisions create ambiguity. Novel decisions lack familiar analogies that can be used to suggest solutions. Complexity makes it hard to know what action is best. Contradictory decisions have several competing interpretations. Some decision makers respond to this ambiguity with fear or denial. Fear leads them to sweep away ambiguity by making silly commitments. Smithburg's concerns about a hostile takeover, and his future, prompted him to jump at an ill-advised acquisition. Others ignore evidence that an early commitment may be ill advised and that the situation is spinning out of control, as did top decision makers at Nestle.

Observers and higher-ups see that something is amiss and call for action, creating pressure. Decision makers attempt to show that the situation is under control by jumping on the first answer that crops up. Asking a task force to look for answers leaves the situation ambiguous. Critics ask, "When will the answer appear?" The decision maker wonders, "How do I deal with critics until then?" An opportunity that pops up sets aside such pressures, but such a remedy often proves to have minimal benefits and limited use.

### Misused Resources

No money was spent on setting directions in the debacles. The ready-made idea seems to be free. Problem solving seems timely and pragmatic. Neither provides a direction that indicates what is wanted as a result.

The telescope decision started with an answer and never looked back. The Astronomy Department chair and the university president saw the telescope as a good idea and then matched it to their long-standing problem of reputation. Arena proponents bought a "build it and they will come" homily to attract a major league sports team.

Decision makers in the Shell, Waco, and Quaker debacles dabbled with problems. Smithburg assumed a problem and forged ahead with the first idea he came across that mimicked his past successes. Little was allocated to direction setting here. Reno spent considerable time assessing possible actions but little time probing what was provoking action. No one in the Waco orbit had any idea what was motivating the Davidians. Resolution is difficult when you do not know what the other party wants. Shell was much more diligent in its problem exploration, looking for ways to responsibly dispose of an obsolete oil rig, but problem analyses misled them. Being clearer about the results others were after could have headed off this debacle.

## Bad Practice

Ready-made solutions and problem analysis have limited successes because both focus on the wrong things. Decision makers who impose an "answer" create an artificial clarity of purpose. The idea is clear and its intended results are implied by the idea's benefits, when (or if) they are fully understood. Many decision makers see a direction as a solution because they do not know what they want until they see what they can get (Wildavsky, 1979). Having an answer sweeps away this ambiguity and makes the action, if not the hoped-for results, clear. But beginning with a ready-made idea is risky when you lack a clear understanding of what is needed. The telescope project was never clear about its aims. If an enhanced university reputation was intended, many less expensive ideas and projects with more impact and less political vulnerability could be imagined. Instead, decision makers explored the virtues of the telescope idea and reactions of key people to it. The more blatant this becomes, the more time and money advocates must invest in defending their idea.

Powerful decision makers impose ideas that seduce them. Seizing such an apparent "opportunity" is seen as a pragmatic way to speed things up and cut costs. When you latch onto an idea in this way, little learning can occur. Stereotyped responses and traditional ways of acting are typically adopted. Such solutions seldom rise above "adequate" benefits and have a limited life.

Focusing on problems limits a search for answers, and these limitations may not be understood because they can be quite subtle. A decision-making effort directed at overcoming a morale problem is limited to a morale-like solution. By naming the type of solution to be sought, search is narrowed and overly focused. Shell's top management focused on ways to make a deep-sea disposal of the Brent Spar palatable to potential critics and salable to others. Reno sought a way to overcome the problem of arresting wrongdoers. Smithburg sought to put Quaker in a defensive posture by taking on debt, which would thwart a takeover.

Problems used as directions are failure prone because defensiveness is stirred up by the problem. People who see themselves as potentially responsible for the problem take steps to deflect criticism. Energy used to defend your actions is drawn away from finding better answers. Nestle's top management spent years defending their infant formula marketing practices. Only a pitched battle between Shell and government leaders, provoked by Greenpeace and the public outcry they fomented, pulled Shell's top management away from a deep-sea disposal of their Brent Spar. Up to this point, all time and effort had been directed at justifying the action. Smithburg took one defensive action after another to defend his Snapple purchase and push blame for its shortcomings onto others. Problem listing is seductive, and decision makers use this approach in one-quarter of their decision-making efforts.

## What to Do

Setting directions with an objective is more effective than following either an idea or a problem tactic. Next let's look at why objectives are effective and how to fashion them.

### Objective Tactics

An objective identifies desired results, such as lower cost or increased market share. An objective works as a direction because it focuses a search on an expected result and thereby gives everyone involved freedom to look at any solution that can realize the intended result. This opens the search up to anything that would provide this outcome.

People have a bias toward action and a fear of being seen as indecisive. This makes objective setting commonly known, but uncommonly practiced. Many of my study participants acknowledge that they had been exposed to objectives during their education, but most are action-oriented and see objectives as an academic exercise. Identifying the desired result does appear to be obvious after a decision is made, and devoting time to something thought to be obvious is irritating. Such decision makers stress the need to "get on with it" and have little patience with objective setting sessions. Also, many decision makers want to be seen as decisive, which creates an artificial pressure for action. This pressure can take several forms. Decision makers are expected to "put their wake in front of their boat." You are pressured by people in an oversight role for assurances that you can deal with a seemingly important claim before much is known about it. By rapidly indicating what will be done, you seem to be on top of things. The press and many others in an oversight role sneer at authorizing a study with objectives: "What, another study? Why can't we do something?" This makes it difficult for you to champion an orderly process that clearly articulates a desired result (an objective) and to wait for solutions. Decision makers who would prefer to follow such a path are often pressured by higher-ups or people in an oversight role to grab at the first idea that pops up. The people creating such pressure act as if everything has an immediate solution. Even when a decision maker knows it is foolhardy to make decisions this way, the pressure for a quick fix often wins out.

Ironically, setting an objective has the opposite effect. Objectives liberate people to search widely for solutions, which lowers the chance of failure. Consider a hospital CEO who must respond to a threat by a large health maintenance organization (HMO) to cut its reimbursement rates. The hospital's proposed service charges, negotiated by the hospital CEO biannually and formalized as a contract with the HMO, have been rejected because the HMO claims that the hospital is overstaffed. To respond to this threat, the hospital CEO identifies a cost reduction target (the objective) and lets departmental managers come up with ways to make the necessary cuts. The cost reduction target directed the search for ways to reduce labor cost. A successful rate negotiation with the HMO resulted when the CEO demonstrated the cuts that were to be made.

All but an overly demanding objective provides such a result. An objective that is unrealistic, calling for more than can be achieved with the time and resources available, can lead to panic-ridden frustrated behavior (Janis, 1989). The chance of success improves when a realistic objective is set. At this point you must be wondering about the "stretch objectives" found in the writings of TQM and re-engineering. My reading of this literature suggests two explanations. The cases cited in TQM and re-engineering are mostly anecdotal and seem to have one common element—poorly used resources. For example, long-distance carriers Sprint, AT&T, and MCI were not satisfied with Bell Atlantic's time to hook up new customers. Thirteen hand-offs and seven information systems caused repeated delays as people coordinated with one another or waited for replies, producing a fifteen- to thirty-day waiting period. The objective selected, which was close to ten hours of actual work, is hardly a stretch. This result is explained by redeploying the resources found in unneeded or inefficient procedures, not stretch objectives. On the other hand, the continued use of stretch objectives in stressed companies that are short on resources may be one cause for the erosion of morale and growth of apathy found in many of today's companies (Kelley, 1992).

## Finding an Objective

Identifying an objective can be difficult. Many decision makers are primed to think solely in solution terms. And there are no tests to determine whether the "correct" objective has been identified. The dual challenges of dealing with the solution centeredness of people and identifying an objective are considered next.

### Uncovering a Tentative List of Objectives

The idea tactic illustrates how people displace to solutions. Many decision makers are decidedly solution centered (Shull, Delbecq, and Cummings, 1970), which provokes the premature commitment blunder. Solution-centered preferences are deeply rooted, and it is often best to accept and work with such preferences rather than to try changing them. To do this, a variation on the group process described in Chapter 4 is offered to uncover a tentative list of objectives. This indirect route has been shown to be effective in my past work.

First, participants in a group are asked to identify solutions. People are prone to do this. They may insist on doing so in your decision as well, so allow participants to displace to solutions. But make a deal. Ask the group members to also write down the results they expect for each solution that they uncover. In the silent generation phase, each group member lists solutions on the left side of a page and the result that this solution is expected to provide on the right until all solution ideas are exhausted. In the listing phase, the facilitator uses two sheets, recording solutions on one and expected results on the other. This decouples solutions from expected results. The facilitator then helps the group prioritize the expected results that were uncovered.

If the expected results that are offered are connected to the solutions, the facilitator can show that broad scale solutions fit only with broad scale expected results but that narrow solutions can be fit in many places. This illustrates how a narrow objective limits search. The demonstration shows that a narrow objective is less desirable because it excludes many kinds of solutions. It also shows how a broad scale objective expands a search. Finally, this approach plays into the task of finding appropriate objectives, discussed next.

Individuals can apply this approach to uncover candidate objectives as well. List solutions that have cropped up from your own ruminations, the claims made, the ideas offered by stakeholders, and other sources. When this list is complete, list the results each solution can provide. This gives you a list of tentative objectives for the next step of the objective setting effort. When comparing the hoped-for results, look for a broad objective and a narrower one to see the scope of solutions that would match each. This gives you some guidance as to how broadly you want to pitch your search effort.

## Selecting Objectives

The difficulty of objective selection can be best demonstrated with an example. Consider an organization in which decision makers have a cash flow concern because the company's receivable and payable accounts are unbalanced. Should this be attacked with an objective to increase cash flow or should an increase in revenue serve as the objective? If the revenue-generation objective is addressed, a redesign of products and services might be considered, along with marketing to find new customers. If the cash flow objective is addressed, solutions take shape as ways to balance the flow of funds in the company. These solutions are very different and illustrate how an objective can narrow a search or broaden it.

**The Hierarchical Relationship of Objectives.** Objective selection creates a paradox. Each objective identifies a system. Every system is part of a larger system and contains many smaller ones, so all systems have a hierarchical relationship. Choosing the scope of a system to be addressed is similar to choosing an objective, but it is not clear which system should be selected. To overcome the paradox, two tests are offered. You may choose to limit your purview to those systems over which you have control, or you may select some that stand out from the others due to their seeming urgency and importance.

To make this choice less arbitrary, system theorists look for an objective that identifies a system that is both larger and smaller than the focal system. Looking at objectives in this way can be justified on two counts. Virtually everyone recommends developing multiple options because decisions with multiple options are more successful. Dual objectives encourage this. Also, when options stem from broader objectives, it opens up inquiry. Options that balance accounts payable and receivable are quite different from those that increase revenue. The DIA decision seemed to identify lots of options, but each was a variation on the new airport theme. Options that are broadly defined, as in the previous example, overcome this difficulty.

Consider a Toyota dealer who had been getting troublesome signals after a long period of sales growth. Declines in the closing ratio (a measure of lost sales) were noted and profit had leveled off. The owner attributed this to staffing difficulties. Growth had added salespeople who lacked encul-turation into Toyota's way of doing business, suggesting that training was lacking. This seemed unlikely to me. To break out of this bind, the training direction was expanded and narrowed. The narrower view focused on the behavior of salespersons, attempting to identify things that were turning off customers. Remedies would be limited to ways to modify the undesirable behavior. A broader objective was set to look for ways to expand profits, bringing into view options such as promotions, buyer incentives, cost cut-ting, and pricing policy. This allowed me to open up the search without ignoring the owner's wishes.

Note how objectives in the Toyota decision have a hierarchical rela-tionship. The owner must find ways to overcome behavioral problems to do training, and training must be in place before promotions, cost cutting, and the like will work. Creating objectives that uncover options in this way brings to light hidden difficulties that have eluded decision makers and must be rectified to ensure success.

***Creating an Objective Hierarchy and Using It to Uncover Objec-tives.*** You can use a laddering technique to create a hierarchy of objectives and interpret it to find the most appropriate objectives to follow. This technique helps you around two difficulties: (1) people who become fixated on a particular objective and (2) arranging a large number of objectives, uncovered by a group process, to reveal their relationships. In both instances one needs to construct a hierarchy of possible objectives to find the broader and narrower ones. The laddering technique provides a way to expand a pool of objectives and give them the needed logic. The objective suggested by a powerful stakeholder, or one that has been assumed without much thought, can be used as a starting point.

My analysis of Ford's transformation in the 1980s shows how to apply the laddering technique (Nutt and Backoff, 1998). In the 1970s the Ford Motor Company found itself in decline, with a critical leadership decision to make (Pascale, 1990). According to industry observers, the decline was prompted by a management that stifled new ideas, lagging productivity, disputes about the type of leadership needed, lack of cross-functional cooperation, an emphasis on control, a silo mentality, and Ford's reputation as a "bad place to work." A visionary leader, Don Peterson, fashioned a remarkable turnaround for Ford. Peterson's tenure was marked by fostering a team approach in top management to deal with the difficulties at Ford. Spreitzer and Quinn (2001) point out new concerns that stemmed from perceptions about who got what during the Peterson era. Key middle managers were found to have blocked further change because they had smoldering grievances and because they were excluded from Peterson's teams. New difficulties emerged due to slow sales and cost reductions that squeezed tradition-ridden work units. This suggests that further transformation at Ford depends on addressing these overlooked difficulties.

A compromise that trades off pay with reduced job demands provides a place to start and simulates the situation wherein an objective is suggested by a powerful stakeholder. To construct a ladder, the facilitator looks for the objective of this trade-off: Why compromise by adding people and cutting salaries, asks the facilitator? An answer might be to reduce job stress. This identifies the most basic objective. The same question is posed again: Why reduce job stress? An answer might be to motivate middle managers. By continuing in this way, a ladder is created as shown in Figure 6.1.

The ladder addresses why and how questions in a hierarchy of objectives. Moving up the ladder answers the "why" question (reduced stress produces more motivated middle managers). Moving down the ladder

*Figure 6.1*
## THE LADDERING TECHNIQUE AT FORD

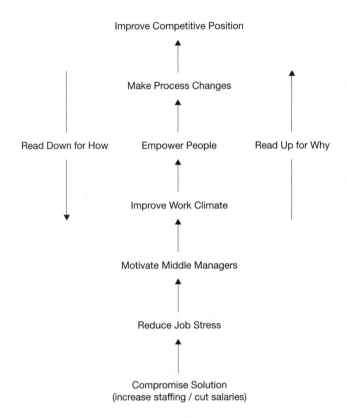

answers the "how" question (one motivates middle managers to help rid them of job stress). One motivates to improve climate (why), and an improved climate can motivate (how). Improved climates empower (why), and empowerment improves the climate (how), and so on down the ladder.

By moving up the ladder, participants can be shown larger spaces or larger systems in which actions can be sought. A bigger space is better because it has fewer constraints (Rothenberg, 1979). Participants in a development effort who see how a broad scale search can open up the decision-making process to more possibilities are more apt to adopt a broader objective to guide their efforts.

It is recommended that participants explore the scope of actions open to them before selecting an objective to guide their search for solutions. If only one is used, the broadest feasible objective is always best. Better yet, objectives that are broader and narrower than the one initially adopted can be used to initiate a search for a string of actions, or options "broadly defined," to make needed changes.

## ▼ Key Points

▼ Decision makers drawn to power and repelled by ambiguity find it difficult to set a direction.

▼ Avoid using an idea as a direction. People are drawn to the idea—either to support or to resist it. Debates about what is needed get lost in debates over the merit of the idea, making purpose unclear and argumentative. Hold back ideas until a thoughtful direction is set that indicates the desired result.

▼ Resist analyzing problems. A problem direction narrows search to the vicinity of the problem. For instance, the problems of excessive absenteeism entice one to look for who is absent in order to hand out rebukes. Such an approach is not likely to discover the causes of absenteeism, such as jobs that lack challenge.

▼ Forget about uncovering problems and go directly to objectives. Setting objectives is more effective because it opens up the decision process to new possibilities. This opening up enables a decision maker to move away from stereotyped responses and traditional ways of acting.

▼ State objectives in performance terms to provide a target.

▼ Use objectives that are narrower and broader in scope than the focal objective to expand the pool of options. This can bring to light a series of actions needed to be effective. Such actions overcome hidden difficulties that have eluded people's attention and must be dealt with to ensure good results. Guide the overall effort with the broadest objective that people will accept.

▼ Unrealistic objectives, given time and budget constraints, reduce the chance of finding answers. Objectives that call for big results are less apt to be taken seriously when time constraints and budgets make such results seem out of reach. Leaders who treat objectives in a cavalier manner are less likely to elicit the support they need to find a useful remedy. The objective must appear to be attainable to realize a good outcome.

# Traps in Limited Search and No Innovation

## CHAPTER 7

"Keep your options open" is sage advice. When making a big ticket expenditure such as buying a car or a house, we identify several options before settling on one. Yet many decision makers making weighty decisions drastically limit their search. Others embrace an idea found in a claim, as in the telescope and arena decisions, and avoid search altogether. Both the idea in a claim or the pet idea of a zealot drive out search. The traps of limiting search are considered in this chapter along with best-practice search approaches. The role of innovation and ways to interject new ideas into the mix of options is also discussed.

Opportunistic behavior drives out search in nearly 40 percent of the decisions explored. This behavior stems from the pull of a quick fix and the push of a pet idea. The quick fix and the motivations behind adopting an idea found in a claim were described in Chapter 6. Here we consider zealots, decision makers, or key players in the organization's orbit who advance their pet ideas. AmeriFlora, profiled in Tables 7.1 and 7.2, illustrates how this decision pushed aside search and became a debacle.

## AmeriFlora

Columbus, Ohio, set out to celebrate the five hundredth anniversary of the "discovery" of America by Christopher Columbus with the largest Quincentennial in the United States. A world class event was proposed to celebrate a discovery many believe took place centuries earlier. Civic leaders envisaged a World's Fair, but John W. Wolf, a well-known Columbus busi-

| Table 7.1 FLOW OF EVENTS IN THE AMERIFLORA DEBACLE | |
|---|---|
| **Choices** | |
| Actions before | Hold World's Fair-like event to commemorate the Quincentennial |
| | Flower show idea |
| | Form commission |
| | Elicit public and private funding |
| | Select Franklin (Wolf) Park as the site |
| Pivotal decision | Host international flower show |
| Actions after | Dispose of assets |
| | Sell park |

nessman and community power broker owning much of the local media, soon took over. Motivated by his wife's desire for an international flower show, he called for exhibits and attractions, entertainment, learning experiences, international culture, and a pageant—all set against a backdrop of gardens and floral displays. He deftly maneuvered the other local power brokers into picturing the event as an international Garden Exposition, which became known as AmeriFlora. Wolf then offered his leadership and formed a board of trustees made up of local CEOs and others with contacts and leverage to oversee the Columbus Quincentennial Jubilee Commission. The commission claimed that AmeriFlora would provide these benefits:

▼ Increase international awareness of Columbus and Ohio
▼ Provide economic benefits to local citizens that would extend into the future
▼ Establish Columbus as a tourist destination
▼ Foster visitors' learning about the environment

An international flower show, something never before attempted in the United States, was seen as an attention grabber that would draw lots of tourists and bring lots of attention to the city. This would help Columbus realize the big city image local power brokers desperately sought. The event would offer entertainment and educational benefits and leave the

| Table 7.2 | |
| --- | --- |
| **THE AMERIFLORA DEBACLE** | |
| Claims | City must be leader in commemorating the Quincentennial of Columbus's voyage |
| Core concerns/considerations (a) Recognized | Improve city image |
| (b) Hidden | Lack of interest in event |
| | Ticket sale prospects |
| | Coming out for Wolf |
| Directions | Flower show (breakeven) |
| Options considered | Flower show |
| Extent of search and innovation | None |
| Use of evaluation | Attendance estimates |
| Impact of evaluation | Demonstrate feasibility |
| Barriers to action | Extent of public support |
| Ethical concerns | Using public money for personal aims |
| Barriers to learning | Secrecy and control limited community involvement |

infrastructure improvements to the city. The timing seemed good, coinciding with the Quincentennial of Columbus's voyage and focusing attention during 1992 on the biggest city in the United States that bears his name.

Personal interests were also at play. Wolf had wielded power in city matters for years but had done so out of the spotlight. Observers writing in *The Other Paper* and the *Columbus Monthly*, local media not controlled by Wolf, called the event a "coming out" for Wolf. According to local critics, Wolf used the Quincentennial to reassert his community leadership just as another local power broker, Les Wexner of Limited Stores—who enjoyed the spotlight as much as Wolf had shunned it—emerged as the spokesman for a new city image. Wolf opposed Wexner's ideas for development of the Scioto riverfront and pushed his own agenda, including his wife's dream of an international flower show in Columbus.

By 1990 the commission had garnered a $300,000 planning grant from the state of Ohio. All public moneys were to be spent on structures and other things the public could use after the event was over. Cost overruns were to be covered by the private sector partners, presumably the commission's member organizations. The city of Columbus, Franklin County, and the state of Ohio were asked to ante up $29.8 million for capital improvements. Sponsorships and private donations were placed at $20.5 million with sources such as legacy donations, grants, philanthropy, and in-kind services. Estimates for revenues were $30.8 million, including $25.1 million in ticket sales from the projected 2.6 million to 5 million visitors, and $2.4 million in concessions.

Like the Millennium Dome, controversy plagued AmeriFlora, and costs steadily rose. Estimates of $77 million quickly jumped to $83 million. By 1991 the budget had grown to $93 million, prompting questions about where the money was to come from. Plans to collect $1.5 million from each of the eleven companies in Columbus were overly optimistic. Critics in *The Other Paper* and the *Columbus Monthly* claimed that donations in the range of $600,000 to $900,000 would be unlikely, $1.5 million impossible. The control demanded by power brokers on the commission and Wolf's well-known style of issuing directives turned people off. Decision-making secrecy made a shared vision impossible to realize. The aims of leaving behind an impressive park with a monorail, a tower, and new buildings to commemorate the Quincentennial were changed and many dropped by the commission without any citizen involvement—hardly a basis on which to create a shared vision. The connection to the Columbus voyages seemed an afterthought, and only a small bust and an abstract sail were offered to commemorate the Quincentennial.

The commission dictated AmeriFlora's location. Franklin Park was selected because it had a high wall to prevent people from looking without paying and because a number of existing structures could be used to cut costs. But Franklin Park was located in a declining part of the city, which raised questions about the security of visitors and its appeal to them. Many believed the banks of the Scioto River would have been a better location. The Scioto site was safe and easily accessible. It also offered a start toward the downtown makeover desired by all, fostered investment in an abandoned high school on the banks of the river, and encouraged maintenance of the displays and structures after the event. Wexner's advocacy doomed the riverfront site. Also, Franklin Park was formerly Wolf Park, an old Wolf investment turned over to the city that needed sprucing up after neglect by city and county officials. This, and support of the river site by a Wolf adversary, made the Franklin Park site non-negotiable.

When the site for AmeriFlora was announced, it prompted immediate opposition. Residents were concerned about the effects of the event on their communities. The commissioners dismissed this and offered to paint people's houses to spruce them up, if the commissioners could pick the colors. The commissioners ignored the concerns expressed by local residents about traffic, safety, parking, and alcohol sales. In response to this, Columbus residents became skeptical about the event and had little interest in going to it.

Commissioners used event planning to take a number of junkets. At one point a delegation of twenty-four people toured Europe visiting flower shows in England, Germany, and France. The costs were folded into the AmeriFlora budget. Wolf handpicked a director that had no experience with flower shows. The director made multiple trips to seventeen countries, often accompanied by staff, to recruit exhibitors. This director and several others, who also lacked experience, came and went without providing much insight into what they had learned about recruiting participants. In the end, success in recruiting exhibitors was modest at best, and the early claims of thirty to forty exhibitors dwindled to seven. Such events in Europe typically have twelve or more exhibitors.

AmeriFlora was an event that never happened. Ticket sales of 2.6 million to 5 million were way off target, as critics had suggested. Similarities with the Millennium Dome are striking. The stated aim of city image enhancement shifted to one of economics. Actual costs came in at $95 million, making it essential to increase sales. Many tickets were given away to create the appearance that tickets were being sold. People quickly learned there were free tickets and became even less inclined to pay for them. Decision makers never made the connection between ticket price and sales, setting ticket prices at $19.95 and parking at $6. The public might have attended in greater numbers had tickets and parking been made affordable. Columbus residents pay only $5 to go the Ohio State Fair and nothing at all to go to the Park of Roses. Free concerts were booked to stimulate attendance. The Hot Summer Nights series did help sales, but it was not enough. Total revenues were $65 million, leading to a $30 million loss. Government put up $30 million and private sources $8 million, so only $21.7 million was realized in ticket sales. This was $11.1 million below the projected $33.8 million. The final attendance figures of 2 million fell far below projections and estimates of 1.75 visits for Columbus residents were far too optimistic. More attention to price elasticity might have increased attendance. According to surveys, attendees were happy with the event but felt they paid too much.

Little of the infrastructure remains. No funds were available to maintain the buildings, so most were designated for give-aways. Budget cuts for higher education dried up funds needed to dismantle and move the buildings, preventing local universities from taking advantage of these offers. The buildings were torn down and sent to junkyards, and today the park shows little evidence of the event. Maintenance costs proved to be excessive, and no one stepped forward to shoulder the costs to maintain the exhibits so most have disappeared. Public officials have little to show for their $30 million investment. The park and the remaining conservatory buildings were sold to recoup part of the losses, and the public must now pay a fee to visit.

What prompted the AmeriFlora debacle? First, members of the greater Columbus community were not involved. The hoped-for cooperation and unity had no chance to materialize given the autocratic, secretive, and self-serving style of the organizer. Wider sponsorship and enrollment were needed to get the community behind AmeriFlora. Flower show aficionados criticized the event, but attendees who had never seen one liked it. Those who went to the show considered the festival culturally enriching and educational. This suggests that more community support could have saved the day by creating more interest in the event. Lower ticket prices would have attracted more visits. National publicity was deficient. The lack of visitors outside the greater Columbus area failed to give the city the hoped-for positive exposure. A river site would have been easier to reach and a better candidate for a lasting capital investment—if only Wexner had not supported it.

Ethical questions lurk as well. Wolf's flower show idea seemed to be a solution looking for a problem: Let's use the desired flower show to celebrate the Quincentennial. This made Wolf seem to be a self-righteous advocate, protecting vested interests by restoring his old park and putting his stamp on the community.

What can be learned from this? Artificial deadlines and group think cajoled the commissioners into buying an idea without giving it much thought. When this happens, no one probes with questions. Conflicting information is discounted or dismissed. Also, AmeriFlora's aims were never clear. The commemorative aim got lost as the flower show was pushed. Being clear about what you want is essential to realize good results. The aim of community involvement was subverted by Wolf's need for control, prompting antagonism and symbolic pacification rather than inclusion and cooperation. Getting people to buy into ideas without some role in their development is notoriously tricky and prone to failure. The need to cultivate local support was never understood. Dealings with neighbors were adversarial and used intimidation. These much-publicized battles were seen as power brokers bullying citizens. Concessions were too little and too late. Economic goals emerged as the aim when losses became a possibility, raising still more questions about the motives of the AmeriFlora organizers. The event's directors became scapegoats and were sacked or resigned, taking with them information that could be used to learn.

## Ready-Made Ideas Displace Search

Decision makers in the debacles either stumbled on an idea, as the university president did in the telescope decision, or offered a pet idea, as Wolf did in the AmeriFlora decision. Wolf's pet idea for a flower show was successfully sold to community power brokers so no search for ways to commemorate the Quincentennial was ever made. The traps of limiting search and innovation led the AmeriFlora team to an event no one wanted and few attended that squandered the investments paid for by the taxpayers and local companies. Many debacles stem from pet ideas. Choice opportunities entice people to bring out self-serving ideas unrelated to any need or priority (Starbuck, 1983). Resources are then mobilized to justify the idea, keeping one from looking into other possibilities. Decision makers who do not push their own ideas are often seduced by the ideas of subordinates or others with an agenda. This resembles the "garbage can" theory in which solutions and choice situations meet due to accidents of timing (March, 1994) and the ready-made approach noted by Mintzberg and colleagues (1976).

Pet ideas that can come from the decision maker, a subordinate, or others with an axe to grind take shape as an idea tactic. As described in Chapter 6, the idea is both a direction and a search result. Resources are used to validate an idea that captures the fancy of a decision maker and to promote it. The idea tactic is rarely successful (Table 7.3). Launching a search will produce better results. Let's see how this can be done.

| Search Tactics | Frequency of Use | Adoption[1] | Perceived Benefits[2] | Development Time[3] |
|---|---|---|---|---|
| *Table 7.3* **SUCCESS OF SEARCH TACTICS** | | | | |
| **TACTICS FOUND IN DEBACLES** | | | | |
| **Idea[4]** | 28% | 41% to 58% | Adequate | 8.5 months |
| **TACTICS WITH SOME SUCCESS** | | | | |
| **Simple Benchmarking** | 19% | 50% to 59% | Good to Adequate | 7.5 months |
| **Single Cycle Solicitation** | 20% | 51% to 63% | Good to Adequate | 11.8 months |
| **Innovation** | 20% | 51% to 63% | Good to Adequate | 15.3 months |
| **BEST PRACTICE TACTICS** | | | | |
| **Integrated Benchmarking (with staff support)** | 6% | 57% to 71% | Good to excellent | 9.8 months |
| **Repeated Solicitation** | 3% | 100% | Good | 6 months |
| **Innovation (with objectives and multiple options)** | 4% | 73% to 82% | Good | 7.9 months |

(1) Adoption rates indicating the range of decisions sustained for 2 years to those that were fully put to use.

(2) Based on the evaluation of stakeholders.

(3) Time measured from point where claims were made until solution was proposed.

(4) The idea in an "idea direction" failed in 17 percent of the decisions, shifting to one of the search tactics to find a replacement idea. An idea cropped up in 8 percent of the decisions after a problem or an objective had been set, so no search was conducted.

# Ways to Search

Decision makers not sidetracked by a ready-made solution use two search tactics, solicitation and benchmarking. Both are more successful than the idea tactic.

## Single Cycle Solicitation

Solicitation is used to get ideas from outsiders. A request for proposal (RFP) is sent to vendors when needs seem clear and to consultants when needs seem vague or uncertain. In the DIA, decision makers used an RFP to seek airport designs and to identify a vendor for the airport's baggage handling system. Vendors or consultants offer prepackaged ideas and show how they meet the organization's needs. For instance, the controller in one of my cases sent out an RFP to solicit software packages for automated billing, evaluating the bids by comparing costs and capabilities. A single cycle solicitation obtains a single round of bids.

Success rates for the single cycle solicitation tactic are noted in Table 7.3 and, as you can see, not all single cycle solicitations are successful. Consider the moves made by Allied Van Lines to alter a lease. Allied's World Headquarters Building, in suburban Chicago, was eleven years into a fifteen-year lease when the landlord offered the company a new lease with lower rates, prompted by recent rate declines. Allied became suspicious, and company officials decided to test the arrangement by searching for market information about similar leases. Using information from their search, Allied presented a counterproposal calling for $5 million less in lease costs than that proposed, 30 percent ownership of the building, and a thirty-year lease to accommodate the joint ownership. The search for terms suggested that Allied did not trust their landlord, yet the landlord believed he had offered a very fair package. Thinking that a trust relationship had been broken, the landlord leased the building to another party who had made a slightly better offer. Had the negotiation not broken down over issues of trust, the landlord would have taken a bit less in revenue from Allied to retain an "old and valued customer."

In the Allied decision, the solicitation tactic revealed more than the decision maker wished. Decision makers often fall short of uncovering what is available when using this tactic. People who do not know what they do not know or what they want can be duped. Vendors sell their wares following a "buyer beware" principle. A failure to see whether such systems fit with local needs has led to many debacles. Huge expenditures are made for data processing systems and the like even though many system features have little value for the company and someone must be paid to write software to get the system to work.

### Benchmarking

Benchmarking the practices of respected organizations offers another way to search. A high-profile organization is visited to get ideas. Seemingly useful practices are identified, guided by an objective to be met or a problem to be overcome. Recall the production planning decision in Chapter 1 in which someone who had installed a system for a leading competitor was hired to eliminate stock-outs. In addition to "hiring a solution," single benchmarks are derived from site visits and from descriptions published in periodicals and books. Decision makers say that they copy the practices of others to be pragmatic and to cut costs. As one of the participating decision makers noted, "Why rediscover the wheel when someone may have done it for you?"

The search steps found in a benchmarking tactic differ from those of idea or solicitation. The idea tactic seeks a ready-made solution in a claim or in a pet idea. Benchmarking looks at the business practices of other organizations for ideas. Solicitation develops a statement of needs to uncover ideas and has an assessment step. Benchmarking looks for ready-made solutions and lacks an assessment step. The decision maker makes a plant visit to observe a practice thought to be useful and makes a judgment about its value, so a formal assessment seems unneeded. Decision makers using the single cycle solicitation tactic conduct formal assessments. The success rate of benchmarking is shown in Table 7.3

## Blunders that Lead to Limited Search and No Innovation Traps

Traps that limit search and innovation are found in premature commitments, misused resources, and questionable practices. Let's see how these traps arise in the debacles.

## Premature Commitment

The oft-observed rush to judgment limits search. In three of four decisions no new ideas are discovered. In two of three decisions the tactics used to search limit learning. Even when a search is carried out with benchmarking or solicitation, there is pressure to act quickly. Decision makers with a low tolerance for ambiguity fear that decisions "in the making" pose threats. This prompts them to push for answers, limiting the time spent searching. Stepping into the unknown is resisted, so the ideas considered are typically variations on current business practices.

A more subtle push to limit search comes from "group think" (Janis, 1989). Groups and teams can have a downside. As cohesion develops, the goodwill fostered creates shared stereotypes, beliefs, and self-censorship among team members, making it hard to disagree. Maintaining goodwill takes on such importance that all suggestions that differ from conventional wisdom are censored. To maintain harmony, people subordinate their ideas to serve what they think are the interests of a controlling body, as in the AmeriFlora decision. Discussion to suggest new ideas is censored before it can begin.

A team or group working together gravitate toward a compromise. People are subtly pressured to buy into the emerging consensus, creating group think. Buy-in is valuable during implementation but can be counterproductive when ideas are being sought. Here diversity, not agreement, is valued. Team members who give up competition to out-do others also give up the competitiveness needed to uncover new ideas. Anyone offering a new idea is treated as a deviant who fails to help the cause. When this kind of censorship develops, no one will speak up to question the pet idea of the zealot, the first idea offered by a vendor, or the first benchmark that shows up. The idea of a flower show took on a life of its own because no one on the leadership team questioned it or offered any other way to commemorate the Quincentennial. Offering another idea could have led to conflict, which is avoided at all costs once group think takes over.

There is less need to manage social and political forces during a search. Consensus can be subordinated to finding good ideas. Conflict can actually be helpful if kept within reasonable bounds. The widely held maxim of stirring the pot to get ideas is a reflection of this. The social and political forces that prompt conflict are more apt to arise as claims are considered and as ideas are being evaluated, but these forces are less apt to surface as ideas are being uncovered. A claim or an evaluation creates commitment to action that some may disagree with. The ideas uncovered in a search are just possibilities, without a commitment to act on them.

People's subjective notion of time also limits search. The wait for an answer can seem indeterminable if one believes there is danger in the wait. At the first sign of unrest, decision makers feel an urge to calm troubled waters, and this urge is very hard to resist. To head off unrest, a decision maker jumps on the first bland alternative that comes along—one with no bad features but no good ones either (March and Simon, 1958). This shuts off discussion about what to do. It is just this situation, with its moderate level of perceived conflict, that can increase the chances of finding a good idea (Fredrickson, 1985).

Crisis and its urgent need to take speedy action rarely occur. None of the decision debacles considered thus far required immediate action, although some of the decision makers behaved as if this was the case. Only one in ten decisions has significant urgency, and only one in a hundred can be called a crisis. Were it not for their devastating consequences, the attention devoted to decisions with urgency and crisis would be out of place (e.g., Staw et al., 1981).

Studies of crisis decisions reveal still another downside to making premature commitments. A panic-driven search in which people find it impossible to be vigilant information processors can result when anxiety and stress are pushed to the brink by a crisis (Janis, 1989). Needs are exaggerated, and time horizons shrink. This situation becomes more intense when objectives are not clear or when people have personal aims that conflict. People who see themselves as winners and losers enter the fray to protect their interests or to limit their losses, further complicating the situation. When the search fails to find a way to wiggle out of all this unpleasantness, a pattern of behavior called "defensive avoidance" is produced. Warning signals used to fashion a claim are distorted, going well beyond original interpretations to take on a far more ominous tone. Decision makers in such situations grope blindly for a way out of the morass. The only priority is to fend off the dogs snapping at their heels. During this period of groping, repeated failures to find an acceptable course of action produce "hypervigilence," and the decision maker's ability to handle information declines abruptly. Panic prompts simplistic ways of thinking and a frantic search for a remedy. This can lead to some very poor choices that, as we look at them later, have obvious lapses of logic.

Consider the Carter rescue mission debacle. Islamic militants in Iran had taken U.S. diplomats and embassy employees hostage—a violation of law in every civilized country across the globe. The media, led by ABC and its new late night news program *Nightline*, created intense pressure to gain the hostages' release. ABC officials saw an opportunity to hype their new program. Night after night Ted Kopple, *Nightline's* talking head, ticked off the days that the hostages had been illegally confined, producing unprecedented pressure to gain their release. In a classic example of hyper-vigilence, Carter authorized a rescue mission. The plan called for helicopters from an aircraft carrier to assemble in the Iranian desert, then fly to the Iranian capital of Tehran some thousand miles away and take the hostages by force, if necessary, returning the way they had come. No one questioned the mission because the need for action, any action, had become more important than taking a responsible action.

## Misused Resources

Decision makers allocate more time and money to support a search than to investigate claims or to develop objectives. Even so, in nearly three of ten decisions no resources are allocated to a search and decision makers limit the amount spent to search in four of ten decisions. As a result, two of three decision makers spend very little to search for new ideas. Vast sums are spent on the analysis of pet ideas, but comparatively little to find new ones. Nearly everyone who has studied decision making recommends uncovering several alternatives before selecting one and keeping your options open, but these maxims are seldom followed. Decision makers rarely give anything but a single idea serious consideration before a choice is made. Four of five decision makers consider just one idea before acting.

## Questionable Search Practices

Effective decision makers uncover a number of ideas to find one with a decisive advantage (Eisenhardt and Zbaracki, 1992). Several search initiatives are needed to uncover the required number of ideas before a quantum shift in understanding about what to do can occur. Benchmarking and single cycle solicitations truncate search and limit learning. Learning is the primary reason to do a search, so anything that limits learning is undesirable. Search tactics that can expand a search are needed.

## Better Ways to Search

The blunders made during a search are less apt to be fatal than ignoring concerns, deferring implementation, or letting people guess at the hoped-for result. But a careful search can help a decision maker recover from accepting claims without investigation, ducking social and political forces, or taking directions for granted. Good search practices improve the prospect of success even more if a decision maker has dealt with these political and logical issues. To do this, best practice search tactics, which improve on soliciting and benchmarking, are offered along with how to apply them. Innovation is also considered, indicating when to innovate, how to improve the success of an innovation attempt, and how to kindle people's creativity.

### Integrated Benchmarking

Benchmarking exports the practices of an organization or work unit thought to be a high performer. Developmental activities are confined to making changes that would allow the idea to be successfully applied by the borrowing organization. This can fail when there are difficulties in fitting the benchmarked idea to the borrowing organization's situation. Consider a top manager of the University of Minnesota's Medical Center who visited the University of Iowa Medical Center to study its corporate and governance structure. The visitor enumerated the functions of trustees, the prerogatives of its medical staff, and the mechanisms of accountability for state and federal funds. Unfortunately, these arrangements offer little guidance to the University of Minnesota's CEO in devising a governance structure. Factors that played a role in creating this structure are unique. The University of Iowa Medical Center has a statewide monopoly over tertiary care treatment for the poor, giving it control over substantial amounts of revenue. The structure that evolved to fit this situation offers no guidance in forming a governance structure for the University of Minnesota, with its more competitive environment.

It is better to look for ideas in several organizations, seeking best practices to be amalgamated into a plan; this is called *integrated benchmarking*. This tactic can be illustrated by a reorganization in which the organizational arrangements used by similar successful organizations are sought. To restructure the organization, practices and procedures pertinent to the circumstances faced by the adopting organization are identified. The reorganization plan integrates the best practices and procedures found. Integrated benchmarking is rarely used but produces superior results (see Table 7.3).

Limited knowledge of system analysis and access to practices to copy restrict the use of integrated benchmarking. Decision makers seem to know little about systems analysis and other techniques needed to create the "systems synthesis" required to amalgamate business practices from several sources (Weinberg, 1985). Generous staff support increases adoptions of benchmarking by more than 50 percent and bumps up benefits, but twice the time commitment is required to realize these improved outcomes. If integrated benchmarking is to be used, staff support is essential. Decision makers may have limited access to relevant practices to model, and high-status organizations may be locked in fierce competition with the decision maker's organization. Looking carefully to find relevant business practices in noncompeting organizations may help here. Still, there are better ways to search.

### Repeated Solicitations

In a multicycle solicitation, decision makers set out to learn about possibilities and to apply this knowledge to fashion a series of more sophisticated searches. Each new search incorporates what was learned in earlier searches. The initial search uncovers available ideas, and subsequent searches exploit this knowledge by writing an RFP that recognizes cutting-edge capabilities. The Department of Defense (DOD) uses a variation of this approach to procure military hardware. Defense contractors are asked for "concept designs" of fighter planes, radar, submarines, missiles, and the like that can outperform hardware currently in use. DOD pays for these designs to learn about possibilities and asks for new bids on promising ideas. The new RFP incorporates a better understanding of pertinent developments in design, metals, propulsion, electronics, and the like.

A repeated solicitation calls upon you to engage in a process of reflection in which possibilities are carefully studied as understanding about possibilities grows, offering opportunities for learning. Unlike the DOD, you do not have to pay a cent for all this additional information. Vendors are typically willing to offer up their ideas without cost. The time investment to collect this free information pays dividends by improving benefits and adoption prospects, and by saving time. A time savings is realized because the repair of a favored alternative occurs less frequently and takes much less time and effort when it does occur. Taking the time to learn pays big dividends (Kolb, 1983; Pettigrew, 1987).

Repeated solicitation produces superior results (see Table 7.3), but despite its clear superiority this tactic is rarely used. Decision makers shy away from repeated solicitation because it seems overly complex and time consuming. These perceptions prove to be counterintuitive. My studies show that repeated solicitation is both effective and efficient. This tactic has few time demands and is easily justified, given the superior results produced. You can argue for a multiple solicitation tactic to higher-ups reluctant to try it by citing its success record.

### Innovation

A custom-made solution that requires innovation is sought in one of four decisions. Decision makers look for a new idea without any references to ready-made plans, the practices of others, or the ideas of vendors. Staff groups, such as research and design or engineering, or consultants are asked to create a new procedure or to devise a new product or service. Innovation is also applied to fashion marketing programs, controls, products, and services with original features distinct from those found in the practices of others.

Overall, innovation has only modest success. The prospects of a successful innovation improve considerably when an objective is used to guide the design effort and when multiple options are developed (see Table 7.3). Objectives clarify what is wanted, making the search for a new idea more purposeful and thereby more apt to be successful. An innovation attempt can wander without this direction, which reduces the chance of success. Innovation has gotten a bad name because 40 percent of the innovation attempts are directed by a problem or failed to have a clear objective indicating what is wanted as a result. Problems unnecessarily narrow the search for new ideas, and an ambiguous objective makes the results expected of an innovation argumentative. Ambiguous or missing directions lead to a dramatic decline in the success of innovation attempts, which has made innovation appear to be overly risky. Multiple options help as well. At first this may seem foolhardy as the costs and time required increase for one new idea, let alone several. My studies find that seeking multiple options during an innovation attempt is both efficient and effective.

People are reluctant to seek innovation because it seems chancy compared to benchmarking or solicitation tactics. Pragmatic motivations are stronger than the urge to be innovative. This is unfortunate because failure has less to do with the risk of innovation than with how innovation attempts are carried out. In addition to poor direction and limited idea generation, poor results stem from poor practice. Decision makers attempting to innovate are rarely schooled in good innovation practices (a clear-cut failure of our business schools) and have limited access to people who are, which stems from hiring practices. Subordinates who are asked to come up with an innovative solution often have no idea how to proceed. Consultants are even more prone to failure than in-house staff when they offer ideas based on the wants of their clients instead of their needs. The demands for repeat business force consultants to be very sensitive to what their clients say they want, making it difficult to critique these wants for fear of offending the client. Let's turn our attention to ways to increase the prospects of success for an innovation attempt.

## Finding Innovative Options

Innovation demands creativity, yet hard-bitten executives find creativity and creativity aids foolhardy (Starbuck, 1983). The high jinks found in the research and development lab are believed to have little use in the rough and tumble world of making tough decisions. Company leaders privately acknowledge the need for new ideas but shy away from introducing arrangements and approaches that can stimulate creativity in management initiatives, such as decision making. As Tichy and Devanna (1990) note, it is culturally illegitimate in many organizations to dream about the future.

An idea cannot be considered until it has acquired sufficient detail and coherence to be rigorously evaluated.

Such views prompt the poor practice found in many innovation attempts. Those seeking to introduce innovation must climb a slippery slope fashioned by the prevailing attitudes of their leaders. The suggestions offered here provide a path up such a slope that has a lower profile and thereby more chance of being tolerated by the innovation-averse superior. The steps call for a "safe space" and a "new space" to encourage and facilitate creativity.

A safe space offers an environment conducive to uncovering new ideas. Without it people's creative juices can be stifled. The safe space offers a haven where one can speculate about possibilities, and it protects people from the urge of higher-ups to prematurely evaluate their ruminations. *New space* refers to the incubation period required to uncover new ideas. Creativity aids provide a new space that allows this incubation to occur. The creativity aids suggested here are designed to help you avoid the negative images that have discouraged innovation in the past and to encourage good practices. The procedure skirts the image of wide-eyed, off-the-wall behavior abhorred by many and lets people speculate without premature evaluation. Such practices are now being touted under the rubric of "knowledge management" (Dierkes et al., 2001): Old wine in new bottles, but the bottle is fresh so the bad taste left by experiences with "creativity people" is avoided. This is my aim as well.

### Safe Space

Innovation requires an environment that minimizes control and gives people the latitude to speculate. New ideas are more apt to emerge when limits that restrict people's thinking are removed. New ideas are less apt to be realized in a critical and defensive environment (Ray and Myers, 1989). Decades of research show that incubation must occur before innovative ideas surface. Also, to be successful, people must be encouraged to go after new ideas, avoid premature evaluation, and uncover several ideas (Goldberg, 1983; Stein, 1975). To apply these ideas, you must give people permission to seek something new and different, empower self-managed work groups, provide resources, and set in place supportive structural arrangements (Behn, 1991). These actions create a safe place for people to dream about the future. There are three key moves. To provide a safe space, you must create a protected work environment, find people with creative urges, and legitimize speculation about new possibilities by targeting some current practices of the organization for modification.

**Protected Environments.** Work environments often discourage innovation. In the past several years, much has been written about the disadvantages of overly hierarchical organizations with power and decision-making prerogatives concentrated in just a few people at its apex. Such organizations have a "control orientation," which encourages the status quo and discourages new ideas (Neuman, 1989). The forces pushing for the protection and continuation of old business practices are quite strong. A different organizational arrangement is needed to cope with them.

This can be done in several ways. Disney has its dream room. Limited Stores have breakout sessions to make important decisions. Motorola pioneered the use of self-managed work groups. Ford and the automotive industry have platform teams. The common thread is that people are taken from their jobs and put into a new space that simulates an "adhocracy" (Mintzberg, 1985), in which leaders indicate expected results (the objective) but not the means to produce the result. Because such teams gravitate toward the new idea and feel the pull of its attraction, little attention is paid to current business practices. This fosters radical ideas that depart from current business practices. This approach has facilitated highly creative environments essential for organizations that sell the products of innovation, such as Hewlett-Packard (pre Carly), 3M Company, Disney, Intel, Limited Stores, and JPL.

A similar arrangement, on a smaller scale, is needed for the innovation decision. Pull people from their jobs on a temporary basis to offer ideas. This is similar to the practices found in total quality management (Sashkin and Kisner, 1993) and re-engineering (Linden, 1994), which call for teams to be trusted to dream up change. Such teams are behind many of the successes at General Electric, Ford, and Motorola. "Leaderless organizations" such as Orpheus, the symphony that operates without a conductor, demonstrate what is required to empower people. Orpheus provides quality performances without sacrificing the satisfaction of its players, a rare achievement within the world of domineering despots who lead many of the world's symphonies.

Reproducing the elements so successful at fashioning creative motion picture ideas in the Disney dream room (no accountants, no criticism) would have been a breath of fresh air when making big ticket decisions such as EuroDisney. Why do Ford officials resort to tactics that would repel their platform teams when they make a product recall decision? A team-like self-managed work group is used to make only one of five decisions. If you create a team that reproduces the beneficial effects of self-managed work groups, you will increase your chance of being innovative.

*Find and Unleash Creative People.* Both team makeup and empowerment are crucial. A team member's creative instinct is more important than knowledge of the decision to be made. People with creative instincts "think outside the box." Such individuals set the tone and prompt others to do the same. People with inhibitions that limit their creativity should be avoided. The extrovert who must talk to think is a poor choice as a team member as are people whose training and inclinations coax them to evaluate, such as accountants. A person's behavior is also telling. The best predictor of future behavior is past behavior. People who exhibit an affinity for coming up with new ideas are the best candidates for such a group. Also, be on the lookout for right-brain thinkers with this trait and avoid left-brain thinkers who approach everything with a critical posture. People with the Myers-Briggs type of intuitive-feeling-perception (NFP) are good candidates (see Nutt, 1989, for details).

Kelley (1992) shows how "exemplary followers"—people who are action-oriented independent thinkers—become alienated when their ideas are blocked. Some become rank pragmatists who "go along to get along" by taking just enough action to appear supportive. Others become dependent and uncritical thinkers, producing passive and conformist followers who do only what is asked of them. People who have been disempowered in this way grow comfortable with overlearned practices that require little effort and resist change (Neuman, 1989).

Kelley maintains that giving people the latitude to take action in the organization's interest develops exemplary followers. He finds that 80 percent of the positive changes made in organizations stem from the exemplary follower. If you develop people in this way, you will have a rich resource for your organization to tap. Commitments to value change and empowered people are closely related (Neuman, 1989; Walton, 1985). To create such empowerment, take steps to find people who can become exemplary followers and put them in an empowered position with a safe space.

**Discredit the Past.** Many organizational players see their task as the maintenance of what is and their role as one of stabilization. When this becomes the dominant view of people in an organization, routines designed to regulate and control current business practices will systematically derail any search for new ideas. To protect the safe place, draw the organization away from existing practices by destabilizing them (Miller, 1990; Nystrom and Starbuck, 1984). Shed some existing activities that are strongly identified with current ways of doing business. This "letting go" enables people to discard defensive routines designed to protect a current practice that you seek to change and breaks the tie to the old way of doing things. By loosening old commitments you allow some current practices to die, creating a space for new practices to emerge.

Discarding routines that maintain old ways of doing things is both symbolic and instrumental (Jantsch, 1975), signaling that the old business practices can be questioned. Discarding old commitments also helps to destabilize routines, opening up people to new ideas such as partnering with a different set of customers or suppliers to produce new strategic alliances. Discredit projects and activities that maintain current suppliers (e.g., purchasing agreements or sole-sourcing with strategic partners) and customers (e.g., dealers and franchises) to destabilize old commitments. Put all such practices up for discussion and possible modification.

## New Space

Putting people in a cognitive new space gets them into a mental state in which they are more apt to find a creative idea. Do not draw on the ideas of others with an adaptation, as in benchmarking. To innovate, a more generative process is required that puts a premium on finding something new.

Let's list what works. Just ask. People are more apt to move away from current practices and the conventional to the novel and unconventional if you merely ask them to be creative. A chain of such ideas may prompt an idea that meets the objective in a novel way and also offers competitive advantage. Studies of creativity stress the importance of incubation. The "skunk works," which Peters and Waterman (1982) credit with finding many of the creative ideas that gave first mover advantage to companies like 3M, Intel, and Hewlett-Packard, provides many opportunities for incubation. Anything that puts people in a reflective mode has this effect. Consultants who run effective retreats encourage people to take long walks, without their cell phones, and reflect on the issues to be considered by the gathering. The hassles and routine processing in the normal work day drive out creative thoughts. By putting people in an information-rich environment, in which they can neither write nor talk, information can be considered in a unique way and creative ideas will emerge. Such an arrangement frees the mind to roam and limits intrusions that drive out creative thoughts. Devices such a storyboarding, night notes, and similar vehicles have these qualities (Nutt, 1992). Ask people to identify where creative ideas emerged for them. The shower, a steam room or a hot tub, and the like are often cited. To get the creative minds of people to work, provide a chance to reflect during work hours. The longer the incubation and the more frequent its use, the better the result. Devices that encourage this create a new space for ideas to emerge.

People who study creativity in individuals find that the emotive safe space coupled with the cognitive new space draws people toward finding innovative (new to the company) or radically innovative (new to the industry) ideas. To break old stereotypes during an incubation period, ask team members to make the "strange familiar" and the "familiar strange." These maxims are widely supported (e.g., Morgan, 1988, 1993; Ray and Meyers, 1989; Woodman et al., 1993). Two search aids are offered here to help you organize a team's efforts and provide a vehicle for incubation: group management and multiple perspectives.

### Group Management

Team management returns us to some of the recommendations offered in Chapter 4 to uncover claims that called for a silent reflective group process (SRGP) to facilitate consensus. An SRGP also allows the creative ideas of people to emerge (Delbecq et al., 1986), as follows:

1. Ask team members to reflect and identify ideas that meet the objective and to list these ideas without discussion.
2. Have the facilitator record these ideas, one idea at a time.

3. Discuss, elaborate, and consolidate ideas.
4. Identify ideas to be considered further.

The silent reflection period offers a kind of incubation that helps team members come up with new ideas. The act of going inside to come up with a new idea makes the familiar strange, helping people to move away from the conventional and toward the novel. The longer the period of time allowed for silent reflection without distractions, the better the result. Asking members to prepare their lists at home, under quiet conditions with no distractions, can be useful. Then repeat this at the beginning of the group meeting to expand each person's list. A silent listing step provides people with a safe space and encourages a new space by giving each person time to reflect and time for incubation to take place. The steps in an SRGP adhere to the dictum of "quantity breeds quality" and avoid premature evaluation, which is needed to stimulate creativity in people.

## Multiple Perspectives

Linstone's (1984) multiple perspectives make the familiar strange by breaking old stereotypes. A decision is examined from several unique perspectives to set aside people's biases and to broaden their view. Technical, personal, and organizational perspectives provide a means to uncover options from three different angles, illuminating different views of what is possible.

**Technical Perspective.** The technical (T) perspective offers facts and economic realities posed in terms of statistical comparisons, quantitative measures, and countable attributes. Emphasis is placed on the amount saved, projected profit, or level of quality achieved. Other measures commonly applied in the T perspective include an adherence to preset specifications, such as army ordnance judging a rifle in terms of its bullet speed, cost to manufacture, and reliability.

**Personal Perspective.** The personal (P) perspective looks at the decision through the eyes of the people who are affected. This brings out individual concerns such as job security, opportunities to demonstrate competence, or means for advancement. Because this perspective is highly idiosyncratic, it can be quite elusive. The P perspective looks for individuals who see themselves as benefactors or victims, doers or users, and the like, as well as "hidden movers." A hidden mover has disguised power in the organization that can enable him or her to retard, or even prohibit, a decision from becoming a reality and to push others. A hidden mover may be a gatekeeper and a power broker, as well as being an individual with a stake in what is to be done. Such individuals often prepare policy statements and standard operating procedures (SOPs) that set the tone of the organization. People who occupy these positions over long periods of time acquire considerable influence and can help one navigate around rules and procedures. The personal perspective is important because the organizational perspective often swamps personal concerns.

**Organizational Perspective.** The organizational (O) perspective looks at things through the eyes of the organization. This treats the organization as an entity prone to in-fighting among collections of power centers, with people poised to fight off competitors and to maneuver to claim credit. The actors in an organization have goals as well as strengths and weaknesses, which lead to shifting alliances and coalitions to push their interests. Seen from the O perspective, organizational rules and unwritten treaties are put in place to guide a decision process through periods of questioning and controversy. It is this process, as much as the end result, that is important. Rules, codes, agreements, and policies must be followed to ensure that checks and balances in the organization have had a chance to function. Seen from the O perspective, rational analysis can disturb the status quo and become a disharmonious voice. The voice breaks down the cohesion carefully constructed in accord with the treaties negotiated to take care of procedural matters in an organization. In the O perspective the views of the historian and the political scientist have more salience than do those of an economist.

## Examining the Debacles

Linstone's insight is that one of the perspectives dominates and the others get overlooked as decisions are made. Viewing a decision from all three perspectives opens up a search. Let us revisit the debacles to see how a single perspective was dominant and how other perspectives could have been used to open up the search effort.

### The Dominant O Perspective

The Waco and AmeriFlora decisions had a dominant O perspective. The Waco debacle sprang from seeing things solely from the point of view of law enforcement agencies: the ATF, FBI, and the justice department. Protecting the reputation and prerogatives of these organizations swept out P-based concerns about the Davidians' motives and T-based concerns about the feasibility of storming the compound and the loss of life that was likely from such an action.

Wolf 's agenda to assert his community leadership was disguised by the vision of a flower show, and this vision duped the AmeriFlora leadership team. The team allowed Wolf to incorporate them into the organization he created to make his flower show vision a reality, and they bought into the values his organization represented. With the leadership team in his pocket, Wolf hired people to implement his flower show vision and his unspoken community leadership aspirations. The Quincentennial became a ruse to create a leadership team that would endorse his agenda, mobilize support for it in the community, and create an organization that would resonate to what he wanted. As you would expect, the organization's rules and procedures mirrored Wolf's values and were devoted to making the flower show a reality, thereby asserting his community leadership.

A similar chain of events takes place when a company is founded to realize someone's vision. The founder asserts what the organization is about and its mission, values, and the like. Rules and procedures are put in place to help make the vision a reality. Anything that distracts or speaks to things peripheral to the vision is pushed aside. Such arrangements persist long after the founder has moved on, and they become part of the furniture of a company—used but not recognized as posing limitations and restraints on possibilities.

Let's look at the AmeriFlora decision from each of the three perspectives (Table 7.4). To open up a search, a team of local citizens with ties to various parts of the community could have been formed to look into ways to celebrate the Quincentennial. Conducting a search with each of the two missing perspectives would break away from stereotypes and provide a bigger arena in which to search. The team would be divided into two groups, one for the T and one for the P perspectives. Each group would

| | | |
|---|---|---|
| | *Table 7.4* | |
| | **AMERIFLORA** | |

| | Technical Perspective | Organizational Perspective | Personal / Citizens' Perspective |
|---|---|---|---|
| Core concerns | People hired to manage lacked expertise/experience to produce AmeriFlora | **Objectives were similar but plans for what Ameri-Flora would be (e.g., flower show vs. entertainment) were not considered** | Residents felt betrayed by the city<br><br>Concerns not listened to<br><br>General public felt it was not their event |
| Objectives | Profit or breakeven for sponsors and government funding (public and private money) by marketing and promotion to create high attendance | **Image, reputation**<br><br>**Infrastructure**<br><br>**Positive impact on the community** | Voice in decisions<br><br>Maintain neighborhood<br><br>Be left alone |
| Criteria | Breakeven | **Visibility** | Local support |
| Alternatives | Disney-type entertainment<br><br>Reduce scope of event so that it is manageable<br><br>Alternate location | **Flower show** | Use Franklin Park but develop programs that meet residents' concerns<br><br>Alternative location |
| Consequences of alternatives | Smaller target population or a more expensive, larger target population<br><br>Reducing scope may change the nature of the event (good or bad) | **May not create hoped-for image** | Programs cost money, but may avoid many problems<br><br>Residents of alternative location may have similar concerns |
| Implementation barriers | Manipulation of information<br><br>Lack of knowledge, had to rely on outsiders | **Fuzzy vision makes planning difficult** | Limited choice of alternatives<br><br>No dealing with resident problems or concerns of public |

then be briefed on the current status of search using the core concerns, objectives, and criteria implied by the favored option: a flower show. This process is outlined in column 3 in Table 7.4.

A team using the T perspective would develop ideas with a technical viewpoint, drawing on the core concerns, objectives, and criteria suggested by technical considerations. Some possible ways to present the technical perspective are outlined in column 2 in Table 7.4. Using an SRGP, team members would list their ideas for ways to meet a technical objective of a break-even cost, ignoring the consequences and implementation barriers for the moment. In step 2, one idea from each list would be recorded, followed by a discussion and a selection of ideas that seem to merit further consideration. To separate idea generation from evaluation, a second meeting would be held to uncover consequences and implementation barriers for the T ideas that appear to have merit. This is done by silently listing consequences and barriers for each of the ideas. Next, the consequences and barriers for each idea would be listed under each priority idea that emerged. This is followed by priority setting to identify the consequences and barriers that seem most salient for each idea. These steps would produce a list of T-based ideas and an evaluation that adheres to the creativity steps of many ideas and deferred evaluation.

The P team would follow the same steps but use a citizen's perspective, looking for ways to bring about community support (see column 4 of Table 7.4). Once they complete these tasks, the P and T teams would be asked to uncover O consequences and implementation barriers in a separate effort using the SRGP format. Table 7.4 shows some possible outcomes had these multiple perspectives been applied to AmeriFlora.

## The Dominant P Perspective

The telescope, EuroDisney, Denver International Airport, Quaker, and Nationwide arena debacles illustrate a dominant P perspective. The telescope debacle was born of an agreement between the department chair and the university president as a way to improve a low-quality department. The financial stress on the university that this would impose (the T perspective) and the needs of the institution (the O perspective) were ignored. Walt's Dream and Eisner's commitment to it guided EuroDisney. Top management accepted this and gave little consideration to financial feasibility questions (T) about hotel occupancy and even less to their prospective French and European customers (P). The arena's backers shared an aim to make Columbus a big time city. A major league sports team was seen as the only way to do this. The prospects of making money with plan A (Issue 1) and plan B indicate some of the concerns that arise from a T perspective. The O perspective would draw Nationwide back to its core business, which does not include a running sports team or funding an arena, businesses they know nothing about. Both the T and O perspectives were treated superficially in the arena decision, and other ways to make Columbus a big league city were never considered.

Smithburg, at Quaker, let concerns about the seeming erosion of his visibility and viability (P) draw him toward an acquisition that he could turn around to rekindle his fame. The technical issues of competition and potential market share were ignored. No due diligence (T) was carried out, which made the company look foolish as a turnaround was attempted. An organizational (O) perspective that could bring out the likelihood of synergy was ignored as well. The independent bottlers and distributors for Snapple, with their contracts firmly entrenched, made synergy with Gatorade and its centralized production and distribution systems impossible.

Quaker's board could have developed the O and T perspectives more fully to uncover additional options. Knowledgeable insiders and outsiders could have been identified by the board and formed a team. This team could be divided into two groups, with one group asked to develop the T perspective and the other the O perspective. To open up the search, the groups would be provided with core concerns, objectives, and criteria, with the Snapple purchase as one option. The two groups would identify alternatives, consequences, and implementation barriers for the O and T perspectives as described previously. A number of options based on the T and O perspectives could be created in this way with clarity about how to realize them. The O and T teams would be asked to uncover P consequences and implementation barriers in a separate effort. Table 7.5 shows some possible outcomes of such a search.

Table 7.5
QUAKER PURCHASE OF SNAPPLE

|  | Technical Perspective | Organizational Perspective | Personal Perspective |
|---|---|---|---|
| Core concerns | New competitors entering sports drink market<br><br>Most Quaker products in mature phase | Current distribution network not sufficient for Gatorade distribution<br><br>Internal product development lacks creativity and innovation | **Smithburg losing visibility as Quaker products lose appeal**<br><br>**Threat of takeover may cost Smithburg and board of directors their jobs** |
| Objectives | Protect Gatorade<br><br>Get new products to market | Gain access to new channels<br><br>Find alternatives to current R&D focus | **Re-create glory of Gatorade acquisition**<br><br>**Protect jobs** |
| Criteria | Market share<br><br>Consumer response | Market share<br><br>Perceived innovation | **CEO and board have jobs**<br><br>**Top news coverage**<br><br>**Excitement internally** |
| Alternatives | Improve distribution<br><br>Develop brands internally | Increase distribution channels internally<br><br>Increase distribution by acquiring external firm<br><br>Increase marketing programs | **Acquire glamorous brand**<br><br>**Defensive restructuring** |
| Consequences of alternatives<br>　Pro | Gain market penetration for Gatorade<br><br>Short-term company stability<br><br>Gain market share of a proven product with no R&D costs or uncertainty | Increase market penetration<br><br>Increase sales<br><br>Increased brand awareness and market perception of Quaker | **High visibility**<br><br>**No takeover** |

(continued on next page)

*Table 7.5 (continued)*

|  | Technical Perspective | Organizational Perspective | Personal Perspective |
|---|---|---|---|
| Consequences of alternatives<br>Con | High cost<br><br>Glamorous brand not available | Increased logistics requirements<br><br>Excessive acquisition costs<br><br>Limited manufacturing and distribution synergies | **Acquired company could flop**<br><br>**May not stop takeover**<br><br>**Lose autonomy and maybe jobs**<br><br>**Lower share value** |
| Implementation barriers | Competition (Coke & Pepsi) fight for market share<br><br>Must continue to support mature products<br><br>Barriers to market penetration | Distribution locked up by competitors<br><br>No profitable brands for sale<br><br>Barriers to market penetration | **Shareholders**<br><br>**Market response**<br><br>**Board appeal** |

## The Dominant T Perspective

BeechNut, Nestle, and Shell's disposal of the Brent Spar illustrate decisions that became debacles by emphasizing the T perspective. BeechNut's debacle was born of top management's blind rush to avoid a $3.5 million loss. Organizational concerns about image and long-term viability were ignored, as were the potential personal losses that could be incurred by key players. Had top management looked at how things could backfire and create huge problems for them and the organization, the unfortunate chain of events that followed could have been avoided. Nestle was preoccupied with its market share position and failed to see how its critics (P) and their point of view could damage the organization (O).

To dispose of the Brent Spar, Shell officials focused on costs and other tangible measures of difficulties (T), such as the loss of life during onshore dismantling. The consequences of maintaining or dismantling the Brent Spar dominated top management's thinking. This led them to the deep-sea disposal option, as the other options uncovered were found to be expensive and dangerous. These considerations were based on quantitative assessments, and none of them addressed the public's view (P), which Greenpeace managed to ignite. The public's perception of big oil and its lack of responsibility had tainted Shell and made it vulnerable to a cause celebre born of frustration with the irresponsible acts of oil companies and the oil industry. Greenpeace was able to mobilize these concerns and mount a campaign against deep-sea disposal and the precedent it would set. Shell's management saw things differently, as noted by its attention to matters of liability and what is and is not legally allowable (O concerns). This, however, lost out to arguments about the cost and the technical difficulties of maintaining or dismantling the Brent Spar.

To develop a broader set of options, the P and O perspectives could have been developed by Shell's top management. To open up a search, teams would be formed to develop the P and O perspectives, with the T-based option of a deep-sea disposal as a point of departure. Two groups would be formed as before, and alternatives, consequences, and implementation barriers would be identified for the P or the O perspectives as described previously. A number of options based on the P and O perspectives with clarity about how to realize them could be created in this way. The O and P teams would then be asked to uncover T consequences and implementation barriers in a separate effort. Table 7.6 shows some possible outcomes of these three perspectives.

## Finding Innovative Ideas

To uncover innovative ideas, follow the steps in an SRGP guided by the three perspectives. Give each of the three teams core concerns, objectives, and criteria for one of the perspectives and ask team members to identify new ideas that can meet the perspective's objective. Examine ideas that seem meritorious and worthy of more careful development to uncover likely consequences and implementation difficulties. Then examine the ideas from each perspective and look for a synthesis that can deal with the claims and meet the objectives identified for the T, P, and O perspectives. Encourage other opportunities for creative thinking as well. Assign ideas that seem feasible to the evaluation stage, described in the next chapter.

| | Table 7.6 SHELL'S DISPOSAL OF THE BRENT SPAR | | |
|---|---|---|---|
| | **Technical Perspective** | **Organizational Perspective** | **Personal Perspective** |
| Core concerns | **Need to inexpensively dispose of the Brent Spar** | Meet environmental regulations<br><br>Maintain good corporate citizen image | Fear of contamination<br><br>Precedents set |
| Objectives | **Limit environ-mental damage**<br><br>**Minimize cost**<br><br>**Ensure safety** | Minimize liability<br><br>Enhance image | Prevent ecological damage, precedent |
| Criteria | **Cost**<br><br>**Number of injuries**<br><br>**Amount of envi-ronmental damage** | Reputation<br><br>Fines<br><br>Lawsuits | Amount of damage<br><br>Probability of future dumping |
| Alternatives | **Continued maintenance, refurbishment**<br><br>**Deep-sea disposal** | On-site disposal | Quid pro quo (allow dumping for stricter future regulations) |
| Consequences of alternatives | **Exorbitant future costs** | Loss of reputation<br><br>Potential legal problems | Loss of moral credibility |
| Implementation barriers | **Government support fickle** | New and stricter environmental regulation | Public and envi-ronmental group support |

# ▼ Key Points

▼ Provide sufficient time and money to allow a careful search.

▼ Avoid jumping on what appears to be a good idea early in a search effort. Conspicuous alternatives and the first workable alternative that appears will prematurely stop a search.

▼ Resist copying the practices of a single organization unless the fit is clear. Adapting the ideas of others will increase cost and the prospect of failure unless the idea has a good fit with the proposed user's environment.

▼ Avoid ideas that are variations on existing practices. This practice limits innovation and makes it likely the concerns provoking action will recur.

▼ Do not expect vendors to tailor their off-the-shelf ideas without an incentive to do so. Suppliers and vendors force-fit their stock solution to your RFP, and the fit can be more apparent than real.

▼ Develop more than one option. Multiple options allow a comparison of benefits and make it easier to defend a preferred course of action. Multiple options also provide the opportunity to combine the best features of the options into a hybrid that has superior features.

▼ Create ideas by using each of the three preferred search tactics. Each provides a different kind of solution. A multicycle search uncovers off-the-shelf technology that can be locally useful. Integrated benchmarking fashions solutions from an amalgamation of the best business practices of others. Innovation offers new ideas.

▼ Use innovation to uncover at least one idea that will be given serious consideration.

▼ Group process and multiple perspectives are more apt to uncover innovative ideas.

▼ To innovate, use objectives broadly defined, as described in Chapter 6, to direct the search for ideas from the T, P, and O perspectives. Examine the ideas that emerge, seeking a synthesis in which the best features of several options are combined to create a superior plan.

# The Traps in Misusing Evaluation

## CHAPTER 8

Promoting a preferred course of action with a defensive evaluation and disregarding its risk invites a debacle. Decision makers who set out to support a preferred idea get drawn into a defensive evaluation. Because the products of a defensive evaluation are shallow and predictable, clever wordsmiths must work their magic to justify the data to be collected. Vast sums are spent to find evidence that validates what a decision maker wants to do or must support. Little, if anything, is spent on claim investigation, implementation, direction setting, or searching for new ideas. A direction that specifies expected results cuts the ground from under a defensive evaluation by making its self-serving intent evident, so decision makers in the debacles were careful to evaluate a preferred course of action without them.

Defensive evaluations that lack a clear direction produce argumentative and misleading conclusions. Without a direction, different people see different things to be measured. Ford officials focused on the cost of a recall, indicating that this was all that mattered. Critics contended that more should have been spent on measuring the consequences of *not* fixing the defective gas tank. Shell officials had staffers evaluate the cost of disposal, assuming that *their* disposal cost was the primary concern. Shell's critics contended that costs to society had been overlooked. An agreed-upon direction would have broadened the scope of these evaluations and made them work for, instead of against, the company.

Defensive evaluations are misleading, many intentionally so. Pena spent huge sums documenting the merits of a new airport and nothing on determining the benefits of reworking Stapelton. This gives the appearance of trying to mislead, even if Pena believed a new airport was the best option. Disney staffers were told to analyze the French deal, but nothing was spent to find out what other countries would offer. This closed off offers that could have provided a better deal. To defend tax support for the arena, its backers offered dubious studies of economic activity supposedly stimulated by sports arenas in other cities. If an enhanced business climate is the goal, would anyone have an arena at the top of their list? Clarity in one's direction exposes the real purpose of a defensive evaluation—an attempt to mislead.

Evaluations carried out in the debacles said nothing about risk. Ameri-Flora's proponents, like the Millennium Dome supporters, made favorable assumptions about ticket sales to conceal the project's risk from the public officials asked to fund it. Disney's analysis of the French deal drew top management away from questions about its risk. In the other debacles, both benefits and risk were ignored. Smithburg did nothing to measure the benefits or the risk of a Snapple purchase, and OSU officials made the telescope decision without either type of evaluation.

Evaluation offers valuable insights when used to compare the benefits of options and to uncover the risk in these options. Let's see how this is done in practice, what prompts success and failure, and what amount of risk was present in the courses of action followed in the debacles. First, a discussion of best practice and tactics to avoid when making evaluations is offered, following the format used in previous chapters. The debacles are then revisited to show you how to identify and measure risk, and how to use it to evaluate your options.

## Evaluating the Merits of Options

Evaluation is used to document the benefits of proposed ideas. Evaluation tactics used by decision makers differ in the type of information collected and how an inference is made. The track record of these evaluation tactics shows that some work better than others. Let's consider what works best, what to avoid, and how each evaluation tactic is carried out.

## Best Practice

Analytic and bargaining evaluation tactics have excellent track records once a clear direction has been identified (Table 8.1). Each provides convincing information to support a proposed choice, which is more apt to lead to successful implementation of a beneficial idea than are other evaluation tactics.

**Analytic Tactics.** In an analytical evaluation, data is gathered from archives, pilot tests, and simulations, and inferences are made from the data using analytical tools. Archival data extracted from records can be manipulated to estimate the benefits of options. Data sources include the organization's files and databases, supplier and vendor documents, bids responding to RFPs, and standard reference sources (e.g., Dun's, Value Line). To create summative information from the archival data, such as projecting revenue from potential oil sites using historical data on yields from comparable sites, cost-benefit studies, Pro forma income determinations, multiattribute utilities, and the like are employed. Data also can be obtained from pilot tests that try out an idea in a field setting to estimate benefits. A plan to sell an intimate apparel line in Lane Bryant, a subsidiary

---

*Table 8.1*
### SUCCESS OF EVALUATION TACTICS

| Tactic | Frequency of Use | Adoption[1] | Expected Benefits[2] | Installation Time[3] |
|---|---|---|---|---|
| **MORE SUCCESSFUL** | | | | |
| Analytic | 39% | 64% to 75% | Good | 9.6 months |
| Bargaining | 13% | 65% to 74% | Good | 5.8 months |
| **LESS SUCCESSFUL** | | | | |
| Subjective | 32% | 37% to 65% | Good to Adequate | 10 months |
| Judgment | 16% | 36% to 47% | Adequate | 7.5 months |

(1) Adoption rates indicate the percentage of decisions sustained for two years and the percentage that were fully put to use.

(2) Based on the evaluation of stakeholders.

(3) Time measured from the end of development to the end of implementation attempts.

of Limited Stores, was tried out in a few stores to determine sales, turns (inventory turnover), and demographics to forecast profit. Simulations construct a mock-up to produce performance data, such as tracing the steps in a proposed scheduling system for an automotive plant to find where costs could be reduced and output increased.

*Bargaining Tactics.* Evaluation via bargaining brings stakeholders to agreement about the choice to be made by finding a course of action that all can support. Ranking or voting follows a period of negotiation and information sharing.

Evaluative bargaining is typically carried out in a group made up of stakeholders who vote, rank, or prioritize ideas after discussing performance-related data. This is illustrated by a brokerage firm that has its key associates review and discuss the bids vendors offered to integrate their client base and then rank the proposed systems. To facilitate bargaining, data may be gathered from potential users to get feedback on their views of what does or does not work, and why. For example, ideas to increase the productivity of customer service activities were presented to airline clerks, asking for a list of each plan's strengths and weaknesses. The group examined these views to find key areas of resistance and perceptions about matters of importance to the clerks and selected the system with the broadest base of support. Giving people a voice is key. Users and stakeholders in a position to block a decision are less inclined to do so if asked about their preferences before a decision is made.

### Tactics to Avoid

In nearly half of their decisions, decision makers rely on subjective or judgmental tactics to do an evaluation. Subjective and judgmental tactics restrict the information used to justify a preferred course of action and are often unsuccessful (Table 8.1).

*Subjective Tactics.* Decision makers who cull from archival data the most persuasive and compelling arguments supporting a preferred course of action use a subjective approach to evaluation. Objective performance data are given a subjective interpretation. A value judgment is made that interprets the meaning of performance-related data to create new information. This "new information" is then used to argue for the adoption of an idea. Officials in an online information service company examined the benefits of developing an international market in Pacific Rim countries for computer services in this way, finding the proposed new market hard to service, due to time differences, and inferred a low use. Ideas may be labeled as effective if developed by well-regarded people or used by well-regarded organizations. Norming in this way attempts to show that a proposed course of action follows what others are doing, as when CompuServe officials selected a plan to solicit customers by drawing on an approach used by company founders.

Decision makers relying on subjective interpretations often seek confirmation. A consultant or an internal expert may be summoned to add an aura of expertise to the interpretation. The expert is made aware of the preferred choice and then asked to fashion arguments that support it, such as having sales people offer arguments supporting strong sales for a proposed new product. These arguments are pulled together by the decision maker to bolster his or her line of reasoning. Decision makers fashion arguments that include the expert's credentials. People seldom see all this as convincing. Arguments that support a favored idea get dismissed if they appear self-serving, and experts and expert testimony is frequently discounted. Outsider views had less credibility and carried less weight than decision makers in the debacles realized.

***Judgmental Tactics.*** A judgmental tactic is used when a proposed action is defended with assertions about one's knowledge of comparable decisions. This is done by contending that one has the insight to make the choice without offering specifics. No attempt is made to collect performance data. Choices are made intuitively by drawing on experience and knowledge. Decision makers using this tactic identify a favored course of action without offering arguments or information to back up their choice and then push ahead to implement it. The president of the Anthony Thomas Candy Company found a packaging reseal, bought it on the spot, and gave it to a product line manager to implement. The president made a judgment and told people to comply. This makes a judgmental evaluation an extension of the idea tactic. To find a preferred course of action, a judgment is made that draws on unspecified personal beliefs and experiences of the decision maker, displacing both direction setting and search.

Such judgments can seem visceral and capricious to observers, and evaluations made in this way have a poor track record. Pushing an idea without offering a justification makes a decision maker's motives suspect. Suspicion creates an atmosphere that makes success problematic. Some do this to avoid disclosure of markets to be exploited or the new features of products. Others use it to hide a vested interest. Both yield the same result—a perception of fewer benefits and a greater chance that implementation will be blocked.

## Evaluation Blunders

The urge to cut decision-making time and cost plays out one last time in the evaluation of options, which again leads to premature commitments, misused resources, and bad tactics.

### Premature Commitments

Subjective and judgmental evaluations often follow an idea tactic in which direction lacks clarity. Judgmental evaluations offer the idea in place of supporting arguments. Smithburg relied on his judgment to push ahead with the Snapple acquisition. The CEO at BeechNut did likewise, hoping to dispose of the tainted inventory before anyone was caught. OSU officials made a snap judgment to support the telescope, which they later learned to regret.

People who fear that opposition can spring up with little warning use evaluation tactics to marshal supportive arguments quickly and then forge ahead. This often triggers an idea-imposition process, as noted in Chapter 3, incorporating a subjective evaluation tactic. Arena supporters had to offer some kind of defense for their idea, as did the AmeriFlora proponents and the law enforcement people at Waco. In each case, decision makers wanted to act quickly before opposition materialized. To defend a desired course of action, data are found to make the best case for adoption. Data that fail to support the idea are ignored or hidden.

Analysis and bargaining seem overly time consuming to decision makers. You may be surprised to find that this is not the case. Table 8.1 shows that subjective evaluations take more time to carry out than either analysis or bargaining because arguments are provoked by the interpretations that are made. Decision makers must then backtrack to collect more data from archives or experts, or support from power brokers, to turn aside opposing arguments. Collecting data and supporters to counter each objection as it arises drags things out to the point that either an analysis or bargaining could have been completed.

Judgmental approaches are fast but failure prone. Judgment creates an image of caprice. Decision makers who fail to explain the reasons behind their choices encourage resistance, even in a relatively placid situation. They then must resort to an edict to implement the decision because the arguments needed to use persuasion are missing.

Judgmental and subjective evaluation tactics, like so many we have considered, have deceptive efficiencies. The suspicion evoked by a subjective evaluation ends up drawing out the effort and lowering its prospects of success. A judgmental evaluation is somewhat efficient, but not effective due to the resistance it provokes.

### Misused Resources

The cost of analysis or bargaining may seem daunting, and spending as little as possible is always preferred. Taking things into one's hands with a judgment or a subjective evaluation appears to keep evaluation costs under control. It also heads off the critic demanding to know how much is to be spent on involving people to ruminate about benefits and consultants to carry out an analysis. Decision makers in the telescope, Quaker, and BeechNut debacles skipped evaluation altogether, thinking they could defend their choices with the aura of their position and its prerogatives should opposition materialize. But their power proved to be inadequate, leaving these decision makers with little to defend their choices. When power was used a bit more astutely, as in the AmeriFlora, DIA, and Waco debacles, cost again became an issue, and subjective interpretations of data blocked a careful analysis or a consensus-building effort.

Like beliefs about the time required, the costs of a judgmental or a subjective evaluation prove to be deceptive. If you invest time and effort in bargaining or analysis today, it increases your prospects of success later on.

### Poor Practice

Analysis and bargaining work better than judgmental and subjective evaluations because each helps to manage forces that can block a decision. Controversial decisions can be kept under wraps until arguments that support them are tested and confirmed. Analysis can be used to ratify the merits of an idea as well as to choose among ideas, if the direction is clear. Bargaining manages conflicting interests, turning aside games played by people with vested interests. Carefully constructed arguments and consensus about a choice heads off these games.

People resist analysis and bargaining for understandable and for dubious reasons. Analytical evaluations have been known to produce misleading and threatening information. Analysis can be inconvenient as well as nondiagnostic (e.g., March, 1994; Mintzberg et al., 1976). The inconvenience arises from its conclusions: the analysis may not support the idea powerful people prefer. Decision makers who keep their preferences under wraps can control evaluation information. Analytical information is unpredictable and thus a threat to people with such interests. Complex decisions have many value-laden considerations that are difficult to measure. This allows people to seek subjective arguments that support their ideas and to engage in power plays and politicking to see that their idea is adopted. Analysis applied under such conditions creates strife and conflict. Decision makers with a low tolerance for conflict reject analysis to avoid such behavior.

Some benefits are impossible to measure quantitatively. By concentrating on what can be measured, a decision maker loses sight of important considerations that resist measurement. One knows good customer service after experiencing it, but it is difficult to quantify the experience. Many decisions have "soft" outcomes like this that resist quantification. Decision makers who commission an analysis in such a situation get little of value for their time and money. Generalizations are then made contending that analysis has limited use. Despite its limitations, analysis is more successful than either the subjective or the judgmental approach.

Bargaining requires participation, and participation creates commitments. Asking people their views conveys an obligation to consider these views. A perceived loss of control results. Many avoid participation because it conjures a vision of people with little real responsibility pushing wild-eyed ideas. Such ideas are believed to have little practical value and yet must be dutifully considered, if not outright adopted. Because of this, many decision makers use participation only when their power limitations force it and rarely use it proactively (Shamir et al., 1993). Table 8.1

shows that bargaining is both efficient and effective. The cooptation effects of bargaining, which entice the people involved to go along with an agreed-upon course of action, increase the prospect of adoption. A negotiated decision reconciles the conflicting interests of stakeholders, ensuring its acceptance. Concerns about wild-eyed impractical ideas are also groundless. Choices that stem from bargaining produce good benefits, which reach or exceed other means of making a choice, and are quite efficient.

Subjective and judgmental tactics are prone to error. Both place too much emphasis on intuition and too little on careful inference with good data. Intuition, or knowing without conscious reasoning, serves people well in creative tasks, but those same intuitive powers fail when concrete estimates and evaluations are required. People have difficulty making accurate predictions about things such as benefits and costs because base rates and dilution effects create estimation biases (Hogarth, 1980; Nisbett and Ross, 1989).

Base rates are derived from your observations. Vivid target cases or seemingly relevant anecdotes can push aside projections based on the base rate found in a summation of your experiences. Even when this is avoided and the base rate is used, people write off best and worst case outcomes. This discounts the possibility of a really good or a really bad outcome. The expected value is distorted because the up and down sides are ignored when making a projection. Nearly all of the decision makers in the debacles fell victim to this base rate distortion as they made assertions about the merits of a favored idea.

Dilution results when diagnostic and less diagnostic information are mixed. People relying on their experience to make a judgment have difficulty separating the relevant from the nonrelevant experience. The cues that include less relevant information dilute the more diagnostic situations and events. Previous park problems distracted Disney executives and kept them from thinking about difficulties the new park could bring. Windfall outcomes suggest that good practices were followed. But as in Quaker's purchase of Snapple, when things turn out well, success may be due to luck. Base rate biases, dilution, and windfalls create errors in evaluative judgments.

## Managing Uncertainty and the Risk It Creates

Benefits are difficult to estimate because of uncertainty. Most projections have a range of equally likely values, creating uncertainty in the amount of benefit, costs, and other outcomes that will be realized. This uncertainty creates risk. Decision makers in the debacles either suppressed risk or became overwhelmed by it. Overly confident decision makers suppress risk. Decision makers in the EuroDisney, telescope, Quaker, and AmeriFlora decisions made overly optimistic forecasts that suppressed risk. Decision makers in the arena decision and, as we shall see, in the shed load decision made overly pessimistic forecasts and became overwhelmed by risk.

In the debacles, decision makers misjudged the amount of risk in the choices they made, either disregarding uncertainty or overreacting to it. Uncertainty is brushed aside when point estimates are made midway in a range of equally likely values for benefits and when benefits that resist measurement are ignored. Both moves simplify things, but both get decision makers into trouble. Eisner accepted reports based on a single "most likely" estimate of hotel occupancy and attendance. Both estimates proved to be overly optimistic. Looking at a best case situation and ignoring worst case forecasts for occupancy and attendance swept away the risk in the French deal. BeechNut's top management assumed that they could dump the tainted juice and escape any penalties in doing so. Had they explored how large these penalties could be, or even the least worst case estimate of them, they might have taken a different tack. To appreciate the amount of risk in such decisions, the best and worst case range of values that represent possible forecasts of benefits are considered in the evaluation. This is done by incorporating the best and the worst case estimates in a predicted payoff. To see how faulty assumptions about risk crop up, and their consequences, let's look at a New York City blackout and its financial impact.

## The New York City Blackout

On a hot summer day in July, 9 million New Yorkers were left without power in the wake of a summer storm. It took twenty-five hours to restore full power. Under the cover of darkness, the city's criminal element went on a looting spree, trashing buildings and city infrastructure, leading to social, economic, political, and personal losses totaling $28 million (more than $100 million in today's dollars). Consolidated Edison paid out $10.6 million in service restoration costs, lost revenues, noncollectable accounts, and analysis expenditures. The choices that preceded the pivotal "shed load decision" and those that followed it are shown in Table 8.2. The steps taken to arrive at the decision are listed in Table 8.3.

The fateful day began uneventfully for system operators in the Consolidated Edison Control Center. The weather forecast, one of several things center staff monitor, called for a 50 percent chance of a thunderstorm. The system operator projected electricity usage based on weather reports, available supplies, and seasonal usage data. Should the grid become over-

| Table 8.2 FLOW OF EVENTS IN THE BLACKOUT DEBACLE | |
|---|---|
| **Choices** | |
| Actions before | Prior blackouts in U.S. cities pose concerns |
| | Historical data indicating the frequency of conditions that can lead to a blackout are ignored |
| | Three months prior to the blackout seventeen power interruptions reported to FPC |
| | Summer time peak usage of power |
| | Weather forecast calls for storms |
| | Lightning hits transmission tower, knocking out two feeder lines |
| | Generators revved up to compensate |
| | Second bolt of lightning hits another tower |
| Pivotal decision | Power dispatchers advise Con Ed to shed load (seven calls to take this action made in fifteen minutes). Operator refuses. |
| Actions after | Con Ed personnel cut voltage by 5 percent and then 8 percent |
| | Transmission failures mount and the system crashes |
| | During twenty-five-hour period required to restore power, losses of $28 million to Con Ed occurred |

| Table 8.3 THE NEW YORK CITY BLACKOUT | |
|---|---|
| Claims | Power disruption from lightning striking transmission lines possible |
| Core concerns/considerations (a) Recognized | Maintain power flow |
| (b) Hidden | Avoid blame |
| | When to shed load |
| Directions | Prevent loss of power (implicit) |
| Options considered | Power supplements |
| | Rerouting |
| Extent of search and innovation | None |
| Use of evaluation | None |
| Impact of evaluation | None |
| Barriers to action | Fear of consequences |
| Ethical concerns | No one to speak for the public interest |
| Barriers to learning | Treating blackout as unprecedented, once in a lifetime experience |

loaded, a warning alarm sounds and seven load-shedding switches are activated. To "shed load," the system operator blacks out one part of the city to head off a citywide blackout, allowing the system to stabilize. Load can be shed in about two minutes.

Con Ed supplies power to the five boroughs and to Westchester County, north of the city. The company has a 9.88 megawatt capacity and purchases additional power to keep costs low. Power comes from five feeders operated by three power suppliers via aboveground lines, known to be vulnerable to lightning. Lightning struck at about 8 p.m. The first bolt hit a transmission tower, knocking out two feeder lines. To compensate, Con Ed operators revved up their generators. About thirty minutes later, a second bolt struck another transmission tower, prompting a dispatcher from Albany to advise Con Ed operators to shed load. They refused. Instead they cut voltage by 5 percent and then 8 percent. Failures mounted, but no one was prepared to shed load yet. One system overload led to another and the remaining lines went down, plunging the city into darkness. Had the operator shed load after the first lightning strike, or even after the second one, the blackout would have been contained. The system operator had a window of fifteen minutes to shed load but failed to recognize the seriousness of the situation or the urgency to act. In all, seven calls to shed load came from various sources during this time. All were ignored.

What prompted the shed load decision debacle? Con Ed's system operator refused to act for several reasons. Company officials provide little training in how to recognize a shed load situation, and conditions prompting such an event are rare. Rare events become nonevents without contingency plans and training simulations in how to carry them out, as in any disaster planning. An operator's mind-set of keeping the electricity flowing makes it difficult to turn power off. Training could have overcome this and provided the tools to determine when to shed load. Lacking such tools, the operator worried about being held responsible for a partial blackout and did everything possible to avoid it.

Plenty of ambiguity and uncertainty are at work here. The operator had no way to recognize a shed load event or to distinguish it from other power fluctuations. The consequences of a blackout were equally ambiguous. The system operator had to choose between two actions. Both seemed disastrous for all concerned. Perverse incentives are at work. The operator had every reason to believe that both shedding load and not shedding load would lead to recriminations, or even job loss, a no-win situation for the operator.

Let's return to the fatal fifteen minutes in which the decision debacle occurred. The operator assumed his purpose was to prevent a loss of service, but how to ensure this was not clear. This prompted hypervigilance—with extreme time pressure causing simplistic thinking and a frantic search for a way out of an impending crisis. A short-term outlook keeps power on as long as possible and gives immediate relief. The long-term outcome of a blackout was not on anyone's screen. The shed load option seemed much too risky because its consequences were hard to predict. Con Ed had access to civil disorder costs, but the operator did not. It is foolish to expect an untrained system operator to make a systematic and rational appraisal of options in a crisis. The personal needs of the operator swept aside organizational and technical considerations. Concerns about personal responsibility and avoiding blame overwhelmed questions about losses for Con Ed.

There were missed opportunities. A similar situation in upstate New York twelve years earlier should have given Con Ed a heads up. Insurance institute documents prepared in the wake of this earlier blackout found that economic losses in future blackouts could run from a low of $2 million ($10 million in today's dollars) to a high of $44 million ($200 million)—compelling reasons to avoid another blackout. Con Ed learned enough to put a shed load system in place but failed to take steps to ensure that it would be used. Operators were not trained. Con Ed failed to provide straightforward procedures, checks and balances, and responsible parties to make the shed load decision. People can do such a job if they are trained to deal with emergency situations.

No displays of company power status showed shortages and where they were occurring. Miscommunications were likely because Con Ed and its power suppliers lacked knowledge about power source availability. There was too much reliance on a single route for power, as in the prior blackout. Dispersed power sources would have helped Con Ed hedge a disastrous situation. Utility interconnects are voluntary, leaving backup negotiations in the hands of the power companies. In the past, the Department of Energy (DOE) responses to mediate such discussions had been slow and overly bureaucratic, leaving no one to speak for the public interest. The crisis could have been averted, or limited, if the power plants supplying power to Con Ed had a policy of staggering their service requirements. Three transmission lines with a capacity of nearly 4.0 megawatts were not being used the night of the blackout. Better coordination could have made them available. But the power companies were not tuned into one another's emergency needs, so these standby reserves were not shared. Power reserves were inadequate. A few years earlier, due to uncertainty and cost, Con Ed reduced its reliance on gas turbines by 80 percent by not staffing them after 8 p.m. This cut peak load protection by nearly 50 percent. Reserves were adequate for the expected air conditioner drain on power on a hot summer day, but not for a disaster. Con Ed restored gas turbine staffing to twenty-four hours a day to get a little positive public relations in the wake of considerable bad press, even though twenty-four-hour coverage is not necessary and is very costly. All this suggests that Con Ed was discounting the chance of a blackout event to nearly zero.

In the three months prior to the blackout, seventeen power interruptions—losses of more than a 100 megawatt load for fifteen minutes or more—were reported by the Federal Power Commission (FPC). None led to a blackout, but all stemmed from a combination of natural causes, equipment failure, and human error—the very same things that caused the blackout in New York City. Things that could provoke a blackout were known and occurred on a regular basis. Information systems to track them and call attention to dangerous events could have been constructed with the technology of the time. The FPC reports twenty to fifty such events each year and finds that events that can spark a major power outage can be expected every five to ten years.

Con Ed overlooked warning signals. Historical data indicating the likelihood of a blackout were available. Thunderstorms are not uncommon, nor are breakdowns of lines and switches. The relationship between temperature in summer and power usage is well known. Looking at all this in a crisis is impossible. Rules governing action must be fashioned before a crisis, not during one.

Several ethical issues can be spotted. Con Ed serves two conflicting groups: its customers and its stockholders. Actions taken to benefit one, such as cost cutting, are not apt to benefit the other. A utility such as Con Ed must balance these interests, and regulatory agencies are put in place in part because of these conflicts. The public interest is not being served by a regulatory agency when its oversight ignores questions of public safety. Con Ed's management had no preventive maintenance, inadequate power backup, and no disaster plan. None of these management gaffes and shortcomings was recognized by Con Ed's oversight bodies.

Con Ed responded to the public outcry that followed the disaster by claiming that they had been victimized by an "unprecedented series of events." Two towers being struck by lighting in a twenty-minute period was called a "once in a lifetime experience." As the FPC data show, these events can be expected far more often than Con Ed's claims suggest. There had been twenty such instances in the previous fifteen years. Con Ed seems poised for damage control, not for learning and corrective action.

Con Ed's semipublic status as a utility prompted an investigation. Several commissions and review boards were appointed to look into the disaster. New York City's Special Commission of Inquiry into Energy Failure attributed the blackout to Con Ed's management. They found that no amount of equipment could prevent another disaster if Con Ed officials continued to use poor judgment. The committee called for reform in the regulatory process to ensure that Con Ed would be held financially accountable for its actions. Con Ed was not allowed to recover the $10 million in compensation paid out to its customers with rate increases. Out-of-service plants could no longer be included in Con Ed's rate base. This gave Con Ed an incentive to keep plants running efficiently and to sell the reserve capacity. Con Ed agreed to improve on the accuracy of its power forecasts and instituted a "storm watch" procedure that modifies the balance of power when a thunderstorm is predicted to stress power generation and lowers the reliance on transmission lines. A computer then offers contingency plans.

Con Ed managers were contacted to determine the current criteria for shedding load. Company officials were not willing to answer questions. This may be due to concerns about legal liabilities or to a lack of learning. Many years later it is still not clear whether Con Ed has shed load procedures in place or what they might be.

## Estimating Risk

Risk can be incorporated into evaluations analytically or graphically. An analytic approach determines the net payoff for each option being considered by weighting optimistic and pessimistic forecasts of key factors according to their chance of occurring. Forecasts for factors such as sales for a new product, occupancy for a hotel, bank rates to finance a building project, number of rain days for a ballpark, and attendance at an event would be treated in this way. This weighted average of the best and worst case forecast incorporates risk into the evaluation of options.

The logic is like that found in making wagers. If the chance of winning $2 is 50 percent, the expected amount of one's winnings is $1. What one can win is discounted proportionately to the chance of winning it. If the unfavorable sales forecast has a 20 percent chance of occurring and the

| Table 8.4 |||
|---|---|---|
| **NEW YORK CITY BLACKOUT** |||
| **CON ED COSTS** |||
|  |  | **Blackout** | **No Blackout** |
| **Options** | Shed Load | –$512,000 | –$512,000 |
|  | Wait | –$10,600,000 | 0 |
| **SOCIETAL COSTS** |||
|  |  | **Blackout** | **No Blackout** |
| **Options** | Shed Load | –$1,000,000 | –$1,000,000 |
|  | Wait | –$310,000,000 | 0 |

favorable one an 80 percent chance, the expected payoff is determined by multiplying each forecast by its likelihood and adding the result. This weights the optimistic and pessimistic forecasts by their chance of occurring to incorporate risk. Making such an evaluation requires likelihood estimates that are seldom known with any precision. A graphic approach treats these values as unknowns. Uncertainty is estimated by identifying the amount of risk in getting a hoped-for payoff. The graph shows the payoffs and their risk, and decision makers must ask how much risk they can accept to go after a higher payoff option.

Risk can be graphically represented using the information available at the time each of the debacles occurred. Beginning with the New York City shed load debacle, let's examine the amount of risk in each of the courses of action selected. (See Appendix 2 for additional details on how these risk estimates were calculated.)

## The Shed Load Decision

A shed load decision poses an excruciating dilemma for a Con Ed operator. Shedding load would deny power to many customers, which runs counter to company mandates to keep the power on no matter what. If a shed load decision proves to be unwarranted, such an action could put the operator's job in jeopardy. Con Ed's management failed to provide their operators with decision rules to help make them make this difficult and weighty choice.

By identifying the consequences of available options and measuring the risk in each, guidelines can be created to manage risk in a shed load decision. A blackout threat has two options: shed load or wait. Each option has consequences that stem from an uncertain future event—a possible blackout. Uncertainty flows from the possibility that things may snowball and cause a citywide blackout. Instead of estimating the probability of such an unlikely event, it is more useful to estimate the amount of risk in each option. The likelihood of the blackout event is treated as an unknown. To incorporate this into the evaluation of options, the outcomes of the shed load and wait options shown in Table 8.4 are weighted by their chance of occurring, solving for the unknown risk of a blackout. The results are shown in Figure 8.1. The horizontal axis covers all possible values for the likelihood of a blackout event. The likelihood of a blackout, ranging from none to certain, is incorporated in the projected losses for the shed load and wait options.

The top portion of Figure 8.1 considers the decision from Con Ed's point of view. Looking only at company cost, the shed load option is preferred when the chance of a blackout exceeds 4.8 percent. This is denoted by the point where the lines depicting the costs of the two options cross. The shed load option produces a better payoff for Con Ed (less cost in this case) whenever the chance of a blackout exceeds 5 percent. This suggests that the operator should be ready to shed load for ninety-five of one hundred situations in which conditions arise that can cause a blackout. Not much decision risk here. Con Ed has considerable incentive to see that load is shed when a risky situation is encountered.

To take a societal point of view, the cost of looting, lost business, insurance claims, law enforcement, and the like must be included in the estimates of cost. If load is shed, the cost of law enforcement to police the affected area would be incurred by society. This is shown in the bottom portion of Table 8.4 and presented graphically in the bottom part of Figure 8.1. Considering societal costs provides an even more convincing argument to shed load as a precautionary measure to prevent an even bigger disaster. The shed load option is preferred when the chance of a blackout exceeds three chances in a thousand. This would call on Con Ed to

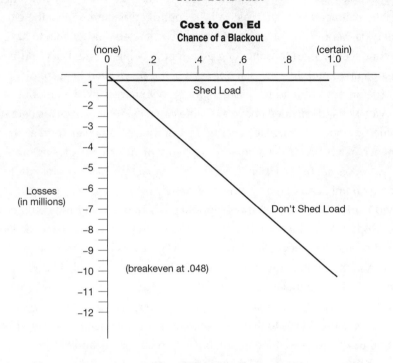

*Figure 8.1*
**SHED LOAD RISK**

**Cost to Con Ed**
Chance of a Blackout

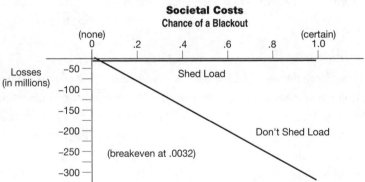

**Societal Costs**
Chance of a Blackout

have its operators ready to shed load in nearly every major storm, something the operators could not fathom. The risk of shedding load is far below
what Con Ed officials believed about blackout risk at the time, and seem
to believe even today. The implied sanctions and implicit incentives in
place to keep service on no matter what are ill advised and must be

changed. To avoid another debacle, Con Ed officials must craft guidelines that tell their operators the amount of load to shed and when to shed it. The public will need education as well. To control crime and protect the citizenry, law enforcement agencies in the area affected must be told to have a contingency plan to police the area that is being blacked out and be geared up to mobilize the plan for each of the seven shed load areas.

The amount of load to be shed can be determined by the amount of service being demanded above available capacity. Total capacity is determined by power ratings for each feeder and reserve power source. The chance of a blackout event increases when switches are not closing properly, feeders are being pushed beyond their capacity, reserve power fails to come on line, and lightning strikes. When this string of events is noted, a shed load decision is warranted. Several types of decision rules could be developed. Shed load could be called for when any feeder exceeds its short-term emergency rating. Such a decision rule is in use by other utilities. A fault line tree could be constructed that shows the likelihood of a system collapse sufficient to cause a blackout. Such a tree would take some work to construct, and analysts would have to experiment with the conditions noted previously to discover where its system vulnerabilities lie. This could pay dividends in the future for Con Ed customers and for the company's bruised image. Con Ed has the capacity to do this but, as yet, fails to see the risk in this decision realistically. Another debacle seems likely.

### AmeriFlora

The AmeriFlora decision in Chapter 7 is similar to many decisions made by U.S. companies that forecast sales to estimate revenues and make pricing decisions to influence buyer behavior. Data describing cost and revenues for the AmeriFlora decision can be found in Table 8.5. The implied objective for the "hold event" option called for a breakeven. Let us see if this assumption is realistic.

Costs can be estimated from other such events, but revenues have considerable uncertainty because it is difficult to accurately forecast attendance. The consultants, who had a good track record for estimating attendance figures for similar large U.S. events such as state fairs, put attendance between 2.6 million and 4.6 million. An attendance range of this magnitude made ticket revenues sufficient to cover costs very uncertain.

*Table 8.5*
**AMERIFLORA**

|  |  | REVENUES[1] | |
|---|---|---|---|
|  |  | Favorable | Unfavorable |
| **OPTIONS** | Hold Event | $6,100,000 | -$27,800,000 |
|  | Cancel | 0 | 0 |

(1) Balance of revenue less projected costs

Donation revenues were also uncertain. Critics called the organizers' fore-cast of $30 million in private donations overly optimistic. With some forty contributors, $200,000 per firm was seen by critics as a more realistic esti-mate. There was no reason to challenge public donations because $30 mil-lion had been budgeted by public organizations at the time. Commission sales, such as memorabilia and food items, were but a small part of the

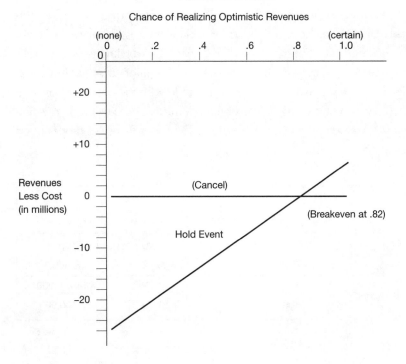

*Figure 8.2*
**AMERIFLORA RISK**

total revenue picture, so they are ignored here. Risk in this decision stems from whether a breakeven can be expected, given what was known about costs and revenues at the time. To determine the break-even risk, the chance of realizing enough revenue to cover costs is treated as an unknown (see Table 8.5). Figure 8.2 shows that a breakeven occurs if there is an 82 percent chance that the more optimistic attendance forecast will be realized. This means that if one hundred similar events were held only eighteen would break even. This puts the chance of success at 18 percent. A break-even outcome should not have been expected because Ameri-Flora was riddled with risk. If a break-even outcome was the expectation, a risk assessment argues against holding the event.

## The Telescope Decision

The telescope decision from Chapter 6 demonstrates how a poor choice was made because decision makers failed to see the amount of risk in their preferred course of action realistically. When risk is considered, the telescope project would have been easy to rule out, reducing embarrassment all around.

Data describing the revenues and costs for the project are shown in Table 8.6. The major uncertainty in this decision was the amount of grant revenue that could be expected if OSU went ahead with the project. Estimates by the department chair ranged from $2 million to $4 million annually. To make the revenue values compatible with the one-time cost of a telescope, present worth values of the optimistic and pessimistic revenue streams are computed (see Appendix 2). The payoffs of the dropout and participate options are shown in Figure 8.3.

| | | Table 8.6 THE TELESCOPE CONSORTIUM | |
|---|---|---|---|
| | | GRANT REVENUES[1] | |
| | | Optimistic | Pessimistic |
| OPTIONS | Participate | −$4,400,000 | −$14,700,000 |
| | Drop Out | −$3,100,000 | −$3,100,000 |

(1) Present worth of annual revenues from grants less annual operating costs and one-time share of telescope construction cost

Figure 8.3

**THE TELESCOPE RISK**

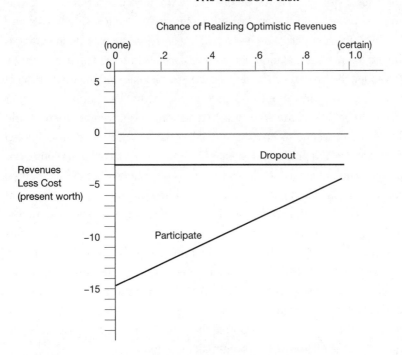

The decision is clear cut. The dropout option has a bigger payoff no matter what is assumed about the likelihood of realizing an optimistic amount of revenue from grant awards. The best case forecast for grant revenue leads to a $1 million subsidy for the department by the university. The subsidy increases to nearly $15 million if grants prove more difficult to obtain and the pessimistic level of revenue is realized. Losses are realized no matter what is assumed about the level of grant support. To propose such a project to the board of trustees, university officials should be clear about its likely costs. The risk assessment shows that the university would have to absorb losses between $1 million and $15 million to realize the departmental reputation objective.

## The Nationwide Arena

The Nationwide arena decision from Chapter 5 calls for a comparison of two options: seeking a tax subsidy (plan A) and private financing (plan B). Instead of using a "do nothing" option to create a baseline for comparison purposes, the two options are compared to see which has a better payoff for Nationwide. With a 90 percent interest in the project, Nationwide was the key player, and the analysis concentrates on Nationwide's costs and benefits. The company also had a parking garage, which company officials hoped to put to use. Nationwide and its partners dreamed up a tax subsidy to reduce the project's risk, but by doing so they labeled the arena project very risky. Worries about poor attendance at hockey games and other events to be held in the arena raised questions about whether there would be enough revenue to cover costs. Table 8.7 summarizes data collected from articles and publications examining the tax proposal at the time. It is assumed that company leaders would prefer a course of action that offered the best profit prospects. To focus on the downside, as the people at Nationwide appeared to do, the likelihood of low attendance is examined.

The risk found in Nationwide's private finance and tax subsidy options is shown in Figure 8.4. The tax subsidy option will always produce a profit, no matter what level of low attendance is assumed. This option leads to a modest profit even if the pessimistic attendance projection is certain to occur. Nationwide is guaranteed of making a profit with a tax subsidy. Limiting its share of profits by adopting the subsidy option, however, substantially reduces Nationwide's profit-making potential.

The private finance option has almost no risk, losing money only when there is a 92 percent chance of low attendance. One must believe that low attendance plagues more than ninety-two of one hundred such projects to discard the private finance option. Clearly this is not the case. The NHL calls for 12,000 season tickets to be sold to grant a franchise to ensure that an owner will be profitable and their franchises viable. Profit potential is another reason to prefer the private finance option. If anything close to the

| | | LOW ATTENDANCE | |
| | | Certain | None |
|---|---|---|---|
| OPTIONS | Private finance[1] | −$3,100,000 | $38,800,000 |
| | Tax subsidy[1] | $6,500,000 | $11,500,000 |

*Table 8.7*
**NATIONWIDE ARENA**

(1) Estimates are present worth of annual revenues based on best and worst case estimates of attendance at all events less operating costs and lease expenses or one-time construction costs.

*Figure 8.4*
**NATIONWIDE ARENA**

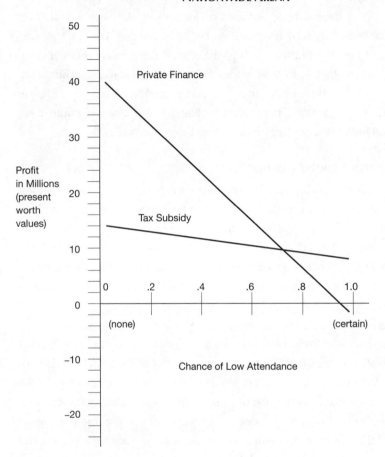

optimistic attendance figure is realized, Nationwide would make substantially more money building the arena on its own than with a tax subsidy
and revenue sharing. The NHL has all but ensured that there will be little
chance of low attendance, making the private finance option very low risk.
Nationwide's concerns about risk were way off base. Had company officials
explored this risk, they would have seen that a tax subsidy to fund the arena
was not needed and that the public furor over it could have been avoided.
Even very risk-adverse CEOs should find such arguments convincing.

Nationwide's goal of being seen as community minded was dashed by
the failure of company officials to see the arena's risk realistically. Nation-

wide asked taxpayers to underwrite any possible loss in a profit-making venture when such a loss was very unlikely. It remains to be seen if lingering ill will toward the appearance of duplicity by Nationwide will lower attendance and thereby revenues. As Hunt observed at a recent meeting, the fickle fans in Columbus will give a team no more than three years to be a winner—that is, to qualify for the Stanley Cup playoffs. Failing that, owners will find their arena empty. By understanding the amount of risk in the courses of action open to them, Nationwide officials could have avoided the ill will that may erode attendance and profits.

## The EuroDisney Location Decision

The decision to locate EuroDisney near Paris had two key uncertainties: hotel use and park attendance. Not all park visitors would stay overnight, so each can affect revenue independent of the other. Disney officials wanted to ensure that the park would yield a profit, but they overlooked the risk in the assumptions made for each of these key factors. Table 8.8 shows the present worth estimates of Disney's share of the discounted revenue streams over twenty years based on best case and worst case assumptions of ticket sales and hotel stays, less the company's $200 million investment.

The chance of favorable revenues being produced by ticket and hotel sales is shown in Figure 8.5. Losses can occur when both hotel and attendance forecasts prove to be unfavorable. Profits are very sensitive to the assumptions made about hotel occupancy and less sensitive to those made for ticket sales. Favorable occupancy rates are more important in the profit picture than promoting attendance, something the park's developers did not anticipate. Favorable hotel utilization made the revenue picture look good; unfavorable utilization made losses likely. Attendance revenues are

| | | ATTENDANCE | |
|---|---|---|---|
| | | Best | Worst |
| **HOTEL** | Best[1] | $92,000,000 | $77,000,000 |
| **OCCUPANCY** | Worst | $9,000,000 | –$6,000,000 |

*Table 8.8*
**EuroDisney Location Decision**

(1) The data represent present worth of Disney's share of revenue less Disney's investment of $200 million.

*Figure 8.5*
**EURODISNEY RISK**

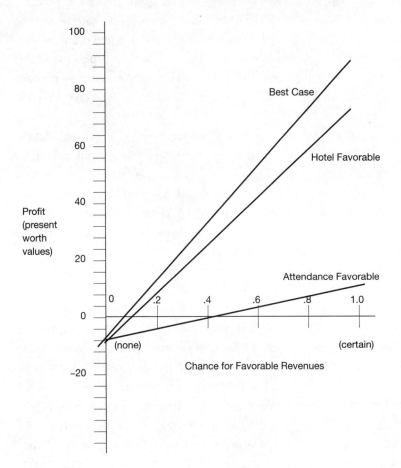

less dependent on favorable projections and have less impact on profit. Disney expected 73 percent hotel occupancy and assumed a worst case occupancy of only 60 percent. Occupancy averaged 36 percent, and the company lost $630 million in the first full year of operation. Disney continued to lose money at a rate of nearly $1 million a day for some time.

In making the hotel occupancy projections, Disney officials overlooked that Paris has lots of cheap rooms and is just a forty-minute train ride away. Park visitors could stay in Paris and make the park a day trip. Hotel revenues were crucial for the Paris location to be profitable, and Disney's overly optimistic estimates of hotel revenue proved to be their undoing. The risk in these projections went undetected. Seeing this risk graphically, as shown in Figure 8.5, would have raised questions, perhaps prompting Disney officials to rethink their Paris location decision and evaluate locations in other countries. At least the French deal, which demanded that Disney construct the hotels, should have been rethought and perhaps renegotiated because it put more risk on the company than company officials anticipated.

Revenues are discounted over a twenty-year period, suggesting that the present worth of the project is low compared to Disney's outlay of $200 million. Disney's best case projection has a 4 percent return, and the worst case outcome is far below that. The payback period of 4.7 years is also based on a best case forecast of revenues. A longer payback period would be unheard of for a project of this size, yet this was likely given what could have been known about risk at the time.

### BeechNut Apple Juice and Ford Pinto Decisions

Another kind of risk is illustrated by the amount of liability insurance to buy. The magnitude of a big loss from a lawsuit is unknown and difficult to forecast. Decisions to install safety equipment in a factory, air bags in automobiles, and product recalls face a similar difficulty. The cost of the insurance, the safety equipment, the air bags, and the recall are known, but the cost of failing to take these actions are not. Decision makers who try to balance the cost of acting against the cost of not acting are stymied by not being able to estimate the loss they would incur if they fail to act. Risk in recall decisions stems from difficulties in making an accurate esti-

| Table 8.9 BEECHNUT APPLE JUICE | | Caught | Escape |
|---|---|---|---|
| PAI Lawsuit | Cooperate | $3,500,000 | $3,500,000 |
| | Stonewall | $3,500,000 + X | 0 |

Note: $3.5 million is value of tainted inventory; X represents the unknown losses due to fines and legal damages if caught trying to sell the tainted product.

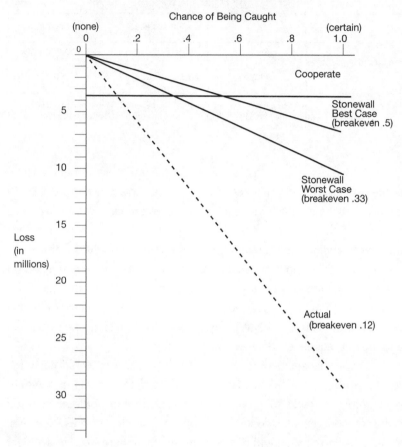

*Figure 8.6*
**BeechNut Apple Juice Risk**

mate of the magnitude of possible losses. Let's look at how this unknown cost played out in the BeechNut and Ford recall decisions.

To dispose of $3.5 million in tainted inventory, top management at BeechNut stonewalled a recall. The decision in dollar terms is shown in Table 8.9. In the table, X represents the unknown cost of litigation, fines, and other penalties, including lost sales. If caught, the company would have to pay this amount and would have to forgo dumping their inventory, worth $3.5 million. If not caught, the loss would be zero. Cooperating has a $3.5 million price tag due to the inventory cost.

| | | An Accident | No Accidents |
|---|---|---|---|
| | *Table 8.10* **FORD PINTO** | | |
| **Ford's Position** | Fix | $137,000,000 | $137,000,000 |
| | Delay | $137,000,000 + X | 0 |

Note: $137 million is cost to repair vehicles in a recall ($11 each with 1.5 million light trucks and 11 million cars on the road for $137 million); X represents unknown losses in litigation following one or more accidents.

To uncover risk, worst case and best case assumptions about the value of the expected losses are made. As Figure 8.6 shows, just above a 50:50 chance of getting caught yields a loss for the company, with a best case assumption about the magnitude of the loss. A worst case assumption finds that the financial loss is greater for the dumping option if the chance of being caught is one in three. Clearly, BeechNut made a very risky decision in selling the tainted apple juice inventory. The actual outcome was disastrous for the company. Fines and penalties exceeded 5 percent of the total baby food market. BeechNut badly misjudged the risk in their decision and the consequences that their actions could bring.

Ford's top management faced a recall decision. They could delay the recall, hoping no accident that involved the defective gas tank would occur, or fix the tanks. The repair cost of $137 million would be incurred if the "fix" option was adopted. Ford officials saw this cost as excessive. Waiting has no cost, should no accidents occur. If there were an accident involving the gas tank of a Pinto, Ford would be forced to fix the tanks and incur losses due to litigation. The decision in dollar terms is shown in Table 8.10.

The best and worst case outcomes can be found in court records. Ford estimated a loss of $49.5 million, based on NHTSA data. This data considered only the costs to society of an injury or a loss of life, not the losses that would be incurred due to litigation. Litigation costs could be substantial, because Ford had covered up the vulnerability of the Pinto to a gasline break in an accident. Eight of eleven Pintos experienced a potentially catastrophic tank line rupture in company tests that simulated an accident (Denhardt, 2000). Ruptures were prevented in test cars that had

*Figure 8.7*

**FORD PINTO**

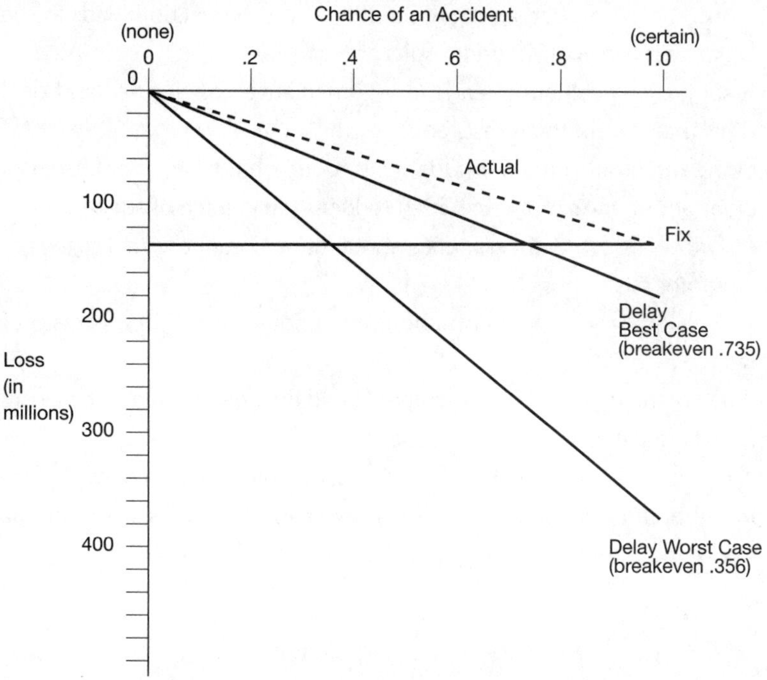

Chance of an Accident

the protective device. If all this were revealed in court, losses in legal terms would be much greater than the estimates.

The worst and best case assumptions appear in Figure 8.7. Ford's overly optimistic best case estimate of their losses led them to delay a recall. A more realistic estimate shows that Ford badly underestimated their potential losses in such an event. Ford escaped these losses by a stroke of luck. Just prior to the fatal accident, bad press had convinced officials to issue a recall. By adopting the fix option—however belatedly—Ford was able to win the lawsuit and experienced no losses other than the costs required to fix the tanks. Industry observers claim that Ford dodged a bullet by failing to make a worst case estimate of their losses. In the Firestone tire recall Ford was not so lucky. Industry observers place the cost of litigation at $50 billion. You can recall a lot of cars for that.

## ▼ Key Points

- ▼ Using analysis or bargaining to identify a course of action leads to successful decisions, if desired results are clear.
- ▼ A subjective evaluation leads to argumentative conclusions and decisions that are apt to be resisted.
- ▼ Using intuition to make a judgment about what to do prompts suspicions about one's motives, which reduces the chance of success.
- ▼ Risk flows from the uncertainties about future conditions that make precise forecasts impossible.
- ▼ A decision maker's intuition about the amount of risk in a decision is often way off base.
- ▼ Many of the debacles seem avoidable had the amount of risk in the preferred course of action been understood.
- ▼ A graphical analysis makes risk understandable. When the level of risk in the options being considered is understood, options with minimal risk or those with the most potential payoff can be identified.

# Ethical Traps

A person's ethical stance is rooted in his or her standards of fairness and justice. What one believes to be fair and just is imposed on a decision and how the decision is made. Decision makers apply standards of fairness and justice to what they see, which may or may not capture what actually takes place. Both the appearance and the reality of an ethical lapse can spell trouble. A decision seen to be threatening to an organization's image or to its traditions of fair play provokes strong reactions. Concerned individuals may be moved to use any means at their disposal to prevent the erosion of image or a departure from fair play. A lack of vocal opposition can be misleading. People file perceived ethical lapses on a personal scorecard, providing an ongoing read of management's moral compass.

The decision debacles illustrate ethical lapses, their consequences, and how they can trap decision makers. To dodge an ethical trap, you need both awareness and a means to cope. Awareness can be gained by uncovering the motives behind ethically questionable positions. To evade this kind of ethical trap, you must counter the often implicit incentives that encourage people to hold these positions. Situations in which people have opposing ethical positions pose a second kind of trap. To navigate around this trap, you must look for the values behind the opposing views. Once these core values are understood, you can seek actions and practices that recognize them and can alter your course of action and your decision approach to remove objections and affirm core values.

## Types of Opposition

Opposition can break out in the wake of an ethical lapse. Critics with leverage mobilize countervailing power and take up positions for a pitched battle. Power is applied either to block the decision or to terminate the flow of events in a decision-making process. Opposition is signaled when attempts are made to slow things down. Knowing that noncompliance will render a decision moot, critics call the decision-making effort ill conceived or downright evil to get others to refuse to act or to comply. If the critic has sufficient power, a counteroffensive may be mounted. In the pitched battle that ensues, leverage determines the outcome. If the protagonists have comparable power, arguments will begin to surface that support the opposing positions. When it became clear to Nestle and Shell that opposition was real and had to be dealt with, company officials began an aggressive campaign to defend their plans. It took a pitched battle to force these positions into the open.

Insiders at Ford had few avenues to express concerns about the recall decision, and people at Quaker had no way to critique the ill-conceived acquisition. People without power who oppose a decision resort to tokenism. Tokenism produces tacit resistance, postures that avoid constructive action, and passive-aggressive behavior. All result in delay and lost energy. When carried out in sufficiently clever ways, procrastination and minimal effort make the costs of a decision seem to outweigh its benefits. A rational decision maker abandons such efforts. Others see tacit resistance and gestures of support as a challenge to their authority. They expose the gesture to discredit and then bowl over opponents, leaving resentment in the wake.

## How Ethical Issues Arise

Ethical issues can erupt at any point in a decision-making effort. Claims can seem wrong-headed and provoke opposition, as in Nestle's infant formula marketing and the DIA. Decision makers feeling pressure to act may barge ahead and run over people whose interests could have been served or preserved. It makes little difference to FedEx officials which truck a driver gets, but it is very important to the driver. An allocation of trucks may seem

*Table 9.1*

## ETHICAL ISSUES IN THE DEBACLES

| Shell's Disposal of the Brent Spar | Waco Siege | Quaker's Purchase of Snapple | Nationwide Arena |
|---|---|---|---|
| Not all deep-sea disposal problems were revealed

Overly optimistic environmental impact estimates

Inaccurate toxic waste inventory | Apprehending lawbreakers took precedence over people's safety

Bogus information provided

Risks to Clinton administration dismissed | Personal interests superceded organizational interests

Scapegoating used to cover tracks | Misrepresented plan options

Traded public schools for sports team

Used public dollars after Issue 1 was defeated |
| **Telescope Consortium** | **AmeriFlora** | **New York City Blackout** | **The DIA** |
| Red squirrel habitat not considered

Personal aspirations of project champions limited options

Big university subsidies required with best case scenario | Public money used to underwrite an event to benefit private interests

Overly optimistic attendance figures | Lax oversight

Blame directed at operators

Public protection still lacking | Business travelers benefited

Taxpayers paid

Politicians decided |
| **Light Rail** | **Ford Pinto Recall** | **BeechNut's Infant Formula** | **Nestle's Apple Juice** |
| Some travelers benefit, rest must subsidize

Build it and they will come mentality known to fail | Profit drove principle

Test data for Pinto covered up

Frequency of problem misrepresented | Product mislabeled

Illegal sales made to developing countries

Looked like a victim to cover up being a villain | Ignored how product was being used

Assumed critics had self-interest |
| **EuroDisney** | | | |
| No alcohol just a ploy

Used any means necessary to sell the idea | | | |

unethical if it overlooks what the drivers believe to be fair. Adopting an idea that pops up outside of a formal search may seem to be a clever way to take decisive action. To others, the idea may raise questions about your vested interests—even if there are none. Whose interests are being served and whose are neglected will always pose an ethical issue.

Reactions to an ethical lapse can provoke tokenism or a pitched battle, depending on the amount of outrage and the power and influence of your opponents. The scale of the outrage that is felt and the extent to which opponents will go to thwart a decision are often underestimated, leading to debacles. Table 9.1 summarizes ethical issues in the debacles considered thus far. Let's turn our attention to how ethical issues arose in a decision to build a light rail system for mass transit.

## Urban Transit Revisited as Light Rail

For decades urban planners have been urging public officials to adopt up-to-date mass transit systems. Planners argue that U.S. cities should have systems like those found in most European cities. San Francisco and Washington D.C., among others, have spent huge sums to realize this aim.

Congestion and environmental decay motivate urban planners. Most American cities are experiencing rapid growth in their downtown areas and a simultaneous increase in the number of person trips by autos. Existing highway systems that serve city centers are reaching capacity. Parking is limited and increasingly pricey. Forecasters predict this will soon lead to unacceptable levels of

- ▼ Congestion, producing more travel time, travel cost, and inconvenience
- ▼ Pollution and noise, increasing environmental stress
- ▼ Gasoline use, producing more dependence on foreign oil

Trends also point to declines in the use of buses and other forms of public transportation. The loss of rider revenues has made public transportation system officials cut back service and call for more tax subsidies. In addition, cities that lack urban transit systems will lose out on federal funds earmarked for such projects.

Planners believe mass transit is the best way for people to access down-town jobs and services and the only way to reduce the pollution and noise that are degrading downtown areas (Dickey, 1983). Automobile-related remedies are neither efficient nor environmentally friendly, yet most fore-casters predict an unbridled increase in automobile use. Only huge invest-ments in urban transit systems, which offer commuting options, will stem the tide of automobiles. Another motivation is to access funds set aside for urban transit to realize a better return on federal block grants. The set-asides for urban transit are also justified as a step toward energy inde-pendence, reducing our dependence on foreign oil. Different parties have a different mix of goals. Federal players with their goal of lessening our energy dependence use federal funding to subsidize urban transit. Elected officials must sort through all this to find the best options open to their city.

Urban planners believe the only remedy is a large-scale investment in infrastructure. But can the dual goals of economics and reduced conges-tion, with the attendant improvements in noise and pollution, be realized? Let's look at the record. Urban transit solutions take two forms: under-ground and light rail. The Bay Area Rapid Transit system, better known as BART, promised an exemplar underground system—air-conditioned cars with carpet, easy ticketing, quiet operation, clean and attractive stations, and service encompassing 123 miles of the San Francisco bay area. BART was to follow the corridor with the largest projected congestion between the two bay area cities of Oakland and San Francisco. The cost, projected at between $590 million and $720 million when first proposed, was to be met with bonds and subsidies to offset operating shortfalls, should they occur (Hall, 1984).

Like so many of the big ticket projects discussed so far, reality has little resemblance to the hype. Costs for BART ballooned to $1.3 billion—nearly double the forecast and $400 million above legislative appropriations. This seemed deadly to planners, who trimmed the planned 123-mile route to 71 miles to keep costs below $1 billion. Design and construction problems forced modifications that cut operating speeds to an average of 40 mph, well below that of autos and below the claimed 70 to 80 mph. Problems encountered in tunneling across the bay, control system design, and sub-contractor coordination hiked the cost to $1.6 billion for the 71 miles of coverage.

BART planners believed a clean and efficient urban transit system would entice people to abandon their cars. They also assumed that people would congregate near BART stations to live. Such assumptions belie long-standing patterns of behavior. There is no evidence that urbanites, for whom BART was designed, will abandon their preference for personal cars and low density detached housing. To justify the cost, the system planners made just these assumptions. It took forty years for the predicted riders to materialize.

In many big ticket projects, forecasts are mere propaganda. When first opened, use was so low that BART ran an operating deficit of $40 million. To offset these losses, the state legislature passed a one-half percent sales tax subsidy in an emergency session. After the dust settled, $2 of subsidy were needed to create $1 of revenue. Taxpayers put up the difference. When BART opened, less than half of the projected riders materialized, and for decades BART remained an inefficient and ineffective solution to urban congestion. The costs of operating BART were twice as high as a bus system and 50 percent greater than using an automobile. Subsidies that covered two-thirds of BART's operating cost were required to keep ticket prices competitive with the cost of commuting with an automobile. Despite the subsidies, urbanites resisted commuting on BART.

What can be learned from the BART debacle? There is no evidence that clean and efficient urban transit will change the commuting preferences of urbanites. The availability of urban transit failed to convince bay area commuters to abandon their cars or to locate near stations to avoid park-and-ride hassles. Only prohibitively high costs keep people from driving. Cost estimates for the system were overly optimistic, perhaps deliberately so. This pattern repeats for nearly every infrastructure project borne of hype. Advocates resort to public relations rhetoric to confuse the issue and distract policy makers. BART proponents said "the question is not can we afford BART but can we afford to not have BART" to deflect hard questions about costs and the prospects of reducing urban congestion at the time (Hall, 1984). Assumptions of no technical snags and no inflation were patently ridiculous. Nevertheless, Washington D.C. and other cities soon set out to create an underground using these very same assertions and assumptions. When challenged, proponents use defensive evaluations based on unrealistic projections buried in masses of incomprehensible detail.

The new bright idea is light rail. Similarities with underground mass transit debacles are everywhere. Planners in Sacramento, California, and Columbus, Ohio, are now entertaining an "over ground" option to cut costs, operating electrical vehicles over reserved right-of-ways for rail and busses. Plans call for developing underused and abandoned rail corridors to connect urbanites to downtown and to neighboring cities. Because a corridor already exists, redevelopment is presented as feasible and low cost. Again, ridership is assumed using a "build it and they will come" mentality.

Facts argue differently. In ten light rail projects, ridership ranged from 15 percent to 72 percent of forecasts, and construction and operating costs were always underestimated. Construction costs averaged 50 percent above estimates and operating costs 100 percent above estimates. These same overly optimistic projections of cost are made over and over again (Pickrell, 1990). Old streetcar corridors were paved over for roads long ago so a light rail service must share city streets with the automobile. The connecting rail beds are even more problematic. Most have deteriorated from neglect and poor maintenance, and all have half-century-old technology unable to support today's high-speed trains. Stations have been lost to urban revival and sappy projects like convention centers. These and other overhyped infrastructure projects of equally dubious value now occupy the land. Finding space to develop a downtown station is difficult and costly. Train right-of-ways are far from where today's urban commuters live, requiring a commute to access them. A park-and-ride approach increases many commuters' travel time and imposes parking hassles. This leads to low ridership, which drives up costs. Taxpayer subsidies are demanded. Sound familiar? The zealot's hype gets translated into tenuous assumptions, defensive evaluations, and a failure to even approach the dual goals of controlling commuting cost and reducing congestion.

Despite all this history, the Central Ohio Transit Authority (COTA) proposed a thirteen-mile rail line, most of it on existing rail right-of-ways and the rest to coexist with downtown Columbus roadways. (Table 9.2 profiles the proposal.) The price tag is $445 million, with an additional $90 million needed to buy land for right-of-ways to connect to the old rail line, hiking the price tag to $535 million. Scores of stations are to be built, many of them curbside in the downtown business area to compensate for the dem-

|  | *Table 9.2*<br>**LIGHT RAIL FOR URBAN TRANSIT** |
| --- | --- |
| Claims | Urban congestion poses economic and social threats |
| Core concerns/considerations<br>  (a) Recognized<br><br>  (b) Hidden | <br>Concerns about access to federal dollars, environment, transit time, energy use<br><br>Proponents' image, hype, modern methods that apply and do not apply |
| Directions | Use light rail technology |
| Options considered | Light rail technology (posture with others, such as traffic control, bus options, and commuter incentives) |
| Extent of search and innovation | Limited to the pro forma options others have uncovered |
| Use of evaluation | Defend the light rail option, demonstrating its features with dubious assumptions |
| Impact of evaluation | Defend the idea by dramatizing questionable benefits and covering up weaknesses |
| Barriers to action | Available funds do not begin to cover the most favorable cost forecasts |
| Ethical concerns | Who pays, who benefits, and who decides |
| Barriers to learning | Fear of failure, inability to reach overhyped expectations |

olition of the downtown rail depot. Others are to have nearby lots for park-and-ride users. The alignment is to follow existing tracks along the major north–south interstate highway. Existing rail companies are to defer right-of-way to the project. Options that call for traffic engineering flow improvements, preferential treatment of cars with multiple riders, peak period traffic management via staggered work hours, and bus lanes and express service are ignored in the COTA analysis because federal transit funding sources do not allow bus–rail comparisons. Because infrastructure projects often attract media attention, they are believed to enhance the image of politicians and others who realize them. Without this feature, appeals to deal with social concerns of noise and pollution are ignored.

Learning is set aside in countless cities as they repeat the same mistakes. Looking at expected use, federal dollars, and other relevant factors, the same conclusions emerge. Mass transit infrastructure is a bad investment. A debacle was avoided in Columbus when local economic conditions tanked and light rail dropped off politicians' agendas. Light rail zealots may not be practical, but they are persistent. Plans have popped up at regular intervals in Columbus over the past two decades. Voters rejected a plan in 1999 only to have COTA planners float yet another plan a mere two years later. Critics claim that $535 million for light rail makes no sense when busses can offer the same service for $95 million. To defend the project a COTA planner said, "intuitively [we know that] people will ride light rail." Yes, but how many, and how much of a subsidy will be required? A longtime COTA critic called the plan the "Barnes boondoggle," after COTA president Ronald Barnes, pointing out that as more people telecommute the need to travel to the downtown will decline and travel to the city edges will grow. Bus service is flexible and light rail is not.

## Ethical Fallout in Light Rail and the Other Debacles

All pricey infrastructure projects pose ethical concerns. Light rail proponents trot out the same old arguments and force fit them to a new city: light rail will encourage business, create jobs, stimulate growth, reduce dependency on foreign oil, and access "our share" of federal tax dollars that will go to others if we do not act. Oh, and by the way, it may even reduce congestion and its attendant noise and pollution. Claims that seem bogus bring out critics. Many arguments born of hype are shallow, illogical, or outright misrepresentations. The very real problems of providing efficient and effective urban transit are swept away by the hype and misrepresentations.

Like the other debacles, light rail prompts concerns about costs and benefits. When cost and benefit seem out of balance, critics come out of the woodwork. Decision makers in the debacles expressed dismay at what was being said, often attributing it to their critics' lack of ethics. Con Ed called the blackout in New York a "one-time event" caused by an implausible series of happenings—two lightning strikes during a peak power use period. Critics saw it differently, lambasting Con Ed officials for their lax oversight. Both Shell and Greenpeace saw the other's position as filled with deliberate errors. Shell officials were shocked at the vehemence and the outright misrepresentations in the claims of their critics. Environmental groups mobilized by Greenpeace believed stopping "big oil" from making deep-sea dumping a routine practice justified any means, even bogus data about environmental threats. Critics saw the FBI and other law enforcement officials as oblivious to the loss of life that would result from an attack on the Branch Davidians' compound. FBI and other law enforcement types were dismayed by what they saw as an unwillingness of public officials to seek swift punishment for lawbreakers who had killed ATF agents just "doing their job." The FBI was shocked by the intensity of the criticism leveled against them in the aftermath of the attack.

Divergent ethical positions provoke strong reactions, with each party vigorously defending the rightness of their position. Some of these positions are heartfelt, but many are born of convenience, habit, and personal interests. Let's turn our attention to the motives behind such positions and to how a suspension of ethics sets an ethical trap.

## How Ethics Are Suspended

Machiavelli may have been the first to advance a "dirty hands" explanation for decisions that ignore ethics. People in power are thought to have dirty, or at least tainted, hands because they deal with unsavory issues. This can trap subordinates who serve the people in power. Dirty hands become "many hands," as underlings scamper to support the boss. Subordinates may feel obliged to use whatever means necessary to help those in positions above them. A less charitable explanation has subordinates posturing for organizational spoils.

Failure to apply personal standards when making decisions at work sets an ethical trap. Some public and private sector managers routinely misrepresent the effectiveness of their departments in legislative and budget hearings, reasoning that they must be advocates. Honesty in conceding that a budget cut would do no harm would make a cut certain but would not entice others to come forward with a similar admission. Managers in firms routinely overstate the accomplishments of their subordinates, thinking that rewards garnered for marginal subordinates create obligations, a form of slack that is stockpiled for times when the going gets tough. In the military, anything below a near 100 percent efficiency rating will damage a military career. This crimping of the evaluation scale makes it impossible to distinguish among officers who have made significant, as opposed to routine, accomplishments, and more important, who you would follow "up the hill" in time of war. People trying to hire someone face a similar dilemma. Letters of recommendation are expected to exaggerate a person's accomplishments. Deciphering such letters becomes a discounting game, with potential employers trying to figure out what is being said by looking for "damning with faint praise" and other cues that suggest reservations. Or potential employers may just read into the letter their own biases about a candidate. Such expectations make it difficult for anyone to be honest, so these practices are perpetuated to avoid damaging anyone.

Selectivity in reporting accomplishments puts on a "best face." Many people believe their employers expect advocacy and that organizations have "special ethics." An organizational objective is treated as a "higher value" in which the ends justify the means. This view has been expressed in various ways, perhaps beginning with Machiavelli, who claimed that the mores and standards of justice applied to one's personal life have no bearing on work behavior. One must be ruthless in the pursuit of organizational interests and use deceit and guile as instruments of action. To do otherwise would betray an employer you are pledged to represent. Perhaps with this in mind, Carr (1978) attempts to reconcile personal and business integrity by advancing the "practical requirements" of business. A double standard of morality is viewed as a practical necessity. How, for example, can one be honest with a competitor or an accreditation review body? Decision makers distance themselves from deceptive practices, such as lying, by treating the situation as a game. In a game, people take steps to win something for the organization, which allows them to evade personal responsibility. People who suspend personal ethics and substitute the ethic to serve the organization are driven by self-indulgence, self-righteousness, self-protection, and self-deception (Carton, 1983).

## Self-Indulgence

The lust for power and the lure of greed corrupts both public officials sworn to a higher standard of conduct and private sector managers expected to act in the best interests of their company. Decisions with questionable ethics can be tempting when they offer power or a lucrative payoff. Smithburg seemed motivated solely by personal gain. He was concerned that a takeover would strip him of the power and prerogative he enjoyed at Quaker. A new board could rein him in and impose approval steps that would slow his drive for exciting new business challenges. Smithburg had grown bored with Quaker and its staid product line—it is hard to get excited about selling pet food—and sought the excitement of splashy deals (Burns, 1996). When the Snapple acquisition turned sour, Smithburg blamed others, contending that they failed to make the hoped-for Gatorade–Snapple integration a reality. The fault lay with Smithburg's failure to uncover the two beverages' incompatible production methods and markets.

Pena engaged in several questionable actions to realize his dream of a new airport for Denver. The campaign to win voter approval was rife with raw politics and big money. Both his objective of securing new airport funding and the means seem tainted. Contracts were given to friends who, in turn, invested in helping the DIA become a reality. The situation ripened to the point that the Securities and Exchange Commission (SEC) questioned whether campaign contributions to Pena and Webb, his successor, were provided in exchange for lucrative legal and securities work in issuing $3.3 billion in airport bonds. A contract was negotiated with a law firm, owned by a close friend of Pena's. City records show the firm was paid $220,000 to act as local disclosure council, and a Chicago firm was paid $367,000 to act as national disclosure council. Both were heavy contributors to Pena's re-election campaign and lobbied Congress for the $500 million Denver received in federal airport funds. One of the bond underwriters, who received $1.4 million from the sale of a $600 million bond issue, was also active in lobbying Congress for federal airport funding. In all, several million dollars in contracts went to firms that appeared to be cronies of Pena and his successors, who then became campaign supporters. With Pena's election closely tied to support for the airport, these contracts posed questions of self-indulgence. And it is rumored that Pena's family owned the land on which the DIA was built.

Wolf's actions to realize AmeriFlora were motivated by a coming out for the long-time community power broker. Historically, Wolf had preferred a low profile and behind the scenes maneuvering; he was rarely seen in community leadership roles. This changed when Wexner, head of Limited Inc., who liked the spotlight, emerged as the spokesman for community renewal. Wolf saw the Quincentennial celebration as a way to recoup lost influence and cement his power with a high-profile role in a major community project. Wolf pushed this agenda and picked people who would be loyal, if not effective, managers. Indulgences become even more blatant when these handpicked people went on junkets to Europe, visiting seventeen countries and billing the project. No accounting for the trips was ever made. At one point, to justify the trips, it was claimed that thirty to forty exhibitors had been recruited. The final total was seven. An international flower show usually has a dozen exhibitors.

## Self-Righteousness

The "rightness" of their cause seduces zealots, and organizations have lots of people with causes. Together they have fashioned a cache of solutions, and each is looking for a home. A solution champion will do whatever it takes to secure the adoption of an idea he or she believes to be right, desirable, or needed. Disney officials became convinced that Eisner's cause was right and acted as if any means available to realize it was justified. The arena's supporters and the telescope's advocates sold their ideas vigorously, if not candidly. Smithburg's success at outsmarting Wall Street convinced him of his ability to pick a winner.

The self-righteous posture struck by law enforcement officials at Waco persuaded them that there was no option other than attacking the compound. FBI officials believed their cause was just: These people cannot be allowed to escape—they killed law enforcement agents. Weak-kneed politicians and political appointees in the Attorney General's office would let this happen. If the FBI was not allowed to assault the compound, the guilty would evade punishment. The longer FBI officials were involved in the standoff, the greater their frustration. To get action, FBI officials called

CJ gas the "least aggressive" approach that could be used and discounted the risks of the gas to children and others in the compound. To push things along, they played on unconfirmed reports that Koresh had molested and beaten children in the compound. FBI and ATF agents were told by higher-ups to support the "official position." Agents appear to have been under orders to describe the standoff in dire terms that threatened public safety if they were to avoid a string of unpleasant assignments. Any means necessary to carry the day. Subsequently, It was acknowledged that Reno's briefings by the FBI contained misinformation. Still later, prosecutors destroyed evidence the Davidian survivors subpoenaed in their legal actions, still believing the cause to be right.

## Self-Protection

People in organizations get caught up in doing what is asked. "Going along to get along" persuades people to support choices they would otherwise oppose out of fear that opposition would be costly to their career. Organizational life reinforces the notion that compromise and accommodation are expected—indeed demanded. This can be pervasive at times, and people who keep faith with their personal ethics are a rarity. Data are fudged to make them support a supervisor's idea. People line up to tell higher-ups what they want to hear. Carried to extremes, this behavior can bring out whistle-blowers who expose ethically questionable practices and cause long-term difficulties for the organization.

Shell officials wanted the case for deep-sea dumping to seem clear cut. Corners were cut and data fudged to remove any doubt about the environmental responsibility of deepwater dumping. The company made inaccurate estimates of toxic wastes in the Brent Spar. Thirty tons of sludge was estimated when the correct amount totaled seventy-five tons. When this came to light, company officials ignored it because a correction would erode their case. The environmental impact of deep-sea dumping was unknown. Nevertheless, to support their case, Shell officials used best case scenarios to predict the rate at which the spar would deteriorate. They worried about bad press but did not see their decision as setting a precedent for all kinds of deep-sea disposals—until environmental groups opposed them. Company officials were furious at the distortions of Greenpeace but did not acknowledge their own errors until forced to. Even with their good intentions, Shell officials appeared to have postured about their environmental concerns to head off questions.

In the BeechNut debacle, LiCari was expected to go along to get along, suspending his ethical concerns about company practices. He went through the motions for a while to avoid being seen as a malcontent that bucked higher-ups. Finally, tension between his beliefs and his suspicions about company practices forced a confrontation that led to his resignation. Later, his whistle-blowing nearly finished the company and ruined the careers of its top management.

### Self-Deception

An advocate role requires subordinates to buy into their superior's agenda. People slide into an advocate posture through many small endorsements over the years. As the endorsements slowly build and take root, people ease into a firm belief that the superior's agenda merits their steadfast support. This kind of self-deception is hard to resist. Being loyal to the boss seems reasonable and expected, but this requires that subordinates treat every situation as requiring them to do whatever it takes to support higher-ups. Because nearly every decision has both communal and personal interests that can be served, there is subtle but very real pressure to look for the superior's interests in a mixed interest situation. Others are expected do the same, leaving some higher body to sort it all out. Justifications include everyone does it, higher authority implicitly condones it, or it is done only when dire circumstances arise.

Nestle officials saw their cause as just and felt that activist groups were making oversimplified claims to attract attention to their movement. Key insiders had immense loyalty to Nestle. They saw Nestle as a moral organization that would not engage in unethical practices. It was easier to see the activists' motives as self-serving, bent on attacking an inherently evil multinational company with no interest in the welfare of third world children. There were two issues: misuse of the product and questionable marketing. One got confused with the other. Nestle officials gravitated toward arguments about product misused and away from whether their marketing was a contributing factor. Initially, evidence appeared to show that infant formula would benefit third world users. Once seduced by this position, it was hard to back away and admit the company's actions were ill advised.

Many small steps were taken until the company's position seemed to be as reasonable at the end of the seven-year boycott as it did initially. To the outsider, there was a clear-cut lapse of ethics in company marketing practices.

Wolf put loyalists in key positions, knowing that loyalists would offer facts and figures that would allow him to make whatever interpretation he wished. Wolf could hear what he wanted to hear. Favorable forecasts of attendance figures were made. The event went ahead with these bloated estimates unchallenged because they confirmed what Wolf had hoped for. The top management team at BeechNut conned themselves into believing they were doing no wrong. People bought the product so it must have value in the marketplace. The adulterated juice posed no health hazard. Company officials convinced themselves that the absence of a health hazard diminished the gravity of misrepresenting the product's contents. Compared to taking a $3.5 million loss in hard times, selling the tainted inventory seemed inconsequential.

Shell's management saw deep-sea dumping as ethical because it was legal. Shell officials reasoned that earlier disposals were incompatible with the Brent Spar situation. No one could show that a deep-sea disposal would cause irreparable damage to the ecosystem. But indications at the time also pointed to growing environmental awareness and more support for "green" issues. Shell officials saw themselves as environmentally responsible but failed to see that the company had been colored by perceptions about "big oil" and its irresponsibility. Shell officials deceived themselves about the prospects of a public outcry and its intensity and the ability of the company to distance itself from the actions of others in its industry. Public opinion vehemently opposed the plan. When a public outcry emerged, company officials could not defend a deep-sea disposal of the Brent Spar with legal niceties. Intense opposition will impact your bottom line.

People who coordinate product recalls at Ford apply two criteria: frequency and traceable causes to design or manufacturing flaws (Denhardt, 2000). Staffers in the recall office at Ford failed to see a "directly traceable cause" because higher-ups at Ford had concealed Pinto's crash test data. The test data showed that eight of eleven of the Pintos tested had "potentially catastrophic gas tank ruptures" and that the three cars that survived the test had gas tank protection devices. Because federal standards that would have ruled the Pinto unsafe would not go into affect for some time,

Ford officials reasoned that the car could be called safe and concealed the test data. The car met legal safety standards when tested. A recall would be costly. The Pinto's profit margins were razor thin. Ford officials adopted a buyer beware principle. They reasoned that a buyer should know that economy cars of the time were made cheaply and not nearly as safe as bigger, more expensive ones. You get what you pay for. Finally, there was the "safety doesn't sell" mentality of the time. Ford officials let these rationalizations justify putting recall benefits in dollar terms. The seeming callowness of putting a dollar value on human life put a big dent in Ford's public image that persists to this day.

People in Ford's recall office engaged in self-deception as well. The job placed heavy time and emotional demands on them. At the time of the Pinto recall, one hundred other recall campaigns were under way and many others had yet to be decided upon. The job required looking at human suffering: burns, injury, and death. Such pictures have a dulling effect after a while, and people's defense mechanisms take over to shield them from the psychic toll. Individuals continuing to work in such a job would find it difficult to believe their employer was responsible for all this death and misery. When the recall office finally learned of the crash data, staffers compared the Pinto to other small cars and concluded that the Pinto was merely the "worst of a bad lot" (Denhardt, 2000). Denhardt also reports that people who held positions in the recall department at Ford, after some time for reflection, feel considerable remorse at their failure to apply personal ethics to their job.

Self-deception also trap light rail advocates. Advocates truly believe in the need for mass transit. These needs are seen as so compelling that questions of financial feasibility can be set aside. This gives the critic a platform to raise questions. The ensuing flap blocks thinking about badly needed urban transit remedies that are financially responsible.

## Traps in Playing Out Ethical Debates Based on Moral Position

People who engage in self-protection, self-indulgence, and self-righteousness ignore their motivations, and those engaged in self-deception have buried them. Decision-makers provoke opposition when they are unwilling or unable to see any point of view but their own.

Advocates of many large infrastructure projects find themselves trapped by a disparity in who pays, who benefits, and who decides. Light rail proponents have a different view than their critics of how to balance these interests. Economists resolve such differences with "externalities." An infrastructure project has externalities if it produces benefits everyone can realize and if it is impractical or impossible to bill for use, such as clean air. To ensure that users pay for the benefits received, public funding through tax revenues or subsidies is required.

Proponents believe the benefits of light rail have externalities; critics disagree. The dispute turns on whether people can or will benefit from a light rail service. The light rail proponent contends that public funds should be used to provide urban transit systems. When commuters use such a system in large numbers, all citizens will realize the benefits of reduced pollution, noise, and congestion. Proponents of light rail use a "build it and they will come" kind of logic. Critics argue that there is no evidence "they will come," which makes the benefit forecasts overly optimistic. Reality is low use. Commuters can come but will choose not to, preferring the convenience of a personal automobile. Without the projected rider revenue, subsidies will be needed in both light rail construction and operation so people who do ride will be subsidized with public dollars. The benefits of a light rail system have externalities that the ticket price cannot capture because people will not use light rail in sufficient numbers to pay for it. Because people's past behavior is the best prediction of future behavior, critics argue that such projects are never feasible. Failing to see these arguments creates the ethical trap for the light rail proponent.

A mismatch among who pays, who benefits, and who decides always raises an ethical issue. Downtown visionaries decide we need light rail, the public pays, and those lucky enough to have easy access ride and benefit. The mismatch sets an ethical trap. Springing this trap created opposition to the Nationwide arena, AmeriFlora, the DIA, and the telescope consortium.

In the Nationwide arena plans, under Issue 1 (plan A) the public was to help pay for an arena decided upon by a "downtown elite" and used by those who could afford to pay the outrageous ticket prices for a major league sports events. The public was to benefit from an arena by being able to live in a major league city, a dubious claim rejected by the voters. In plan B, the taxpayers were billed for the land and improvements without their approval, creating still another mismatch. Both plans prompted an ethical debate because of mismatches among the costs, benefits, and prerogatives to decide.

AmeriFlora proponents made a similar misstep. The public was to benefit from becoming a "destination," from taking the lead to celebrate the Quincentennial of Columbus's voyage, and from the rehabilitation of the old Wolf Park and its remaining buildings plus the new buildings. Others saw such benefits as illusory and the $30 million public price tag as public assistance for a rich power broker. It was Wolf's project; he would reap a lion's share of the benefits. Ethical questions arose when critics revealed who was benefiting, paying, and deciding.

Pena decided that the city of Denver needed a new airport. DIA, like most airports, is being paid for with bonds and complex federal funding mechanisms that demand public dollars and public underwriting. A carrier does not pass on these costs to the traveler because folding gate charges into the price structure of a carrier would cause a huge jump in ticket prices. The public is claimed to benefit from a new airport so these gate charges are not passed on to the air traveler. In reality, it is the employees in local businesses that do most of the flying. Local business leaders want an airport that offers service at below cost for the frequent flyer, the business traveler. Pena decides, Denver area companies get disproportionate benefits, and public dollars pay for the DIA.

The university endorsed a telescope with no hope of ever breaking even. The analysis presented in Chapter 8 reveals that a large subsidy is needed, even if the most favorable revenue projections are realized. When other departments got wind of the plan, they objected to the subsidy because it would draw down funds they depended upon. Again, there is a mismatch. University leaders decided to bill all university departments to benefit the Astronomy Department.

Those who decide and impose costs on others, expecting personal gains, set another kind of trap. Recalls in the BeechNut and Ford cases pose questions of profit taking by selling unsafe products or misrepresenting them. In the acquisition of Snapple by Quaker, Smithburg misrepresented his motives and who would benefit. To push their plan, Shell officials gave inaccurate estimates of the toxic inventory in the Bret Spar and gave best case estimates of rate of deterioration and seepage of toxic waste expected in a deep-sea disposal location. This resulted in understating the benefits of the proposed dumping to the company and in understating the costs to society. Profit appeared to be the driving principle at Shell, a surefire way to bring out opposition. Shell officials created the impression that they had suspended their ethics for personal gain.

## Ethical Rationality

Next, we turn our attention to working out ethical differences before positions harden and become intractable. This calls for ethical rationality to be given status equal to that accorded logical and economic rationality, discussed in Chapters 6, 7, and 8, and political rationality, discussed in Chapters 4 and 5. Logic is used to search for actions warranted by economic realities. Politics is employed to search for actions warranted by self-interest. Ethics guides a search for actions warranted by standards of fairness and justice. Ethical rationality is introduced into decision making with two steps. First, find ways to neutralize the interests that prompt self-indulgence, self-righteousness, self-protection, and self-deception. Second, confront ethical considerations as they arise during the decision-making process. Ethical issues are managed by aligning costs, benefits, and the prerogatives to decide.

### Neutralizing the Motives to Ignore Ethics

An organization's ethical image erodes when company officials slip into self-indulgent and self-righteous postures, when self-protection is forced on people, and when self-deception governs how people get ahead. Zealots prey on the people needed to support their ideas, making their lives miserable until support is given. Zealots create elaborate games to make their ideas seem warranted and that people's support of them is freely given. Decisions become an elaborate pretense in which the zealot directs things from behind the scenes and gives public assurances that mislead to avoid difficult questions. Every decision is compartmentalized so zealots can evade responsibility for their ethical lapses. The game that results may offer an untroubled mind and a secure position for a time. If you play games with ethics, you may dodge responsibility in today's decision but end up with a debacle tomorrow. To stop the gradual erosion of personal ethics, you must insert ethics into the decision-making process. To insert ethics into situations rife with self-indulgence, self-righteousness, self-protection, or self-deception, you must neutralize the motives that pull people toward these traps. Corrective action can be found in eliminating the often implicit incentives that encourage ethically questionable behavior.

*Neutralizing Self-Righteous and Self-Indulgent Behavior.* Exposing vested interests neutralizes zealots. Require zealots to build communal benefits into their ideas and question what appear to be personal benefits. This can be difficult for a subordinate, but a peer or a superior can ask questions to uncover the interests of people who can influence or be influenced by a decision (see Chapters 4 and 5).

Discourage self-indulgent behavior with "fraud by proof systems." Examples include tamper-resistant systems and auditing procedures such as those found in financial management. Safeguards can be found by adapting the inspector general function in the federal government and applying the "ethics in government" act to your company. The most important step that you can take is to make it clear, by actions as well as words, that self-indulgent behavior is unethical and will not be tolerated. This is what Buffett did after he became president of Salomon Brothers, the investment banking division of Salomon, Inc. The company was reeling from illegal trading and a CEO whose slash and burn tactics encouraged subordinates to follow these practices. Buffett charted a new course, making it crystal clear with a startling memo that said, in part, "you are expected to report instantaneously and directly to me, any illegal or moral failure of an employee of Salomon. . . . When in doubt, call me" (Sims, 1991). He included his home phone number to drive home his message. Buffett fired top managers who were tied to ethical wrongdoing to show that actions would follow his principles and that these new expectations would be enforced. Only people who would commit to these ethical principles were hired. By these actions Buffett imprinted on the company his own image as one of the country's most ethical investors.

*Neutralizing Self-Protection.* Show people caught up in self-protection another path. According to studies, people who raise ethical questions in organizations are not subjected to penalties or harassment. Point this out to show that defensive actions are seldom needed. State the ethical positions of the company clearly as Worthington Industries does by printing the "golden rule" and its application to all company transactions on the back of employees' business cards. Another step is to vest mediation responsibility in all your top managers. Demonstrate that the ethical standards of the company have equal standing with economic, logical, and political rationality when making decisions. Reinforce this. Show that ethical questions are always welcome by making such questioning company policy. Include the machinery to pose ethical questions. The "designated ethics official" who provides mediation for disputes that arise in a federal agency offers a model. Dispute channels have an added advantage of eliminating the disastrous consequences that follow whistle-blowing. Such channels provide the means to raise questions and express concerns. Courts rule in favor of companies with dispute channels and against whistle-blowers. People with concerns are expected to use the dispute channels to question proposals. You can target individuals who fail to do so as dissidents and manage them in postincident damage control.

**Neutralizing Self-Deception.** Self-deception is countered by getting people to see that having a reason for a choice is no substitute for choosing right. Subordinates create a deception when they push their own ideas by selectively including what will support their case, leaving everything else out. The deception is justified by mixed motive situations in which someone will benefit—so why not us and not them? The pressure to make choices that will benefit higher-ups in an organization is gradual and insidious, disconnecting the demands of a job from subordinates' personal ethics. To avoid such disconnects, insert ethics as a decision-making criterion having the same importance as economic, logical, and political criteria. Embed standards for fairness and justice into the fabric of your organization by putting them in job descriptions, mentoring, and formal discussions. Show how deceptions work against organizational interests.

An organization benefits when justice and fairness standards seep into its culture. They discourage misleading letters of recommendation and fitness reports as well as bogus threats of dire consequences in capital budget requests. This removes the incentive to ask for more than one needs, expecting cuts. If this pattern of deceit and game playing can be discouraged, you can get a better fix on the true needs of your organization. Legislative hearings, budget meetings, and similar forums will take on increased importance because real needs are being considered.

## Aligning Costs, Benefits, and Prerogatives

People caught up in indulgences, righteousness, and protectionism claim they are serving the interests of their employer. A legal or a functionalist view of business ethics results. The legal view holds that business firms are not a creation of society but an autonomous entity expected to make a profit. Officials in the companies involved in the debacles appear to embrace this view. As Milton Friedman supposedly said, "The business of businesses is business." The functionalist view is even more dogmatic. A form of social Darwinism is advocated, leading company officials to believe they are expected to make a profit any way they can. People caught up in a deception have a different view. They adhere to a variation on fundamentalism that calls on them to do whatever it takes to maximize profit without deceptions. But such individuals deceive themselves about their own deceptions, as in the Pinto recall.

**The Stakeholder View.** People taking a legal, functionalist, or fundamentalist view of ethical standards position themselves to act in their employer's interests. Doing whatever it takes to serve company interests can get you in trouble if your decisions violate the ethical expectations of others. Ethical questions can be turned aside when company interests are repositioned with a stakeholder approach. To do so, consider the obligations you have to a broad array of constituencies. Recognize the interests of stockholders, creditors, employers, customers, communities in which the company operates, the environment, and the general public. Consider the positive and negative effects on each constituency as you make a decision. Attempt to align the costs, benefits, and prerogatives of each constituency. Not all interests can be served, but most can be considered. Such a position shows that you have applied standards of fairness, which often will remove the objections of people who can become opponents. A stakeholder approach discourages incentives that draw people toward indulgence, righteousness, protectionism, and deception traps. If the costs, benefits, and prerogatives of constituent groups can be aligned, ethical issues will evaporate.

*Value-Based Differences.* Ethical convictions about practices to be followed and choices to be made can point people in very different directions. Differences arise because beliefs about what is fair and just can vary from one person to another, making an ethical position value-based (Johnson, 1993; Werhane, 1999). Like claims and the concerns they hide (see Chapter 4), people rarely grasp these values because the ethical position staked out says little about the values that ground it. Emotional outbursts from a concerned stakeholder verbalize an objection but not the values that prompted the objection. When you try to mediate such a dispute, you will find yourself on a slippery slope. Missing value signposts make for an unknown terrain and hard going in an effort to scale the slope and find a mutual understanding.

Shell and Con Ed officials did not grasp their own motives nor their critics' motives, which were also visceral and incompletely understood. The Shell and Con Ed critics were expressing outrage, but the ethical lapses identified in such outbursts reveal little about the value-based positions behind them. The standards of fairness and justice that provoked this reaction are not transparent, and the ensuing debate is forged by the conviction that the other party is unethical. This is sure to prompt conflict, and intractable positions with no way out. Either the powerful decision maker steamrolls the opposition or the opposition brings down the decision maker. Both leave resentment in their wake, which festers to poison the next encounter. To resolve the confrontation, you must see how ethical positions form, how values are hidden in the positions, and what to do to cope.

*How Ethical Disagreements Arise.* Two decisions, both based on true events, show how people can develop very different views of what is ethical and unethical. One deals with performance appraisals and the other with a consultant's study for a company CEO.

A large company with three hundred corporate engineers scrapped its performance appraisal approach and put in its place one that ranked people from one to three hundred, or from "best" to "least best." This was done to precisely draw a line indicating which engineers were to receive rewards, such as salary increases, and to "rank and yank," targeting engineers at the bottom of the list for counseling or dismissal. Such a ranking approach is believed to overcome the deficits in traditional appraisal systems in which the ratings for several criteria, such as creativity, initiative, and appearance, are added up. Engineering supervisors manipulated the traditional appraisal system by rating average people above average on the criteria that count, such as creativity and initiative, distorting the results. A "Lake Woebegone" outcome results in which everyone is rated above average. The new system called for supervisors who had worked with each engineer to share with one another what they knew about the person. A vote was then taken to find the best (number 1), second best (number 2), and so on. This seemed more accurate than the old approach because information must be shared publicly before each ranking decision was settled upon. All of the engineering supervisors had the opportunity to call attention to a high performer, and a comparison of virtues of the engineers was thought to reflect each engineer's true value to the company.

Of course, no system is infallible. All can be "gamed" by clever people. An "old hand" explained how: "I brought up each of my key people early, much before others that I knew were better. I got a crony to second my nominations. (Of course, I seconded his.) Then I argued vehemently for my guy and feigned dismay when others pushed him out. After a few tries, I had built my social credit: I had graciously given way to others and their arguments on several occasions. Then, I could cash in on my social credit and slip my candidate ahead of more deserving people." By graciously accepting each defeat and by looking stricken at his "failure," the old hand built up his stock with his peers to be cashed in later on to push "his people" up in the rankings.

Consider a second case. Here a consultant deliberately prepared a sloppy presentation to trip up company officials according to their biases, keeping them from questioning a proposed study. Words are misspelled early on in the presentation to give the "tidy bowl" types something to criticize. They snicker and point out spelling errors. (Be careful to misspell only words that the tidy bowl type is able to recognize.) A heartfelt thanks puts the tidy bowl types out of the game. No more interruptions from people who can add. Later, an ill-advised substudy is trotted out to give people who hate consultants and question their motives something to bash. After a fight, this part is reluctantly dropped. The study/consultant haters now feel they have done their part by cutting some of the fat from a bad proposal. These deceptions are needed because the study is a ruse. The

CEO has already decided what he wants to do and wants the study to make it seem legitimate. The consultant was hired to carry out a phony study to help the CEO get done what the CEO wanted to get done.

**Hidden Values.** In my executive training, participants are asked if these actions are ethical or not and why. There is seldom an agreement. Typically, half of the executives see the old hand in the rating game as unethical, half as ethical. Arguments in support of the old hand's tactics include building loyalty, protecting one's people, and an expectation of the same gaming by others. Arguments that go the other way cite misrepresenting a person's value to the company and enticing game playing by others.

The reaction to the consultant's presentation is much the same. Half think he is clever and half are appalled. Those who agree with the consultant's tactics believe a consultant must do what the CEO who hired him or her wants. Also, supporting the CEO is seen as an investment to get future business. Others note that the CEO may not be able to disclose his or her plans. Still others assume that a CEO has the knowledge and prerogatives to make such a judgment: a CEO would know what is best. It is the consultant's obligation to do what the CEO asks. People who find these tactics unethical are more suspicious of the CEO's motives. They see the consultant as losing long-term credibility by manipulating people. Others see the tactics as discouraging people from offering potentially beneficial ideas. Again, there is little agreement about what is or is not ethical.

Note how these reactions say very little about values. The values provoking the executives in my classes to conclude that an action is or is not ethical are missing from what they use as arguments. The executives who find actions to be ethical tacitly accept lying as a necessary evil. Executives who see these actions as unethical cannot accept lying. Executives who see the end result as justifying the means resolve a means–ends conflict in favor of ends. Ends don't justify means for others. One's views of means and ends suggest a key value.

The social construction of reality offers additional insights. The appearance of reality is taken to be reality. If people seem to agree that an employee is "bad," no one bothers to collect data to confirm this view. Hearsay is accepted as fact. This "fact" then frames how everyone views the employee. Evidence of a good performance by the "bad" employee is set aside as a "special case." Each positive contribution is drowned by past evidence that disagrees, producing a "yes but" assessment. The executives who work for altruistic people see the old hand and the presenter as having the company's interests at heart. Executives skeptical of the motives of the old hand and the presenter have had different experiences and developed different expectations. Here people are believed to follow their self-interest. Such conclusions are forged by values that call for one to be accepting or skeptical.

None of the decision makers in the debacles considered the ethical positions of stakeholders, nor did they probe for the values behind them. Let's turn our attention now to how this can be done.

## Coping with Divergent Values

Ethical concerns can be uncovered by prodding. Call upon people to reveal their ethical worries as claims are being made, interests disclosed, directions set, courses of action considered, and evaluation data collected.

As the decision-making effort unfolds, ask people to point out anything that has questionable ethics for them. To encourage this, apply a billboard and a moral code test. In the billboard test, ask people to imagine their reaction if the discussion were to appear verbatim in a newspaper. Set the tone by telling people to propose only actions that conform with their ethical standards and object to actions that raise ethical questions in their mind. Introducing ethics is tricky business; there are no moral absolutes. Providing a moral tone allows questions to be raised that bring a borderline action into focus. Ethical issues can be flushed out when a proposed action receives an ethical review. An ethical review makes it easier to overcome the rigidity, dogmatism, and group think that keep people from sharing their ethical concerns.

To pick up on concerns that can escape the attention of insiders, conduct a formal ethical review at two key places in the decision-making process. One is undertaken as claims are being forged, the other when actions are being contemplated. Carry them out with the claim reconciliation and option identification steps described in Chapters 4 and 7.

Polling can be carried out with a mail or telephone survey or in a focus group. For each, the first step is to identify the stakeholders for the decision. Insiders, such as peers, superiors, and subordinates, and outsiders, such as stockholders, board members, creditors, suppliers, alliance partners, today's and tomorrow's customers, as well as representatives of communities in which the company operates and the general public, can be stakeholders. Involve the more important stakeholders as survey respondents or group members. Ask them to review the claims or the options being considered for ethical concerns. To do this, participants are called upon to voice both the concern and the value-based position that prompted the concern. For instance, a person may object to the old hand's tactics in the rating case because it distorts the ratings, and this is not fair. The distortion of results is the concern and the value is fairness.

List the concerns and values separately to decouple them. Examine the values on the list to discover core values that lie behind the stated ones. Core values can be affirmative, such as justice, service, freedom, dignity, honesty, or trust. Or a core value can call for avoiding things, such as omission, deception, manipulation, misrepresentation, lies, veiled threats, cheating, or espionage. Test the core value behind each ethical claim by asking two questions. First ask how the concern in the claim or option evokes the value. Then ask how the claim or option could be modified to affirm the positive values and avoid the negative ones. If value clashes are uncovered, form a broadly representative group. Use the values uncovered to provoke a discussion in the group. In discussion, seek an action (a claim or an option) that will adhere to all the core values identified. If such a discussion is managed carefully, a "mutuality relationship" is created that replaces a self-orientation in which people suspend their ethics.

A dialogue among a community of stakeholders about ethical action will be centered on the management of relationships, where ethics is invariably located. If stakeholders become sensitive to ethical concerns, these concerns are less apt to be set aside to satisfy people's perceptions of their organizational obligations. To do this, make all discussions of what is acceptable adhere to the highest common denominator, not the lowest. Reconcile ethical debates by setting out and then accepting the values behind each position. When you highlight ethical traps in this way, advocacy will be seen in a new light—as a demand to abandon personal ethics. Decision making then becomes self-reflective and thus self-conscious by a focus on "what is right." You can ease unethical actions off the table by showing a proponent how he or she would be seen by advocating such an action.

Ethical issues offer "defining moments" (Badaracco, 1997). In some, one either does the right thing or takes another path. Such decisions have a right and a wrong course of action, and decision makers do or do not adopt ethical principles to find it. Most decisions are far muddier than this, and choices create winners and losers that are less apparent. When the choice is between right and right, some will gain and others will lose. All one can do is balance conflicting interests and uncover the fallout. In a right–wrong choice, decision makers do or do not come clean, as in the BeechNut decision. Here the dilemma is in finding a way to introduce an ethical position.

Why do so many high-level decision makers ignore ethical considerations when making decisions? Why do successful companies allow this to happen? The debacles show that greed and self-interest play a role, but these do not fully explain the absence of ethical considerations. Johnson (1993) finds that many company leaders lack "moral imagination." They fail to see the broader context in which a decision is apt to be viewed and do not apply a "moral point of view" to what they recommend and what they do. This narrowed perspective stems from the paucity in moral imagination, not from the more base motivations of self-interest and greed. To evade the traps set by a seeming ethical lapse, look for the variety of reactions a decision can evoke. Polling exposes other possibilities and consequences, which opens you up to a broader range of issues, consequences, and solutions. A decision can then be made that evades the parochial interests in mixed interest situations, replacing it with a communal one. Without the two ethical reviews, well-intentioned people lose sight of this.

## ▼ Key Points

- ▼ Ethical positions are rooted in a person's standards of fairness and justice.
- ▼ A seeming ethical lapse creates opposition that takes shape as a pitched battle or as tokenism. Both bleed away energy and create delays.
- ▼ Ethics are suspended by people's self-indulgence and self-righteous motives, and ethics are set aside when self-protection and self-deception are required to get ahead.

- ▼ Ethical traps are set when there is an unwillingness to admit that ethics have been suspended and by actions in which there is a misalignment of who pays, benefits, and decides.
- ▼ Ethical traps can be avoided by giving ethical rationality equal standing with logical, economic, and political rationality in decision making.
- ▼ Ethical issues can arise anywhere in a decision-making effort.
- ▼ No tests can be applied to label the positions people take as ethical or unethical.
- ▼ Defining stakeholders broadly and uncovering their value-based concerns about what is ethical shifts the discourse from the lowest to the highest common denominator, seeking actions that embrace the values people believe to be crucial.

# Learning Traps

D ecisions produce outcomes with consequences. Learning requires an assessment of these consequences and the actions taken to realize them. Fire departments learn by reviewing how major fires were handled, examining how firefighters and equipment were dispatched and used on the scene and looking for practices that should be modified. Everyone involved is assembled to determine how the fire could have been fought differently to reduce property losses, injuries, and any loss of life. Surgeons, cardiologists, and other diagnosticians gather regularly to review cases, examining the progress of heart surgery patients, comparing notes about predicted prognoses, procedures used, and outcomes, questioning methods, and sharing experiences. Such reviews are mandatory for in-service training in all U.S. hospitals. The partners of consulting firms debrief consultants upon their return from an engagement, asking probing questions to learn what was done, what worked, and to offer advice. The partners look for ways to use the knowledge gained to serve new clients, to do the same thing at the same price for less cost, and to isolate best practices. The ideas extracted from such sessions codify best practices and how issues, such as downsizing, were resolved. Mckinsey and other well-known consulting companies create "knowledge management databases," archiving best practices and successful recommendations.

Hoping to deflect blame and protect prerogatives, decision makers in organizations maneuver to keep their decisions from receiving a post-mortem. There is also a natural reluctance to reveal information that could expose mistakes and errors. Information is power so people do not tell all they know. Perverse incentives, misleading outcomes, and a "hindsight bias" also coax people to conceal information, forging a climate in which one tells others as little as possible. A climate conducive to information sharing provides companies with a way to dodge these traps. In this chapter, you will see how the three learning traps take root and grow in an organization, ways to root them out, and how to replace them with a climate conducive to learning.

## Perverse Incentives

Perverse incentives coax subordinates to do things higher-ups insist they do not want. A perverse incentive can be implicit or explicit. The explicit perverse incentive rewards the wrong things. The implicit perverse incentive lurks in the climate in which decisions are made.

Explicit perverse incentives stem from things like a reporting scheme that evolves into a ritualistic exercise with little connection to the aims of the organization. Orphanages are discouraged from placing children if their budget is based on census figures. Elaborate placement procedures, complex placement criteria, and lengthy waiting periods follow in the wake of census-based budgets. Members of oversight bodies fail to see that their budgeting practices create a perverse incentive. Seeing low placement rates, they ask, "Why is it so difficult to pry a child out of here?" Finger-pointing starts. Espoused aims (placement) and budget drivers (census) are incompatible, prompting the people being blamed for low placement to take defensive action. Information is hidden or destroyed, making it difficult to learn.

Implicit perverse incentives are woven into the fabric of an organization's climate. This can happen when leaders let unrealistic expectations take root and grow. Subordinates are given an assignment and told to give it their "best effort." Pressure mounts. A hoped-for result becomes an expectation, and everyone competing for choice assignments is pushed to "up the ante." Commitments are made that guarantee a good result, putting the "wake in front of the boat." This can be difficult to pull off because success often depends on things beyond one's control.

In such a climate, higher-ups expect every decision to be a winner and hand out swift reprimands when there is failure. Decision makers observe and learn—they learn that failure is not tolerated. They also see that many decisions, theirs and others, fail. A dilemma results. Failures are unavoidable, but higher-ups expect success and punish failure. This creates a perverse incentive that coaxes people to hide information that could point to a failure.

Decision makers who can shoulder blame do not wait for the second shoe to drop. If an error, a lapse of judgment, or an oversight is traceable to them, they look for excuses and scurry about taking defensive action. Decisions are buried. A defense is prepared for decisions that could be unearthed, shifting attention to favorable consequences and discounting the importance of unfavorable ones. Reports are lost, consequences are buried in a mass of detail, and lines of responsibility are blurred to distract, confuse, and mislead. If this fails, excuses are constructed that rationalize the outcome and how it came about. Soon it is no longer clear what happened or why. Higher-ups hear contradictory tales and must plow through masses of detail, which draws them away from asking important questions. Sorting all this out fritters away time, with dubious benefits. Shrouded outcomes and clever rationalizations hide failure-prone decision-making practices. People who fail to see a decision's consequences have little reason to question decision-making practices. Such maneuvers can deflect all but the really big ticket decision postmortems.

Leaders are blind to these perverse incentives and to their role in creating them. They fail to see how a culture that refuses to accept failure forces subordinates to take a defensive position. This pressure to produce results sets the learning trap. Any admission of error is sure to bring misery, and rational folks avoid misery. Even when there is little chance of hiding an error, rational people do not own up. This creates a powerful incentive to bury mistakes. Because a decision could turn out badly, no one collects information about it. Higher-ups speak glowingly of their decisions when subordinates know otherwise, hoping to deflect questions that could expose them to sanctions. Bad outcomes are revealed in carefully measured doses, if at all. This refusal to face reality is often viewed with alarm by subordinates, who fear that higher-ups are either oblivious or unwilling to deal with the consequences of their actions. Few feel sufficiently empowered to speak out. LiCari did at BeechNut and was forced out for his efforts. Mum was the word at Disney, Nestle, Ford, Shell, and Quaker. To remove the threat posed by decision postmortems, you must break through this veil of fear.

Bennis (1989a) identifies two kinds of climates that are created by the actions of top management, one encourages disclosure and the other discourages it. Mayer, the CEO of Metro-Goldwyn-Mayer (MGM), was frustrated at failures to hear about problems with his films until cost overruns and contract disputes had become intractable and shouted, "Tell me what's going on around here, even if I fire you." Watson Jr. at IBM took a different tact. A midlevel executive expecting to be fired for a multimillion-dollar mistake was given a pep talk. When anxiety got the best of him, he blurted out, "Get it over with, fire me!" Watson responded, "Fire you, I just spent millions educating you!" Unless you work for a Watson Jr. type manager, the reality of organizational life makes it difficult to disclose information that could tie you to a failure.

### Defensive Actions

When perverse incentives are at work, an attempt to do a decision appraisal sets defensive action in motion. To avoid difficult questions, bad news is offset with good news. One deception leads to another. The cover-up with its distorted good news demands concealing actual events and outcomes with misinformation, creating a cover-up of the cover-up. Such behavior is quite rational, but it produces a lose–lose situation for the organization (Argyris and Schon, 1978). To illustrate such a cover-up, let's look at a company manufacturing components of an airframe (Ritti and Funkhouser, 1987). Each division overdesigns its component to minimize the chance that its component will fail. The cumulative effect of all this overdesign makes the airframe too heavy and the U.S. Air Force refuses delivery. Management is unable to find the root cause of the excess weight because each division engages in the same behavior. The "good news" is made public—the part works. The "bad news"—that the airframe is overweight—is covered up. The cover-up grows to include the act of deception; all of the division managers know that the airframe will be too heavy. This is covered up. The cover-up is then covered up, and all of this becomes "undiscussable."

### Discussability

Cover-ups are always two-tiered. Information must be hidden, and the steps taken to deceive others must also be hidden. The need to keep the lid on swamps all other considerations. Higher-ups and people in oversight roles have no idea what is going on. When things become undiscussable, gaps and inconsistencies in reasoning and how the reasoning applies to a decision go undetected. Discussability is the linchpin of learning. Let's see how undiscussability developed during the collapse of Barings Bank.

## The Collapse of Barings Bank

In 1995, Barings Futures Singapore (BFS) went bankrupt, leaving hundreds unemployed and debts of $1.7 billion. The Barings Group was purchased for the token price of one pound by a Dutch banking conglomerate. How did the Barings Bank, a storied institution dating to 1763, come to such a fate? Table 10.1 provides an overview.

The story begins with Nick Leeson, then a young trader with a knack for hard work and for cutting corners. Leeson began work for Barings in the Futures and Options Settlements Section. In his book, Leeson (1996) notes that no one at Barings knew anything about futures trading, and no one asked questions for fear of appearing incompetent. Leeson saw his superiors as fools and the bank's rules as archaic and, thus, easy to circumvent. His first opportunity to do so came in 1990. Management had allowed one hundred million pounds sterling in unclaimed share certificates to build up at the Jakarta office. Management had no idea what to do about this, so it was ignored. Leeson sorted out the mess after a year of effort and was rewarded with the post of general manager of Barings Futures Singapore.

Later that year, Leeson created the infamous 88888 account in the Singapore office to handle "error accounts." The account was originally set up to hold, for later payment, clients' losses from small trading errors made by the bank. The "five eights," a kind of round-off error in a stock trade, indicates how errors occur (Reyes, 1995). The account was cleared quickly as adjustments were made. The London office decided to handle this centrally and ordered all local offices to close their 88888 accounts. Leeson left the account open and used it to successfully hide a twenty-thousand-pound error.

Later Leeson began making unauthorized trades on behalf of the bank, booking the trades to the 88888 account. Initially, he had some success, but by midyear he had incurred one million pounds in losses. His trading

| Table 10.1 | |
|---|---|
| **SECURITIES TRADING AT THE BARINGS BANK** | |
| Claims | Results seem good, no need to monitor means/methods. |
| Core concerns/considerations (a) Recognized | None (head in sand on bank's position and practices) |
| (b) Hidden | Audit irregularities |
| | Profit drives principle |
| | Reputation and image threatened |
| | Risk and gain trade-offs |
| Directions | Make more profit any way you can |
| Options considered | More of the same |
| Extent of search and innovation | None |
| Use of evaluation | Routine audits, external audits, standard reporting procedures |
| Impact of evalution | None |
| Barriers to action | Protecting bank's image and reputation paramount |
| | Resistance to change |
| | Monolithic structure and lack of know-how (incompetence) allows accountability to slip |
| Ethical concerns | Bonuses encourage risky behavior when low-risk investments are bank policy |
| | Accountability ignored |
| | Scapegoating |
| | Evasion of responsibility |
| Barriers to learning | Culture and incompetence |
| | Regulatory and audit divisions of bank unwilling to challenge upper management |

behavior was akin to gamblers attempting to recover their losses with double or nothing bets. The approach failed and produced still more losses. His success in covering up the earlier error coaxed him to hide these trading losses in the 88888 account. Leeson then contrived a series of cover-ups to conceal the losses from auditors and to inflate his section's profits. Barings top management accepted the reported profits and made funds available to Leeson to make still more trades.

Leeson was trading in risky derivatives—financial instruments designed to provide trading parties with a measure of protection against unexpected price shifts—in the name of the bank. Here is how derivatives are traded. The trader lays out a portion of the value of the asset, hoping to benefit from the asset's price fluctuations. Futures and options can be bought. A future's contract stipulates a delivery date for a commodity, such as silver or oats, or a financial instrument at a specified price. Most are cash-settled, without the asset ever being delivered. A buyer receives or pays the difference between the market and the contract price of the asset. An option gives the buyer the right to buy or sell shares at a fixed price at or before a future date, and the buyer pays a fee for this.

Leeson was expected to deal in low-risk derivatives or the arbitrage of derivatives between the Nikkei and Singapore International Monetary Exchange, known as SIMEX, which is risk free. Bank officials should have questioned Leeson's reports because huge profits from low-risk derivative trades were highly unlikely. But times were tough, and new ways to make money were being piloted by other banks. Austere conditions had forced banks to move into stock market investments to supplement the modest fees earned from borrowing from and lending to clients. This may have been a factor in the failure to question Leeson's activities. Instead of questioning, management advanced eight hundred million pounds to cover his position. As Leeson (1996) says, "[higher-ups] all wanted to believe that my profits were real." The bank reinforced Leeson's activities by handsomely compensating him with more than one million pounds annually in salary and bonuses.

Barings' top managers caused the Barings debacle by their lack of oversight. Let's recount the opportunities to take action that were ignored or mishandled. Early on, a Barings' internal audit concluded that Leeson's supervision was lacking. Nothing was done to remedy the situation. At the time, Leeson was sitting on losses of one million pounds. The bank could have been saved had top management acted on the audit report. Leeson's superiors knew of his dual role as chief trader and settlements head but ignored it. The initial audit questioned this, but Leeson's bogus profits made the auditors wary of questioning someone who was creating so much profit. Poor accountability at Barings allowed the situation to ripen. A matrix structure had Leeson reporting to local managers in BFS and to product managers in London. Both assumed the other was accountable for Leeson. The bank had norms for risk position, trading performance, and funding allocation that were to be monitored daily by the bank's Asset and Liability Committee (ALCO). Leeson's huge profits, which exceeded the Barings Group's assets, failed to attract the ALCO's attention. Instead, the preoccupation of ALCO in at least six meetings was finding ways to fund Leeson's trading. Early in 1995 a SIMEX margin call alerted the ALCO to Leeson's trading. At this point, ALCO asked Leeson to reduce his positions, but they never followed up to see that this was done. Leeson's methods were never questioned because his results were good and because no one in London had the slightest knowledge about futures and options. Later, an audit by Coopers and Lybrand uncovered a fifty-million-pound shortfall in Barings' futures operation. Barings officials dismissed it as a routine error. As these events unfolded, it was common knowledge in the Singapore markets and the Singapore International Monetary Exchange that Barings was teetering on the brink of disaster. Early the next year, still another audit blew Leeson's cover and he resigned. Soon after, Leeson was convicted of illegal trading and sentenced to eight years in a Singapore prison, not a happy thought.

Observers believe the Barings debacle could have been avoided had the most basic of control mechanisms been in place (Overell, 1995) and had the bank's climate allowed questioning (Brilliant, 1995). A profit incentive dominated, driving out any other consideration, and greed made bank officials blind to the methods being used (Fay, 1996). Leeson was, in part, a victim of this. Bank officials pushed him to continue his trading and rewarded him for doing so. Such an incentive to perform needs some qualifications and stating them is the responsibility of top management. The climate of the bank also created perverse incentives. Pride and reputation at Barings had dysfunctional consequences. A reputation as being a "cut above" the rest came from being one of England's oldest banks. Top management's pride kept them from asking questions to avoid looking foolish. But they were not above letting Leeson take the fall for their failures. Who should be responsible for a company's make or break decisions?

## Failures to Learn at the Barings Bank

Perverse incentives and cover-ups blocked learning at the Barings Bank. Leeson hid his illegal trading. Bank officials hid their inability to understand the futures trading business. Top management created the incentives that pushed Lesson to do what Baring officials insisted they did not want—high-risk trading. Bank officials baited Leeson with enormous bonuses, but Leeson's own greed pushed him to take the bait. As Lesson (1996) says, "If the market had turned, I'd have made millions and become a hero." Little learning here. All this was made possible by a lack of discussability. Barings' top management failed to see events realistically. Their appetite had been whetted by huge profits. They "did not see that they did not see" that such profits were unlikely. Bank officials could not admit they had no way to tell what was really going on. They covered up their incompetence and then covered up the oversight failures that the incompetence created. Being a "cut above" makes it hard to acknowledge questionable practices. Perverse incentives in the bonus system made a bad situation worse.

The bank's storied reputation belied its top managers' actions. Reputation and profit by any means are apt to be incompatible. Bank officials instructed their traders to trade only low-risk securities but rewarded those who engaged in high-risk trading. Huge bonuses sent a clear message about what was valued. A "greed is good" dictum was being followed. Continuing success made it difficult to raise questions about practices that made the success possible. Barings' officials also postured about their guilt. Checks and balances were not in place. No one in the trading business is allowed to book his or her own transaction.

The regulatory structure in the United Kingdom failed to learn as well. As a key official said, "The events leading up to the collapse of Barings do not, in our view, . . . point to a need for any fundamental change in regulation" (Sraeel, 1995). Such a position makes more of the same possible. Others in charge of regulation have failed to learn as well. A year later, a trader at Daiwa Bank lost millions and did not report it to the SEC, which led to a revocation of the bank's charter in the United States.

The insidious creep of discussability can keep a decision maker from seeing that a situation is spinning out of control. The pattern of deception has good news offsetting bad news, cover-ups of the information dumps, and a cover-up of the cover-ups—all undiscussable. Outcomes and missed opportunities and a summary of the cover-ups and discussability for the Barings Bank and several other debacles are summarized in Table 10.2.

## Rooting Out Perverse Incentives

A simple case is offered to illustrate how people get caught in a discussability trap and what is required to get them out. Imagine that the COO of a company, while doing a performance appraisal of a long-time senior level employee with a record of poor performance, said the following (Argyris et al., 1987): "Your performance is sub-standard and you appear to have a chip on your shoulder. I've heard lethargy, uncommitted, and disinterested used to describe your efforts. We can't have this in our senior level people. I know you want to discuss injustices you believe people have inflicted on you in the past— but this is history and a rehash of history won't get us anywhere. Let's talk about today and your future with the company."

How effective was the COO's appraisal? People in my executive training classes say that his approach had little chance of success, describing it as judgmental, degrading, accusatory, and threatening. They believe that a listener would feel bullied, causing panic and defensive reactions. They see it as counterproductive and unjust to pressure someone without listening to what the person has to say. This can be summed up as a "win" orientation, emphasizing being rational to achieve a purpose while suppressing feelings. One's position is advocated to save face, but this face saving is apt to produce miscommunication, self-fulfilling prophecies, and escalating errors.

When people in my training sessions are asked what they would suggest to the COO who gave this appraisal to improve things, they often reproduce the same kind of appraisal without being aware of it. This illustrates discussability. We can all fall into this trap. To avoid the trap, a new approach is required.

Table 10.2
LEARNING BARRIERS

| | Outcomes | Missed Opportunities | Cover-Ups | Discussability | Other Perverse Incentives |
|---|---|---|---|---|---|
| **Barings Bank** | 1.7 billion pound loss and the bank's collapse<br><br>Barings group purchased for one pound by Dutch conglomerate | Corrective action to recognize and stop trading | Risky trading<br><br>Failure to understand futures<br><br>Reasons for rejecting audit disclosures<br><br>Bonuses for high-risk trading | No one at Barings would engage in questionable practices<br><br>Environment in which people can say one thing and do another | Bonus system |
| **DIA** | Delayed opening<br><br>Controversy over its cost<br><br>Baggage system failures | Using Munich system to benchmark system problems and timelines<br><br>Run conventional baggage handling in tandem with new one | Timelines overly optimistic<br><br>Baggage system design oversights | Can't reveal design oversights<br><br>Tactics used to drum up support in Congress | Accurate cost estimates make project look bad |
| **EuroDisney Location** | Opening with sabotaged systems, bomb threats, transit strike, French farmer boycott<br><br>Ten years to recoup investment | Other locations, other projects<br><br>Put French culture into operations (e.g. alcohol, picnicking)<br><br>Always one park behind | Limiting downside risk also limits upside gains | Can't admit failure to consider French culture<br><br>Decision made for wrong reasons, perhaps no reasons | Eisner wanted the project so others expected to support it<br><br>Walt's Dream |

(continued next page)

*Table 10.2 (continued)*

| | Outcomes | Missed Opportunities | Cover-Ups | Discussability | Other Perverse Incentives |
|---|---|---|---|---|---|
| **Nestle's Baby Formula** | Seven-year boycott<br><br>Lost sales<br><br>Damage to image | Ignore signals of controversy<br><br>Fail to see connection of marketing with improper use<br><br>Use advertising to promote infant welfare | Impact of formula that costs half of a family's wages to use<br><br>"Fact books" ignored safety issues<br><br>Knew of inappropriate use<br><br>Boycott's impact | Can't reveal what was spent to fight boycott<br><br>Open discussion of problem discouraged | Company loyalty as unthinking support of company actions<br><br>Long-standing policies |
| **BeechNut's Apple Juice** | Fines of more than $10 million and jail for TMT<br><br>$15 million in lost sales and lawsuits | Join PAI lawsuit (look like victim, not villain), pay small fine | Using adulterated concentrate<br><br>Hold harmless agreement with U.J.<br><br>Mix so hard to detect<br><br>Reasons for LiCari's poor performance evaluations | Locked into duplicity<br><br>Lied about actions, location of juices, and shipments to developing countries | No agreed-upon test so won't get caught<br><br>Everyone does it<br><br>CEO's promise to maintain company profitability |
| **Nationwide Arena** | Got NHL team<br><br>Appearance of duping public to subsidize private sector project | Nationwide better off building without public participation | Plan B<br><br>Extent of corporate welfare in plan A (Issue 1) and plan B | Can't discuss backup plan as it would reveal a deception | Once committed to a marginally ethical plan, its lack of ethics must be discounted<br><br>Only removal of plan A allowed plan B, which made more money |

| | Outcomes | Missed Opportunities | Cover-Ups | Discussability | Other Perverse Incentives |
|---|---|---|---|---|---|
| **Shell's Disposal of the Brent Spar** | Consumer boycott<br><br>Social consciousness questioned<br><br>Now use stakeholder assessments | Failure to involve a credible environmental group<br><br>Underestimated public outcry to a decision seen as environmentally unfriendly | Errors in estimates of environmental impact | Unable to admit errors or use of best case scenarios | Prevailing norms and values not made public<br><br>Force of public opinion required before company would back down |
| **Quaker's Acquisition of Snapple** | Losses of $85 million<br><br>Financed by selling profitable pet food and bean divisions | Internal restructuring to thwart takeover<br><br>Improve Gatorade's distribution and marketing<br><br>Early divestiture of bad acquisition | Smithburg's motives and faulty decision process<br><br>Terminate those who object | Reasons for acquisition and how decision was made<br><br>Board complacency | Hero image hard to maintain (success the norm)<br><br>Windfall outcome distorts how past practices are seen |
| **Waco Siege** | Loss of life<br><br>Loss of image | Negotiations<br><br>"Violent sect"<br><br>Knock on the door to serve warrant | Motives for armed assault<br><br>Need for rapid action<br><br>Origin of molestation claims<br><br>Koresh knew of attack | Push for vengeance<br><br>Unable to admit tactics may have been wrong | Recriminations<br><br>Law enforcement values |

## The Ladder of Inference

To dodge the learning traps set by perverse incentives, a new way to approach inquiry and its inference making is needed. The ladder of inference calls for one to

- ▼ Provide directly observable data for evaluation
- ▼ Explore these data jointly
- ▼ Look for unintended consequences
- ▼ Develop shared conclusions

The most important step is to agree on the data to be used. Provide directly observable data for the evaluation. Ask the other party if he or she agrees with these data or wants to offer additional data. This can take some time. Allow the other party time to collect data and to offer qualifications, ramifications, and rebuttals to the data provided initially. Second, explore how the data are seen by each party, seeking confirmation from the other. Third, make explicit judgments and state opinions to show when the consequences of the other party's actions were inevitable, but avoid saying it was his or her intention to produce these consequences. This keeps the appraiser from unilaterally controlling things by making attributions about the other person's motives. Encourage the other person to express feelings and ideas along the way. The ladder of inferences calls for data sharing and testing, finding data both parties agree are relevant, making inferences with the data, agreeing on the inferences being made, and developing a shared conclusion.

The aim is drive out perverse incentives, implicit and explicit, and set in their place new incentives that alter the decision-making climate. The hoped-for shift moves from a climate like that at MGM under Mayer to the one at IBM under Watson Jr., which encourages people to find best practices and share them. To learn what does and does not work in the search for best practices, organizations must have norms that stress the common good. Such norms must be created and institutionalized before decision outcomes will be made public for review and comment. Decision makers can then inquire about and reflect on previous decisions in which there was a learning failure.

## Applying the Ladder

To show how perverse incentives can be rooted out and how learning could have been facilitated, let's return to the debacles, piecing together facts available at the time.

**The Barings Bank.** Both internal and external auditors attempted to offer information identifying trading irregularities to Barings' top management. Senior officials could have hired a futures trading consultant to help them make inferences with auditors' data and avoided a meltdown of the bank. Multiple consultants might have been needed here to substantiate what was taking place. If each brings the same message, it would provide confirmation of the findings. When caught up in a knowledge gap, ask for help.

**Shell and Nestle.** Shell officials were candid, to a point. Not all data were revealed and some additional data came to light after Shell had decided on a deep-sea disposal. When Greenpeace challenged the decision, data were offered disputing Shell's claims that a deep-sea disposal of the Brent Spar would have little environmental impact. Greenpeace later acknowledged that they had misrepresented these data to bolster their position. Greenpeace's spokespeople claimed this was justified because their position was right and because Shell's data were also inaccurate.

Shell officials missed a chance to develop shared data about deep-sea disposal. Officials could have offered on-site inspection of the spar by a third party to verify what the company had done to clean it, the sludge that remained, and the toxicity of the sludge. Making this public would have allowed Shell to correct errors in their estimates and take corrective action, such as removing the additional sludge. Each party's environmental impact claims could have been turned over to a project team appointed by Shell, Greenpeace, public officials in Norway, the United Kingdom, and other affected areas. The team could have considered data from each party and from their own experts. By exploring the data about the spar's eventual decomposition and release of any remaining sludge, the team could have made inferences about the environmental impact of a deep-sea dumping. Had such data been allowed to emerge, public support could have been gained and Greenpeace's fraudulent claims exposed. To do so,

Shell would have had to hold their deep-sea disposal remedy in abeyance, pending support by an independent party.

Nestle missed numerous opportunities to learn during the seven-year boycott brought about by their refusal to address perceptions of its marketing practices. At several points along the way, a public hearing could have been staged with impartial experts hearing testimony from Nestle and its critics about their practices, not unlike the Shell situation. Nestle could have set aside unwarranted criticism in this way and gotten a fresh perspective on how company practices were being seen by the public and potential consumers of its products. Showing that the company accepted reasonable criticism and restructured their marketing approach to respond to it could have set a new course before major damage to Nestle's image had set in.

**Waco Siege.** The hostage team and the FBI had different data. Attorney General Reno could have avoided a tragedy by asking each party to defend its data. What makes this a hostage situation, coping with a violent sect or the apprehension of lawbreakers? What evidence did each party have to support the interpretation offered? People in both camps could then have been asked to share their data and suggest actions that *both* sets of data supported. Reno was in a position to insist that no action be approved unless it considered the data offered by both the FBI and the negotiators, not just one or the other.

**Infrastructure Projects.** Pena's critics claimed that a new Denver airport was not needed. To defuse the controversy, Pena could have set up a commission to examine the Stapelton situation. Parties pushing for an airport, such as the FAA, and those criticizing it, the airlines and Pena's political opponents, could have been asked to suggest experts for an evaluation panel. This panel could have weighed data supporting both a Stapelton Airport rehabilitation and a new airport. The question could have been settled by a public report that identified the strengths and weaknesses of the two proposals.

A similar procedure can be used for other infrastructure projects such as light rail, the Nationwide arena, and AmeriFlora. Forming a bipartisan group to examine the need for light rail, or any other large-scale image-driven initiative to be supported with public dollars, allows examination of data from several viewpoints. A conclusion that all the data would support can then be sought. In the process, each party gains insights into new ways of viewing the decision. This approach would help cities see the value of jumping on the "Olympic bandwagon" and other pricey image-conscious initiatives that demand public support. Thinking through what is expected from such decisions sets aside tired, hackneyed arguments and replaces them with a clearer picture of needs and possibilities and the required costs and likely payoffs. The debate becomes more enlightened and the public interest is more apt to be served.

Postmortems of the telescope consortium project show that the university did investigate but learned little about how to fund big science or an Astronomy Department. Reconciling data from supporters and antagonists would have given university officials a better way to manage zealots with an agenda in the future.

**Recalls.** The Ford Pinto and the BeechNut recall debacles are being replayed in the Bridgestone/Firestone and Ford Explorer recalls and countless others. What have Ford officials learned?

The price tag for the tire fiasco has been put at $50 billion in lawsuits and lost sales, but Ford continues to stonewall. Lawyers representing two million current and former Ford vehicle owners argue that a faulty ignition device in Ford vehicles causes stalling. In more than three hundred Ford models made between 1983 and 1995, the ignition was located near the engine block where heat could cause the device to fail and the engine stall. Internal documents show that Ford confirmed the problem and could have moved the ignition module to a cooler spot for $4 per vehicle. Lawyers claim Ford concealed information about the ignition location problem from federal safety regulators. Ford denies that these vehicles stall but has settled dozens of death and injury suits connected with stalled vehicles. Note how history is repeated.

Critics and Ford have different data. There is no attempt to share the data, let alone develop a shared inference about what the data held by both parties suggests. A new ignition system? A vehicle repurchase? There is little chance that any of these options will be adopted until each party learns about the other's views. Finally, after eighteen years of debate, as bad press about the Ford SUV and its tires depressed Ford's stock price, Ford agreed to recall five million cars at a cost of $2.7 billion late in 2001. Still the parties see the data differently. Ford officials contend there is insufficient statistical evidence that the ignition module presents a safety problem. Federal safety officials disagree and claim that data about ignition problems has been concealed by Ford. A joint effort by critics, such as the NHTSA, and Ford each offering data for the other to interpret could speed up recall decisions and save lives. It might even save money. Ford is currently facing $2.4 billion in claims from Bronco SUV owners, $1.7 billion for asbestos related ailments, and $600 million for defective restraint systems. *Consumer Reports* magazine, published by Consumers Union (CU), found nearly ten years ago that the Ford Explorer and Expedition were subject to rollover. Ford denies the claims but has redesigned the vehicles in 2001 along the lines recommended by CU. This puts a new light on the Ford–Firestone tire failure debacle. In the long run it may be cheaper to find accommodation than to fight such claims.

**Disney and Quaker.** The EuroDisney fiasco could have been avoided had Eisner been open to other ideas. A variety of big ticket projects, including parks, could have been sought. Or, if it was to be a park, a variety of park locations could have been put forward. The supporters of each proposal would then make presentations to top management. So far, this process is much like the annual new capital decisions in many companies. The ladder of inference calls for a twist. Proponents are asked to listen to the ideas of others and to present a report that incorporates some of what others want to do in their proposal. The report takes a company perspective, indicating which projects each proponent would adopt and why. Such a process at Quaker would have avoided the Snapple debacle.

## Misreading Outcomes

Windfall successes and bad luck failures also set a trap. A windfall outcome can hide bad practices. The loss of Issue 1 created a windfall for Nationwide because plan B proved to be more profitable than plan A (Issue 1). The decision to push for Issue 1 was hardly a good one, but it produced a good outcome, illustrating how good results can hide bad practices. Quaker's promotion of Gatorade hit the right market at just the right time and produced a windfall for the company, and for Smithburg. Smithburg saw this blind luck as an endorsement of his flaky acquisition practices. Bad luck may accompany good practices and lead to undesirable outcomes. Shell did not duck environmental issues but still got torpedoed by Greenpeace. A far greater environmental threat arose when a damaged oil rig with full tanks was allowed to sink near the shoreline of Peru, but there was no Greenpeace activism. No one could have foreseen how Greenpeace's claims would ignite a cause célèbre that mobilized worldwide public opposition to a legal remedy. Such a chance event can make it impossible to realize a good outcome, no matter what decision-making practices are followed.

Many find it difficult to separate the outcomes realized from a decision from the decision-making practices applied to make it. Bad practices can be present in decisions that turn out well due to good luck, and good practices can be present in decisions that turn out badly due to bad luck. To make a meaningful assessment, we must distinguish between them. There are four kinds of decision postmortems; they deal with context, windfall outcomes, faulty forecasts, and bad decision-making practices. To learn, decision makers must discover which type applies to the decision being assessed.

When practices are appropriate and outcomes good, assessment is directed to *context*. To learn, you must account for the context in which good results were realized, denoting the time, topic, urgency, and other aspects of the situation. Failing to appreciate context can lead you to export a good practice to a situation for which it is ill suited. This type of learning can be difficult. When flush with success, the feel-good aura extends to everything associated with the success, including the practices followed. It is natural for decision makers to apply the practices associated with a success to the next decision without much thought. Disney officials saw past park successes but not the context that made the park appealing. People in Japan, starved for the "Disney view of Americana," were captivated. But the French? Europeans?

Good outcomes are realized when revenues leap far beyond expectations, creating a *windfall*. Windfall successes have little to do with the acts of decision makers or their decision-making practices. An unbiased recall of the estimates made for key factors is needed to detect a windfall outcome. This is rare. It is much too easy to be swept away by the good fortune of sales and other things that far exceed what was expected. Decision makers make the windfall seem preordained and part of their plan and claim credit. When a serendipitous event seems planned, others will be misled and endorse the decision maker and his or her practices. The Nationwide arena backers are crowing about their successful sports team and its average attendance of more than 16,000 per game. One hopes that Nationwide leaders see the flaws in their analysis (see Chapter 8) and avoid them in future projects. Officials in cities looking at a new airport, such as London and St. Louis, should take a careful look at Pena's tactics. The DIA's success, claimed because the airport is now being used, has more to do with the lack of options than with good planning. Smithburg's success with Gatorade had little to do with his personal likes and dislikes. Recall that his due diligence amounted to nothing more than tasting the product. He repeated the taste test approach for Snapple and had quite a different experience. Ford avoided a big loss in the Pinto lawsuit because of sheer luck in jury instruction. Their many very bad decisions on recalls since then are noteworthy. A windfall outcome can keep decision makers from critically appraising their decision-making tactics.

Better *forecasts* are needed when decision-making practices are good and the outcome is bad. Learning stems from uncovering assumptions buried in forecasts to detect risk. This was discussed in Chapter 8, showing how bad assumptions were fatal to the forecasts made in the shed load, EuroDisney, Shell, AmeriFlora, and telescope consortium decisions. Bad forecasts do not condemn the other decision-making practices. The analysis approaches applied by Shell and EuroDisney used good tactics but with bad or incomplete data. One has to look beyond the forecast to see this.

Both *decision-making practices* and forecasts can be faulty. Addressing one without the other leads to incomplete learning. To avoid limiting corrective action to one or the other, check both forecast and decision-making practices, beginning with the forecast and its assumptions. AmeriFlora, shed load, and the telescope consortium decisions all merged questionable forecasting with poor decision-making practices. Each of these decisions was assessed (see Chapter 8) by first discovering how risk was handled in each of the key forecasts. Next, do an appraisal of the tactics used, following the guidelines in Chapters 4, 5, 6, and 7. Then select tactics with a good track record that fit your circumstances.

# The Hindsight Bias

Creeping determinism sets a final learning trap, referred to as the "hindsight bias" (Fishhoff, 1975). Once a decision and its results fall far below expectations, observers find it difficult to believe that the decision maker ignored all those warning signals that are popping up everywhere. People are misled because their memory of what happened becomes distorted. They consolidate to make chance events seem less chancy. With sufficient consolidation, disastrous decisions will seem avoidable. Let's see how this can happen with a postmortem of the *Challenger* space shuttle disaster.

## The Space Shuttle Disaster

Many claim that the *Challenger* space shuttle disaster of 1986, which killed seven astronauts, should have been foreseen. There was a known risk in low-temperature launches. Engineers at Morton-Thiokol, the rocket booster contractor, found that O rings in the rocket booster do not seal properly at temperatures below 50° F. The engineers in several reports documented these concerns, and NASA decision makers were aware of the reports. The engineers also claimed the same situation arose during a previous shuttle launch countdown and that only a last-minute increase in temperature averted a disaster. NASA administrators contended that nothing would ever get launched if they listened to the advice that comes pouring in from all quarters during a countdown.

From the vantage point of hindsight, the shuttle disaster seems preventable. A prior prediction was made and verified, but ignored. An earlier tragedy had been averted because of a chance event, a sudden increase in temperature at the Cape Canaveral launch site. NASA administrators were (and are) political appointees, many with a terminal case of technological ignorance. NASA leaders were unable to understand the engineers, on the rare occasions when they tried. With this background in mind, blame for the shuttle disaster seems to rest squarely on the launch team at NASA.

Before you buy into this explanation, consider how creeping determinism emerged from the hearings investigating the disaster. Once critics listened to the testimony, the risk of O-ring failure became far more certain than it was at the time of the launch decision. Creeping determinism makes the explosion seem preordained, and stochastic events such as the likelihood of O-ring failure appear deterministic. The failure to heed warnings about the risk of a low temperature launch is now taken to be the cause of the disaster, not one of many contributing factors. Other equally plausible explanations, such as bureaucratic smugness and ponderous decision processes, are swept aside (McConnell, 1987). NASA's management had grown from 1,050 employees per launch in 1966 to an estimated 1,850 per launch for the shuttle program. Transactions that once took six weeks take six months. But panels investigating disasters must find scapegoats and fall guys. NASA's top managers were sacked and replaced with their predecessors, who are also political appointees with little technological sophistication. NASA's decision processes remain largely unchanged.

### Why Hindsight Biases Arise

Knowledge of an outcome restricts memory. Instead of recalling the past in terms of the uncertainties present at the moment of choice, people come up with a reconstruction that accounts for the outcome. To make sense of what happened, we revise the history of a decision by creating coherence in the antecedents they have observed and by associating them with the outcome. The Japanese attack on Pearl Harbor seems predictable in retrospect, as does the economic chaos that stemmed from the Arab oil embargo. Decisions in which outcomes are known cause us to see these outcomes as inevitable and clearly related to available cues. When the same decision is described as having an unknown outcome, it produces less certainty and fewer and less intense cue associations.

Making predictions of yet to be realized events is riddled with uncertainty. A decision maker is confronted with many paths, each capturing an important contingency that cannot be fully understood at the time of a choice. To have made more timely decisions concerning gas rationing, for example, would have required accurate estimates of the shortfalls of hundreds of petroleum products and the economic consequences of each—and anticipating totally unexpected events. Consumers reacted irrationally. They lined up at gas pumps with nearly full tanks to top off their tanks, creating a chaotic and explosive situation across the country. Predictions require imagination, flexibility, and a thoughtful response to unexpected events. Hindsight requires little imagination and allows an observer to trumpet a now clear-cut relationship of cues and consequences. You see the cues as causal because they are present when you experience the outcome and its consequences. It is easy to make this association after an outcome is realized because uncertainty about the cue has been washed away. Memory distortions and the lack of surprise make this bias possible.

*Memory Distortions.* Memory plays tricks on us when the outcome of a decision is known, distorting what happened and permitting rationalizations. Blame is quick when there seems to have been an avoidable error, as in the shuttle disaster. Some decisions produce good outcomes for serendipitous reasons. Decision makers become visionary leaders when their decisions turn out to be right and bumbling idiots when they fail. Limited memory capacity creates the need to consolidate events to permit recall. It is expedient to forget attributions that proved to be incorrect. This leads us to bogus linkages between cues and outcomes that persist over time and distort our learning. Knowing how things turned out imbed bogus cue outcome associations in our memory. These bogus associations become firmly implanted and difficult to unlearn.

*Lack of Surprise.* When we see the outcome of a decision, all surprise vanishes. This has two implications. First, a lack of surprise suggests that there is little to learn. The decision outcome is treated as if it were preordained. Second, the causal explanation applied in future decisions is apt to fail. Consider a company CEO reflecting on the costs and benefits of product advertising. If the ads precede an increase in sales, a linkage between the ads and sales can be presumed. Other equally plausible explanations, such as a dedicated sales force and good training, are then discarded, overlooking the role that salespeople and trainers have in the success. Such an after-the-fact connection of ads and sales is a poor way to learn because the connection lacks validation. And people rarely seek out information that tests beliefs formed after the fact about action–outcome relationships. If you attribute your success to your own acts, you may overlook equally plausible explanations for success in your dedicated and hardworking staff. This leads to disillusioned subordinates and missed learning opportunities. Finding other plausible explanations for a success provides you with a more penetrating view of the decision and re-creates the level of surprise needed to learn. The hindsight bias assumes away surprise.

## The Debacles

Hindsight biases plagued the debacles and set traps that limited learning. Civic leaders who supported the arena point to the NHL team now in Columbus with attendance well above the 12,000 per game target and crow about their foresight. An NHL team seems preordained. The Sydney Opera House has become a tourist attraction and was prominently featured in ads for the 2000 Olympics. This viewpoint overlooks the fact that the Opera House is a performing arts center disaster, being too small to stage a major opera, and that ticket holders on a peak day routinely get there an hour late due to parking and mass transit snafus. BART was considered an urban transit disaster until tens of thousands of people, stranded in San Francisco after the 1989 earthquake, escaped via BART. In defending BART, urban transit advocates say that a major earthquake had been predicted for almost a century. But was BART built to rescue people stranded by a quake? In the aftermath of the quake, news media asked engineers looking at collapsed overpasses and bridges if they had been inspected recently—a classic illustration of the hindsight bias.

EuroDisney (now Disneyland Paris) is making money in the twenty-first century. An appraisal would ask if stockholders should have to wait ten years to break even on a $200 million investment. The DIA's baggage system now works, but this success must account for the substantial investment by the city to get it to work. Critics of AmeriFlora said "I told you so" when it became clear that the event attracted little interest and fewer paying customers. All this seems inevitable today, but each must be judged by the facts available when the decision was made.

## Dealing with Hindsight Biases

Decisions must be reviewed with all of their ambiguities and uncertainties to set aside the biases in hindsight. Parole boards are vigorously criticized when a felon is released and commits a crime. Critics ignore evidence of model behavior in confinement and the degree of risk in comparable cases on which the decision to parole was made. To make an unbiased determination of whether a parole is warranted, a review must be confined to the facts available at the time the decision was made. To determine the extent to which error is avoidable, the same doubts faced by the decision maker must be present when doing an assessment. Hearing about a released prisoner who commits a crime removes all doubts and fatally biases the assessment.

There are some key steps to conducting an unbiased review. First, you must disguise the outcome. Identifying the individuals involved will reveal whether or not a crime was committed after the release. People are remarkably adept at gathering facts that are consistent with a known outcome, suggesting that decision makers knew all along of the risks they were taking in releasing a prisoner such as Willie Horton. To examine parole board release decisions, you must reconsider them with the facts available when a release decision is made, such as the record of violent behavior and findings from psychological testing. A reviewer is given access to the same information that the board had access to and is asked to make a parole recommendation. Note how the simulation excludes information that reveals more about the situation than the decision maker (parole board member in this case) could have known. Next, compare the number of people recommended for release who later committed crimes to those proposed to be released by the test group of reviewers who later committed crimes. When you separate chance events from those that were foreseeable, the comparison provides a way to determine the difficulty of the release decision and the degree of precision possible.

Consider a second example in which graduate school admission decisions are tested to learn what precision is possible. Students known to be either "stars" or "admission mistakes" are identified on the basis of job and academic success. The stars and mistakes are characterized with information used to make the admission decision (test scores, grade point average, and other such indicators), deleting names. Members of an admission committee are then asked which applicant should be admitted. The track record of the members of an admissions committee can be assessed according to the precision with which they can identify the disguised stars and admission mistakes as students with or without potential. The members of the committee with the best track record train incoming committee members.

Grant review agencies use similar tactics in a prospective manner. The ratings of individuals serving on review panels are tabulated. Averages of rank scores are compared to the scores of each member to identify who tends to rank high or low. The results of a particular panel can be examined in light of members' tendencies to be harsh or lenient. Panels can be constructed to meet particular aims of the sponsor, such as stringent reviews because of anticipated budget cuts. Shell should try this. Company geologists at Shell are 90 percent sure of a "soaking" site (one that makes money for the company) in their recommendations, but they had it right only 50 percent of the time.

## ▼ Key Points

- ▼ Perverse incentives prompt people to take defensive action. The defense misrepresents outcomes and events. A cover-up of the misrepresentation is created that requires a cover-up of the cover-up to keep the lid on, producing undiscussability.

- ▼ To root out perverse incentives, inquiry moves back to a data collection stage. People are shown the data, allowed to rebut and qualify these data, and offer their own data to find data everyone agrees are relevant. Inferences are made with the pooled data to reach a joint conclusion, replacing individual interests with communal ones.

- ▼ Chance events make it possible for good decisions to lead to bad outcomes, due to back luck, and bad decisions to good outcomes, creating windfalls. Windfalls can be misread to conclude that good practices were used, and bad luck can be used to infer that bad practices were followed. Either can lead to misjudging the value of decision-making practices.

- ▼ Forecast failures must be separated from bad practice to get a fix on failure-prone decision-making tactics that need correcting.

- ▼ The hindsight bias makes an outcome seem inevitable. People see the cues that precede outcomes as clear cut and bad outcomes as avoidable. To assess a decision, re-create the uncertainty and surprise experienced when the decision was made.

# The Lessons: Avoiding the Blunders and Traps

D ecision debacles follow from being caught by one or more of the seven traps set by making one of the three blunders. This book offers a path that avoids the blunders and sidesteps the traps. When you are able to do this, your chance of success increases by 50 percent. In this chapter, the lessons learned from successful decisions are summed up, providing a road map that points toward, but does not guarantee, a successful outcome. The chapter is organized around the moves you can make to avoid the blunders: stay issue-centered, use resources wisely, and adhere to best practices through each stage of the decision-making effort.

## Stay Issue-Centered

In the debacles, decision makers made premature commitments by grabbing onto the first idea that popped up. These hot ideas that promised a quick fix were, at best, misguided, and at worst, wrongheaded. Recall Smithburg's disastrous beverage acquisition, the telescope partnership, Wolf's flower show, Nationwide's try for a tax subsidy, Pena's new airport, the delayed product recalls, and the Paris location for EuroDisney.

Even when decision makers tried to contemplate possibilities before taking action, as in Shell's deep-sea disposal of the Brent Spar and Reno's delay of the assault at Waco, the pressure for rapid action became intense. To deal with this pressure, decision makers must stay "issue-centered" (Delbecq, 1989). The traditions of appreciative inquiry, discernment, and pausing to reflect help you stay issue-centered.

253

## Appreciative Inquiry

Staying issue-centered enables you to maintain an exploratory mind-set. Cooperrider and Srivastva (1987) use the notion of a mystery to make this point. A decision does not pose a problem to be solved but a mystery to be embraced. The urge to "fix" something is out of sync with the needs of decision making. A mystery calls for *appreciative inquiry*, in which skillful questioning is used to get to the bottom of things.

The claims that capture the fancy of a protagonist make up one part of the puzzle. A knee-jerk diagnosis with such information runs considerable risk of missing the point. Important decisions justify the equivalent of a one- or two-day event to uncover what is "at issue with the issue," much like your annual retreat. Appreciative inquiry places considerable emphasis on this kind of discovery. An investment is made to discover what gives life to the issue being contemplated. Pause in the claim reconciliation stage with open meetings and other forums in which stakeholders representing various points of view can do a "data dump" that tells you what they know about the issue. Have everyone else gather to listen. Challenge those listening to reflect and make sense of what is heard. Ask them to look for what is most appreciated—what has given life to the issue—before doing anything else.

## The Discernment Tradition

A call to remain issue-centered in decision making can also be found in the spiritual traditions of *discernment* (Delbecq et al., 2002). The pause to reflect suggests an openness in which answers can be revealed and wisdom gained. The attitude toward judgment is one of indifference. The indifference is to which action, not that action is needed. No commitment is made until there is time to reflect and gain insight. Instead of focusing on making judgments, judgment is suspended so understanding can be gained. To engage in discernment, you must let go of the quick fix. This letting go requires that you set aside urges to calm the chaos, to get people "off your back," and to relax the tension. This will diffuse the pressure to give up your freedom of choice that is brought to bear in many subtle ways. Realize that the reasons for embracing a quick fix are often motivated by fear, greed, or a lust for power. These anxieties are often present and usually exaggerated. Fears become amplified and greed and power needs remain unfulfilled because the quick fix is overrated. The contemplative practice of discernment sets aside the quick fix until the true reasons for acting materialize. This gives you the opportunity to be selfless in your decisions and time to let insights emerge.

Create a safe space in which freedom of choice is possible. Be open, listen to stakeholders, and avoid precipitous actions. Debacles often stem from the dysfunctional behavior provoked by fear, greed, and the need for power. Fears can be confronted, along with the dysfunctional personal needs fears evoke, through discernment. Position yourself "in the decision," accepting the uncertainty of not knowing what is best by agreeing not to screen out messages and to engage in reflective listening. Look for deep feelings about what is right and listen for your inner voice. Take on the commitment to manage an exploratory dialogue with many stakeholders. Manage the dialogue with a coaching or facilitation role. Give up directing events with an emphasis on power and control. These steps will provide a picture of relevant interests and how competing interests can be handled.

### Pausing to Reflect

As the debacles illustrate, the pressures for action become intense. Pausing to reflect in the face of such pressure can be difficult to begin and even harder to sustain. When challenged to "get on with it," remind people of the alternative. Ask them to recall the last time people in the organization found a way to rapidly "fix the problem with (fill in the blank)." Ask how many meetings were called *after* the fix? How many of the quick fix solutions turned out to be bad ideas? How many required extensive retrofits? How long did all this take? Who got blamed and what did all that blame accomplish? Ask the critic to visualize the chaos, the squandered energy, and the smoldering resentment. Ask if spending some time to pause and reflect today is a good investment to avoid all this tomorrow.

## Use Resources Wisely

In the debacles, little time or money was spent on anything but defending the quick fix with a defensive evaluation. The cost of such an evaluation is quite visible so people ask questions. Evaluations become tainted when observers see a preoccupation with what the decision maker wants to do or must do to satisfy others. It is hardly surprising that Pena's evaluations spoke highly of a new airport, or that evaluations spoke glowingly of Eisner's idea of a location near Paris for EuroDisney and of the French deal. Shell officials were preoccupied with the economics of deep-sea dumping, and light rail backers ignored questions of who would ride. Proponents used bloated estimates of ticket sales to justify the Millennium Dome, AmeriFlora, and dozens of similar projects. Even when decision makers had the organization's interest at heart, as in Shell's Brent Spar dumping decision, defensive evaluations will seem self-serving and provoke suspicions. More evaluation is required to deal with the suspicions, as in the Ford and Nestle debacles. Suspicions about the answers offered pose new questions and more defensive evaluations. This cycle of suspicions provoking defensive evaluations grows until huge sums have been spent on evaluation and little on anything else.

This pulls funds away from other decision-making activities. No investments were made to investigate claims and reconcile different views of them in any of the debacles. The pressure to avoid what appears to be yet another round of useless meetings can become intense. Of course, later on, the same critic sees nothing wrong with the millions spent on a useless evaluation. "We were forced into it," is trotted out to defend the expenditures. Yes, but the failure to appreciate the concerns of stakeholders prompts opposition that will later mobilize to require round after round of defensive evaluations. Each round prompts more questions and more evaluations to answer them, until the costs become excessive. Why not deal with stakeholders and interest groups up front and avoid all this? It may even be less expensive.

A key message in this book is to make your decision-making investments wisely. To do so, make most of your investments early on. Spend your time and money to stay issue-centered by uncovering and exploring claims and the concerns and considerations that prompt them. You are apt to uncover ethical issues when this is done, indicating areas of sensitivity. This calls for a search to find values that provoked the sensitivities. If you can show that these values will be incorporated in the action that is adopted, a win–win is possible. This inserts ethical rationality into your decision-making process and gives it equal standing with logical, economic, and political rationality. Also, allocate time and money to two other critical steps. Use groups or network with people who can block the decision to find out their interests and ways to manage them. This puts implementation questions into the mix early on, introducing you to political realities so political rationality can be incorporated in your actions. Set a direction to indicate what is wanted as a result before letting anyone offer up "answers." Knowing what is wanted clarifies your expectations and makes a search more effective *and* more efficient. Your evaluations of remedies become more meaningful, easier to carry out, and much less expensive when this is done. Logical and economic rationality can be inserted into the mix to ensure that actions will benefit the organization. Coupling ethical rationality with political, logical, and economic rationality in this way positions you to find a win–win remedy that is admirable as well as supportable and beneficial to those you must cater to.

## Follow Good Practices

Debacles are riddled with failure-prone decision-making practices. Adopting the tactics in Chapters 4, 5, 6, 7, and 8 and the process recommended in Chapter 3 will increase your chance of success by 50 percent.

The best practices offered here have a flow to them that can be related to the appreciative inquiry stages of discovery, dreaming, design, and destiny (Copperrider and Srivastva, 1987). Discovery occurs as you reconcile the claims of stakeholders and network with people who can block the decision to uncover and appreciate their interests and their ideas. The intent is to create a deeper understanding of the issues that merit management and new insights into how this can be done. Dreaming evokes direction and search. To dream one must have a purpose. To envision "what might be," people elicited to help in the quest must know "for what." To speculate about the future, a direction is required that indicates what would constitute a useful speculation. Such speculations can open up new avenues, such as what would an "ideal" solution look like? Questioning then asks why can't we have such a vision and make it real? Design finds remedies by using the search tactics of innovation, soliciting, and benchmarking. Destiny sustains, empowers, and adjusts according to what is learned. The adjustment connects outcomes and their consequences to the actions taken to produce them, removing perverse incentives and accounting for hindsight biases. The intent is to identify practices that improve your chance of realizing positive consequences.

Best practice calls for a discovery process that emphasizes process stages found to have the greatest impact on success. The discovery process allocates time and money to claim validation, implementation, and direction setting and puts them at the forefront of your decision-making efforts. A premium on learning will result through a discovery of decision topics, barriers to action, and desired results. Use the sequence of tasks called for by the discovery process.

### Find an Arena of Action

Successful decision makers stay issue-centered by going beyond the initial claim. Uncover claims that capture the views of a cross section of important stakeholders to find concerns and considerations that are hidden or resist disclosure. Identify the claims of customers, salespeople, suppliers, alliance partners, and others who may have insights. Amalgamate the claims from such sources to identify the range of claims that are plausible. The concerns and considerations behind these claims paint a picture that indicates what the decision is about.

Find possible arenas of action from the concerns and considerations of stakeholders. Was the EuroDisney decision about best location or whether or not to invest in a park? Was the Waco decision about capturing lawbreakers or hostage safety? Did Smithburg's motivation stem from protecting Quaker's marketshare or from thwarting a takeover? Was the AmeriFlora decision about commemorating Columbus's voyage, making Columbus a destination, or remaking Wolf as a visible community leader? Con Ed never reconciled the "keep the power on" mentality of the company with conditions that called for shedding load. Ruminating about stakeholder claims helps open up these questions to find out what a decision is about—its arena of action.

### Manage Forces That Can Block Action

Implementation brings social and political issues to the forefront by uncovering the interests of people who can block action. Opposition can be expected when these interests are threatened. If light rail is needed, how can we convince others that the need is real and the plan a reasonable one? The arena advocates and AmeriFlora proponents could have taken steps to get the general public and their critics to see their side of the "city image" question and the benefits of such structures and events. You can use participation when interested parties are localized. The university president in the telescope decision could ask key insiders for recommendations that would enhance the university's reputation and standing; Disney insiders could be asked for location recommendations; and Quaker insiders could be asked for ways to cope with a takeover.

## Set Directions

The direction indicates the results wanted, guiding the search for ideas with an outcome in mind. Smithburg's urges were interpreted as the desire for a flashy new acquisition. What about finding an acquisition that maximizes profit? Or one that decreased Quaker's exposure to reduce the threat of a takeover? Profit or exposure reduction, as the desired result, call for very different sets of acquisition targets. Was AmeriFlora about infrastructure, rehabilitating a park, the downtown environment, or a better image for Columbus? What needs are served by infrastructure improvements, park rehabilitation, or an improved downtown environment? Does image as a direction put a different light on the need for infrastructure, park rehabilitation, and the downtown environment? Were AmeriFlora and the arena about city image, enhancing city business, or stimulating growth? Should light rail advocates shift their attention from mimicking European systems to the issues of noise, pollution, and congestion? This would bring out remedies that lower congestion, pollution, and noise rather than accepting the solution advanced by zealots. Did the Barings Bank leaders seek maximum profits or minimal risk? You can't have both, so someone must make a tough decision. Did the university want reputation at any cost or reputation with reasonable cost that exacted no penalties on others? Direction setting clears up these questions by identifying an agreed-upon outcome to guide the search for ideas.

## Search Widely for Ideas

If claim, implementation, and direction have been attended to, the remaining steps are much easier to carry out, and there will be far less controversy in doing so. Clarity about a direction to commemorate Columbus's voyage would have made it easier to search for novel plans and innovative ideas that actually mentioned the voyage, neutralizing critics. Had Smithburg been clear about the purpose of an acquisition, he would have found it easier to uncover acquisition options. The university president could have mobilized departments with a direction of offering reputation-enhancing plans. Seed money to mobilize such an effort would be far less than that spent in a fruitless attempt to revitalize a moribund Astronomy Department. Con Ed has yet to identify when a shed load decision is warranted. A directed search increases the chance of being successful no matter what search approach is followed.

## Evaluate Options

Evaluation is straightforward in a development process. The direction specifies what is wanted, such as lower cost, making a cost criterion an appropriate and reasonable way to measure benefit. This takes away the political overtones of using evaluation to defend a course of action and replaces it with an evaluation that documents benefits and the likely risk in realizing them. Identifying the arena plan with the most profit or the least risk is less controversial than collecting data to make plan A (tax support) look good. Comparing the congestion, noise, or pollution of light rail to that of buses in fast lanes is more apt to be accepted than trying to show how light rail can stimulate business in the greater Columbus area. If a cost-effective solution had been accepted as a direction, an evaluation of the cost effectiveness of acquisition options by Quaker and the dumping options for the Shell Brent Spar would have lacked controversy.

## Confront Ethical Questions

Decisions often pose ethical issues for people. A decision that seems ethically neutral to a beneficiary may have a very different look to others. Questions about ethics arise from a misalignment in who pays, who benefits, and who decides. When large-scale high-cost projects such as the

DIA, the arena, and AmeriFlora are seen as having such a misalignment, opposition will soon follow. Uncovering values behind "ethical positions" helps to reconcile ethical confrontations in which both parties see the other's position as self-serving, as in the Baring Bank leadership and Nick Leeson. Uncovering value-based differences among stakeholders shifts the discourse from the lowest to the highest denominator. Ethical issues can be neutralized by finding actions that embrace the values stakeholders believe are crucial.

## Learn about Missed Opportunities

Learning helps you find what worked, what didn't, and why. Perverse incentives, difficulties in uncovering outcomes, and the hindsight bias complicate learning by hiding the information required to make such assessments. Let's revisit the learning obstacles and how to get around them.

Perverse incentives can be implicit, buried in the social fabric of an organization, or explicit, such as a wrongheaded reward system. Both can be subtle and destructive. Organizational leaders ask for quality, measure cost, and lament that people pay no attention to them. The rewards being handed out by Barings Bank leaders for risk-taking spoke more loudly and clearly than did staid bank policy and its low-risk posturing. A culture that has no tolerance for error can be even more insidious. Both coax people to hide outcomes—and hide the act of hiding them. Outcomes that must be understood to learn become undiscussable. To break out of this, you must set a new tone by invalidating perverse incentives driving behavior. In each new situation, you must confront an implicit or an explicit perverse incentive by seeking shared data and shared inferences with "our data." Many such episodes are needed before you can set a new tone for your organization.

Outcomes that emerge may be misleading. To learn from experience, recognize that good practice does not guarantee a good outcome. Good outcomes can be due to a windfall. Bad luck can dictate others. Bad practice can be continued after a windfall success, as in the Quaker purchase of Gatorade. Smithburg repeated his tactics for the Snapple decision with disastrous results. Bad luck may discourage good practice. In many ways, the analysis done by Shell insiders was commendable. The hail of criticism was unprecedented and said little about the analytical tactics Shell officials put to use. Bad luck is neither a condemnation nor an endorsement of the practices applied.

When seeking to learn from experience, the hindsight bias can mislead you. When this occurs, bad results may seem preordained and the practices used to fashion the decision may appear to be wrongheaded. When we witness a good result, it gets connected to insightful practices. The guy who just won the lottery seems smarter than the rest of us who never put our money in anything with such a low payoff. Such a hindsight bias is caused by creeping determinism. The surprise of whether you won or not is missing because the outcome is obvious. This surprise must be re-created to learn. To do so you must hide outcomes and the names of people and other events that would reveal the outcome, and create a simulation that mirrors the real situation. Use a series of decision-making cases or episodes like this to test a decision process and decision makers to discover what procedures do and do not work and who is good at it. The simulation is based on real events but re-creates the level of risk that was originally confronted. To do this, disguise the outcome and give participants information that approximates what would have been available when such a decision was made. Make comparisons of the success of decisions made by different people. This can be most insightful, showing who has the most success in finding convicts who do not commit crimes when released, students who do well on the job, and the like.

## Summative Lessons

To sum things up, there are several things you can do to improve your chance of success. These suggestions are drawn from my research findings and indicate practices to follow and tips on how to manage a decision-making effort. Following them will have very little cost—compared to the cost of a debacle. Consider applying these actions when you are next faced with making a decision.

1. *Personally manage your decision-making efforts.* The prospects of success improve when you take charge. Delegation to experts or to people who are expected to champion

your ideas may give you time for other things but have an unfortunate fallout. The person getting the hand-off will not have your zeal for the effort, which lowers the chance of success considerably.

2. *Make ethics an ongoing consideration.* Empower people to use their standards of justice. Give ethical rationality equal standing with political, logical, and economic rationality. Consider what people will expect and who will oppose you and that what is given by logic and facts has no more power than people's values, as given by their justice standards. Finding actions that embrace these values paves the way for success.

3. *Uncover the arena of action.* Signals that capture your attention may be symptomatic, misleading, or more urgent than important. Careful probing of the claims offered by stakeholders will provide a window that opens up on a landscape with useful insights into what needs attention. The time spent reflecting on these needs to find what is at issue in an issue can pay handsome dividends. A deeper understanding of the issues that merit attention suggest what the decision is about and provide a defense for the course of action that is ultimately selected.

4. *Deal with barriers to action.* Implementation tactics address social and political barriers to action. Intervention is the best way to manage the social and political barriers that can block a decision. Participation can be recommended when using intervention would draw your attention away from other, more important activities. Avoid edicts and persuasion, even if your decision seems urgent.

5. *Establish your direction with an objective.* An objective that indicates the desired outcome opens up a search to new ideas. An open search pays dividends by reducing the chance of failure.

6. *Stress political and logical rationality.* A decision-making process should be able to think about action and how to take action. Many decision makers are pulled toward idea devel-

opment or managing the politics of the situation. They see the importance of one but not the other. There is no substitute for clear thinking or for diplomatic action. Both thoughtful idea development and adroit promotion are essential.

7. *Identify more than one option.* Several competing options improve results. Discarded options are not wasted. They help you confirm the value of a preferred course of action and frequently offer ways to improve it. Employ one of the more effective option development tactics to do this. Consider developing one option with benchmarking, one with solicitation search, and one with innovation. This opens up your search process to a variety of ideas from different sources. The best one, or a combination of the best features of several, often suggests a solution with compelling features.

8. *Insist on learning.* Treat all decisions as a learning experience, as Watson Jr. did when his manager made a mistake that cost millions. Allow mistakes to be discussable. This will open up information about outcomes that you need to learn. Making things discussable is essential for learning.

# The Decision-Making Research Project

My decision-making research project collected four hundred decisions made by senior managers in medium to large organizations across the United States, Canada, and Europe. The decisions are typical of what those managers in contemporary organizations face every day. Table A lists the types of decisions studied along with some illustrative examples. The decisions were taken from three kinds of organizations: public organizations made up of government agencies funded by tax dollars; private organizations with for-profit firms that offer products and services paid for by consumers; and third sector organizations including private not-for-profit organizations, such as the bulk of U.S. hospitals, charities, symphony orchestras, and professional societies. The results do not vary much between the different types of decisions and organizations.

My primary indicator of success is whether a decision is put to use. Changes in conventional wisdom, awareness, enlightenment, or attempts to legitimize did not count as a success. A management information system (MIS) is called a failure if the organization continues to use the old system, and a merger is a success if it is completed. Each decision was followed for two years to determine changes in use that can occur with time. During this two-year period, some decisions unraveled, being used only in part or not at all. With this information, decisions are classified in the study as successful or not according to their initial use (a trial was attempted), long-term use (decisions sustained for two years), and their degree of sustained use (decisions still in full use after two years). Indicators of each decision's value and the time required to carry it out (duration) were also obtained.

| | | |
|---|---|---|
| *Table A* | | |
| **DECISION TYPES INCLUDED IN DATABASE** | | |
| **Type** | **Percent** | **Example/Illustration** |
| Technology | 20 | Whether to invest in infrastructure, such as machinery or buildings |
| Reorganizations | 10 | Choices among internal consolidations and rearrangements (e.g. combine departments, start a new international department). Boundaries considered the same type of topic focused externally (e.g. combining with another firm, acquiring another company) |
| Control Systems | 15 | Select among options for planning, budgeting, data processing, etc. used to monitor inputs and outputs |
| Marketing | 4 | Price and distribution choices, such as developing new market channels or a new customer base |
| Products and Services | 26 | Select among new product options that can be sold to customers; choose among new service offerings sold or made available to clients as part of a contract |
| Personnel | 5 | Decisions involving job training and assessments carried out to build human resources or to reward them (e.g. benefit plans) |
| Financing (inputs) | 19 | Decisions on how to garner funds, raw material, and other inputs |

Decision-making practices were obtained by interviewing the key participants, including the person responsible for the decision. The moves managers made were uncovered and classified into the tactics that were used to reconcile claims, set directions, find solutions, do evaluations, and implement a course of action. Context was identified with measures of decision importance, urgency, resources available to assist in making the decision, support staff quality, initial opposition, success record of the decision maker, power, and the like. Decision outcomes were then identified, and success was measured by linking tactics and the contextual factors to the success measures with statistical techniques.

**The Database of Decisions**
The database of decisions has several notable features. Twenty-three percent of the decisions are drawn from public organizations, 35 percent

## Table B
### ORGANIZATIONS AND DECISIONS IN THE CASE DATABASE

| Organizations* | Decisions (Decision Types) |
|---|---|
| University Hospital | Scheduling O.R. (control) |
| Ross Laboratories | Infant formula for developing countries (mktg.) |
| Florida Medicaid Division | Fraud management system (control) |
| Ohio DNR | Supporting wildlife programs (input) |
| U.S. Air Force | Procurement (control) |
| NASA | Decompression service (service) |
| Veterans Administration | Restructuring (reorganizing) |
| Burgiss-Niple | Lab for toxic materials (technology) |
| Ohio DOT | Budget system revamping (control) |
| Sisters of Mercy Hospital System | Governance structure (reorganization) |
| Public school system | Redesign curriculum (service) |
| U.S. Navy | Radar development (service) |
| NCR | Cash flow management (control) |
| Korean Tire Co. | Marketing in South America (marketing) |
| Wadsworth Publishing Co. | Republishing books as tapes (product) |
| Nationwide Insurance | Computer system capacity (control) |
| Allied Van Lines | Pricing services (marketing) |
| Marshall Fields | New product line (product) |
| Bank One | Selling Visa cards (product) |
| Fifth-Third Bank | Dropping Saturday service (product) |
| GE | MRP system (control) |
| National City Corp. | Private label credit card (product) |
| Lennox | Recycle toxic waste (control) |
| Electronics | Inventory control system (control IO) |
| Anthony Thomas Candy | New product (product) |
| Delco | Tariff management (control) |
| CompuServe | New online service (product) |
| Bethlehem Steel | Scheduling blast furnace maintenance (control) |
| Battelle | Contract bidding (control) |
| Toyota | Increasing sales (marketing) |
| Large urban city | Creation of retirement center (service) |
| Limited, Inc. | Purchase an information system (technology) |
| American Electric Power | CAD/CAM system (technology) |
| General Motors | Robotic assemblers (technology) |
| Korean Airlines | Staff cut back (control) |
| Huntington Bank | Billing and collections procedures (control) |
| American Telephone & Telegraph | Selling an MRP system (product) |
| 400-bed acute care urban hospital | Add a lithotripsy service (service) |
| McDonald-Douglas | TQM teams (control) |
| 575-bed acute care urban hospital | Select a radiation treatment simulator (tech.) |
| Dunning Lathrup Insurance | Modify bonus policy (personnel) |
| Hertz-Penske Rental | Customer service system (control IO) |
| 1,000-bed university hospital | Purchase a magnetic resonance imager (tech.) |
| 343-bed acute care hospital | Add a pulmonary treatment program (service) |
| City health department | Halfway house for the deaf (service) |
| 500-bed acute care urban hospital | Add open heart surgery (service) |
| 1,000-bed acute care urban hospital | Provide a helicopter transportation service (service) |
| 250-bed rural acute care hospital | Create a detox unit (service) |
| Lane Bryant, Inc. | Intimate apparel (product) |
| For-profit abstracting company | Devise a reference library (product) |

*Some organizations requested anonymity

come from private organizations, and 41 percent from third sector (non-profit) organizations, with a single decision taken from each organization. These organizations are medium to large in size and none are new start-ups (Table B). The decisions involve all of the types of decisions found in the literature (e.g., Hickson et al, 1986). Just 60 percent of the decisions were initially adopted, suggesting that the database contains both good and less desirable decisions.

Data were collected with interviews and questionnaires. Interviews were carried out to identify decision-making practices. Questionnaires

| Table C |  |
| --- | --- |
| SUCCESS MEASURES |  |
| **Measures of Decision Value** (averaged to measure value) | **Scale/Time** |
| *Impact* (extent the decision improved organizational capability) | 5 = made decisive contribution, 4 = helpful in several ways, 3 = helpful in a few ways, 2 = helped very little, 1 = none |
| *Merit* (intrinsic quality of the decision) | 5 = exceptional, 4 = meritorious, 3 = average, 2 = marginal, 1 = none |
| *Satisfaction* (satisfaction with the decision) | 5 = satisfied, 4 = moderately, 3 = neutral, 2= moderately dissatisfied, 1 = dissatisfied |
| **Measures of Development Time** |  |
| Elapsed time measured from initiation to end of development and from the end of development to the end of installation attempts | Months to do each (decision time ranges from one month to eight years) |
| Evaluation of development and installation time | 5 = well above, 4 = above, 3 = at, 2 = below, 1 = well below the time required for past decisions |
| **Measures of Decision Use** |  |
| Initial adoption | Proportion of decisions used after development |
| Sustained adoption | Proportion of decisions still in use two years later |
| Full adoption | Proportion of decisions in full use two years later |

were used to determine values for success indicators (Table C) and for contextual factors. The primary informant (strategic decision maker) is well placed in the participating organizations. Nearly two-thirds (65%) are top executives (CEOs, COOs, or CFOs), and about one-third (35%) are middle managers. Secondary informants are line managers subordinate to the primary informant in 56 percent of the cases, a staff person in 36 percent of the cases, and a task force member in 8 percent of the cases.

**Soliciting Participation.** The project began by contacting people holding key positions in organizations, asking them to participate in a study that sought to improve our understanding of organizational decision making. The study was presented as a long-term project to accumulate a sufficient number of organizational decisions to uncover and appreciate the practices used to make them. A decision was defined as an episode, beginning when the organization first became aware of a motivating concern and ending with an implementation attempt.

To ensure interest and first-hand knowledge, the contact person was asked to select a recent organizational decision for study. All decisions were made within six months of the interviews. A participant was asked to select a decision that had considerable importance to the organization due to the resources required and its consequences. The contact person was then asked to identify three people involved in the decision who could be interviewed, including the person who had primary responsibility for the decision. In most instances, the contact person suggested a decision for which he or she was responsible and became the primary informant. Once these data had been collected, the contact person solicited others to participate. Cases grew in this way over a period of twenty years.

Each informant played a specific role. The primary informant, the decision maker, provided information about the steps followed to make the decision. Secondary informants filled out questionnaires and surveys. One of the secondary informants, selected by the decision maker as knowledgeable, also provided a list of steps as a check. The questionnaire data were collected from secondary informants before the interviews to separate thinking about outcomes from the recall of how the decision was made. Secondary informants provided information about outcomes and the contextual factors by filling out a survey. They were asked to rate the decision's value, and its time, urgency, importance, and so forth on the questionnaire.

Retrospective data can be biased by inaccurate recall due to self-justification, memory lapses, and logical incosistencies. To improve data validity and provide a way around these difficulties, the study included multiple informants and data sources, focused on factual events in interviews, sought convergence in interpretations, and used "second chance" reviews of data to jog memory. Recent decisions were collected to reduce memory failure. The data collection included informants with first-hand knowledge, archival records, and documents, and the sources used (interviews and documents) were cross checked. Emphasis was placed on converging to an understanding of events and not on measuring differences that cropped up along the way.

To enhance validity, two informants were interviewed to uncover the steps taken to make each decision. The interview procedure was devised to deal with the dual problems of what people remember and what they choose to tell in an interview. Drawing on qualitative research principles, informants were asked in separate interviews to recall what first captured their attention. In each interview, questioning proceeded from this point by asking, "What happened next?" For example, after the informants described what had captured their attention, they were asked why this seemed important and merited action. Questioning proceeded in this way, taking cues from the last response to fashion the next query. Information gleaned from the second informant was used to corroborate what the primary informant said.

**Triangulating Responses.** The informants' recall of the steps followed to make a decision was captured in a narrative prepared by the author of about twenty pages that described the choice that was made and the steps taken to make it, as recalled by each informant. Informants reviewed their narratives separately and made any changes they believed were warranted. Then, documents such as notes, proposals, or files that still existed were reviewed. Documents and the steps noted by the informants were compared to find inconsistencies and gaps in the "story" that depicts a decision. These inconsistencies and gaps were explored in a follow-up interview with the primary informant (the decision maker). In this interview, attempts were made to reconcile differences and fill in gaps. Thus, two methods and two types of informant triangulation were used to test the validity of each decision description. A clear picture of the decision, agreeable to the informants, was required to include a decision in the database. As data were being collected, a number of decisions failed to meet the clarity or agreement tests and were abandoned. Summary case profiles were prepared for each of the remaining four hundred decisions (Nutt, 1999). One of the profiles listed the actions taken by tracing the them through a transactional model to see which stages of decision making were activated, how each was carried out, and the order of events (Nutt, 1993). The other profile identified the tactics used to carry out search, synthesis, and analysis in each of the process stages (Nutt, 1984).

### Identifying the Tactics

Tactics were uncovered from the narratives and the case profile data, resorting to my interview notes when additional information was needed. The case narratives provided the core information used to uncover actions taken to make each decision. Data from the questionnaires were used to refine some of these actions, putting them in more precise categories.

Several separate reviews were carried out to identify the tactics. Each case was examined to determine how claims were uncovered, direction set, options identified, evaluations done, and implementation carried out. To improve intrarater reliability, the cases were reclassified to repeat the identification of tactics used in each process stage until there was agreement. To do this, each sort put the cases into tactic categories, new or emergent categories, and an unknown category. The repeats were carried out to see if the tactic categories held up. After several sorts, the previous search outcomes were reproduced by the current one, suggesting that intrarater reliability had been achieved. Interrater reliability was determined by asking a colleague to review the decision summaries and indicate the tactic used in each process stage. Definitions were provided, asking the second rater to match cases with the tactic categories or to an unclassified category. Reliability was computed as percentage agreement. This led to a 90 percent agreement between the two people doing the classifications.

### Success Measures

It was assumed that different decisions (choosing one location or product over another) produce different patterns of success and that these decision outcomes could be identified with sufficient clarity to allow success measurements to be made. Research has shown that different approaches produce different decisions that have different outcomes, so this seemed reasonable. Studies that have tried to trace the impact of a decision to overall organizational performance, such as return on equity, have not been successful.

Decision outcomes of interest are the results of a search (number of alternatives), their value, how long it takes, and disposition or use. Decision value was estimated with data taken from the questionnaires filled out by secondary informants. The informants checked along an anchored rating scale with five anchors indicating their view of the decision's impact, merit, and satisfaction (see Table C). To improve recall and precision, the estimate-reflect-estimate (ERE) procedure was used. First, informants made their ratings. Then the informants reviewed the average of their ratings and heard the arguments from the other rater to call for a higher or lower rating. The raters then reconsidered their initial ratings of merit, impact, and satisfaction. Decision merit was determined by an average of the informants' final rating. This approach was used for these reasons. First, using a secondary informant avoids self-serving assessments by a decision maker. Second, organizations are reluctant to provide objective data about benefits and the like. Third, Alexander (1986) found that a manager's subjective determinations of decisions are highly correlated with objective measures, making subjective measures of value indicative of true value.

Duration is made up of two different time periods. The first determines the time for plan development, from need recognition to the completion of a plan. The second identifies the elapsed time from the end of plan development to the end of installation attempts by the decision maker. The first duration measure is used to determine the time taken by claim, direction, and search tactics because this time interval follows the tactics applied and, thus, could be influenced by it. The second duration measure was used to determine the time taken by evaluation and implementation tactics because this time interval followed the tactics applied. Informant's recall was refined by a discussion of the initial time estimates using the ERE procedure. The average development time and implementation time in months from the final estimates was used in the analysis. The duration of development and installation seem important because decision makers are often under pressure to produce results. More timely tactics would be valued.

Decisions were followed for two years to capture downstream changes in their use. Several kinds of changes were observed. First, some decisions had a limited scale of use, suggesting a partial adoption. Other decisions experienced substantial delays before adoption. Finally, some decisions were withdrawn after performance monitoring, becoming ultimate rejections, and some of the initially rejected decisions were put to use. Using this information, three measures were created called initial, sustained, and full adoption. Initial adoption accounts for whether there was an early adoption or rejection. Sustained adoption identifies whether a decision was still in use after the two-year period. The full adoption measure accounts for changes in adoption and treats partial adoptions as failures, making it a downstream indicator of degree of use. Using such measures seems reasonable because success for an organization stems from putting a decision to use. If a decision is not used, it has no value.

### Analysis

The decision tactics that were uncovered in the studies were linked to each of the success indicators with statistical methods. ANOVAs and MANOVAs were carried out to do this. The success measure (number of alternatives, value, time measures, and adoption measures) served as the dependent variables in these statistical analyses. In these analyses, the explanatory factors were made up of the tactics described in the chapters and the tactics interaction with contextual factors such as urgency, importance, extent of support, and the like. A Duncan Multiple Range Test isolated significant differences in the success for each of the tactics.

A complete list of my publications drawn on for the book from this research is provided in a chapter-by-chapter listing in Table D.

| | |
|---|---|
| | *Table D*<br>**CITATIONS BY CHAPTER** |

| Chapter | Work Drawn Upon |
|---|---|
| 1 and 2 | Nutt, P. C., "Surprising but True: Half of Organizational Decisions Fail," *Academy of Management Executive, 13*(4), 1999, 75–90.<br><br>Nutt, P. C., "Successful and Unsuccessful Tactics in Decision-Making," in V. Papadakis and P. Barwise (eds.), *Strategic Decisions: Context, Process and Outcome*, London: Kluwer Academic Publishers. 1997.<br><br>Nutt, P. C., "Preventing Decision Debacles," *Technological Forecasting and Social Change, 38*, 1991, 159–174.<br><br>Nutt, P. C., "The Conduct of Decision-Making," in E. Johnsen (ed.), *Trends and Megatrends in the Theory of Management*, Copenhagen, Denmark: Bratt International, 1986. |
| 3 | Nutt, P. C., "Types of Organizational Decision Processes," *Administrative Science Quarterly, 29*(3), 1984, 414–450.<br><br>Nutt, P. C., "Planned Change and Organizational Success," *Journal of Strategic Change, 2*(5), 1993, 247-260.<br><br>Nutt, P. C., "Types of Tough Decisions and Processes to Deal with Them," *The Review of Business Studies, 1*(2), 1992, 85–110.<br><br>Nutt, P. C., "Planning Process Archetypes and Their Effectiveness," *Decision Sciences, 15*(2), 1984, 221–238. |
| 4 | Nutt, P. C., "Framing Strategic Decisions," *Organization Science, 9*(2), 1998, 195–206.<br><br>Nutt, P. C., "Diagnostics for Strategic Decisions," *OMEGA: The International Journal of Management Science, 21*(4), 1993, 411–423. |
| 5 | Nutt, P. C., "Contingency Approaches Applied to the Implementation of Strategic Decisions," *International Journal of Business, 6*(1), 2001,1–34.<br><br>Nutt, P. C., "Leverage, Resistance, and the Success of Implementation Approaches, "*Journal of Management Studies, 35*(2), 1998, 213–240.<br><br>Nutt, P. C., "Implementation Style and the Use of Implementation Approaches," *OMEGA: The International Journal of Management Science, 23*(5), 1995, 469–484.<br><br>Nutt, P. C., "Selecting Tactics to Implement Strategic Plans," *Strategic Management Journal, 10*(1), 1989, 145–161.<br><br>Nutt, P. C., "Identifying and Appraising How Managers Install Strategic Changes," *Strategic Management Journal, 8*(1), 1987, 1–14.<br><br>Nutt, P. C., "The Tactics of Implementation," *Academy of Management Journal, 29*(2), 1986, 230-261. |

*Table D (continued)*

| Chapter | Work Cited |
|---------|------------|
| 6 | Nutt, P. C., "The Formulation Processes and Tactics Used in Organizational Decision Making," *Organization Science, 4*(2), 1993, 226–251.<br><br>Nutt, P. C., "Formulation Tactics and the Success of Organizational Decision Making," *Decision Sciences, 23*(5), 1992, 519–540.<br><br>Nutt, P. C., "The Influence of Direction Setting Tactics on Success in Organizational Decision Making," *European Journal of Operational Research, 60*(2), 1992, 19–30. |
| 7 | Nutt, P. C., "Decision-Making Success in Public, Private, and Third sector Organizations: Finding Sector Dependent Best Practice," *Journal of Management Studies, 37*(1), 2000, 77–108.<br><br>Nutt, P. C., "A Taxonomy of Strategic Decisions and Tactics for Uncovering Alternatives," *European Journal of Operational Research, 132*(3), 2001, 159–192.<br><br>Nutt, P. C., "The Identification of Solution Ideas During Organizational Decision Making," *Management Science, 39*(9), 1993, 1071–1085. |
| 8 | Nutt, P. C., "Context, Tactics, and the Examination of Alternatives During Strategic Decision-Making," *European Journal of Operational Research, 124*(1), 2000, 159–186.<br><br>Nutt, P. C., "Public-Private Differences and the Assessment of Alternatives for Decision-Making," *J-PART, 9*(2), 1999, 305–349.<br><br>Nutt, P. C., "Evaluating Alternatives to Make Strategic Choices," *OMEGA: The International Journal of Management Science, 26* (3), 1998, 333–354.<br><br>Nutt, P. C., "Evaluating Complex Strategic Choices," *Management Science, 44*(8), 1998, 1148–1166.<br><br>Nutt, P. C., "Uncertainty and Culture in Bank Loan Decisions," *OMEGA: The International Journal of Management Science, 17*(3), 1989, 297–308. |
| 9 | Nutt, P. C., *Making Tough Decisions*, San Francisco: Jossey-Bass, 1989.<br><br>Nutt, P. C., "The Impact of Culture on Decision Making," *OMEGA: The International Journal of Management Science, 16*(6), 1988, 553–567.<br><br>Nutt, P. C., "Decision Style and Its Impact on Managers and Management," *Technological Forecasting and Social Change, 29*, 1986, 341–366 |
| 10 | Nutt, P. C., *Making Tough Decisions*, San Francisco: Jossey-Bass, 1989.<br><br>Nutt, P. C. and Backoff, R. W., "Mutual Understanding and Its Impact on Decision-Making," *Technological Forecasting and Social Change, 29*, 1986, 13–31.<br><br>Nutt, P. C., "Decision Style and the Strategic Actions by Top Executives," *Technological Forecasting and Social Change, 30*, 1986, 39–62. |

# Estimating Risk

Appendix 2 shows the data that were collected and how estimates and calculations were made to construct the figures in Chapter 8.

## New York City Blackout (Con Ed Costs)

### Data

|                  |            | Blackout        | No Blackout   |
|------------------|------------|-----------------|---------------|
| Con Ed Options   | Shed load  | –$512,000       | –$512,000     |
|                  | Wait       | –$10,600,000    | 0             |

Data represent losses to Con Ed

### 1. Shed Load Loss Estimates

Shedding load results in costs to Con Ed based on the percent of load shed, hours down, and cost per kilowatt-hour of the load shed. The amount of 400,000 KW, suggested by the Albany operator, is used (5% of capacity of 8,200,000 KW). The cost per KWH is determined by hours out of service. 25 hours were required in a previous outage. 5% of 24 hours is 1.25 hours to restore service. The FPC estimates short-term interruptions cost $1.00 per KWH (worse case). Cost is 8,200,000 * .05 * 1.25 hours * $1/hr = $512,000.

### 2. Wait Cost Estimates

Citywide blackout cost was estimated from data offered by the Federal Energy Regulatory Commission on the costs incurred by Con Ed during a previous power failure.

They are (in millions):

| | |
|---|---|
| Net Revenue Loss | $5.7 |
| Cost of Service Restoration | $3.4 |
| Analysis of Blackout | $0.5 |
| Increase in Non-collectable Accounts | $1.0 |
| Total | $10.6 |

## Computations

Risk in the shed load decision is determined with the cost incurred by Con Ed. First, one assigns an unknown P to the chance of a blackout. This can range from 0 (never) to 100 (certain). The likelihood estimates must sum to 1.0 so the outcome will cover all possibilities. This makes the chance of no blackout 1 – P. These values are assigned to the data.

| | Blackout | No Blackout |
|---|---|---|
| | P | 1 – P |
| Shed | –$512,000 | –$512,000 |
| Wait | –$10,600,000 | –0 |

The value of each option is determined by weighting the outcomes by their chance of occurring and summing the results.

Shed $= -\$512{,}000\ (P) + -\$512{,}000\ (1-P) = -\$512{,}000$

Wait $= -\$10{,}600{,}000\ (P) + 0\ (1-P) = -\$10{,}600{,}000\ (P)$

This reduces to

Shed $= -\$512{,}000$
Wait $= -\$10{,}600{,}000\ (P)$

To plot the two outcomes, assign the extreme values of the chance of a blackout, never and certain, to each:

| | Shed | Wait |
|---|---|---|
| P = 0 | –$512,000 | 0 |
| P = 1 | –$512,000 | –$10,600,000 |

These values are plotted on Figure 8.1 by locating P = 0 on the horizontal axis and finding its corresponding value of 0 on the vertical axis, and repeating for P = 1 locating –$10,600,000 at P = 1 on the vertical axis. The points are connected with a straight line to show the payoffs for the no shed load option. Repeat for the shed load option, drawing a horizontal line at –$512,000 on the vertical axis for the shed load option. The lines cross at the break-even point, indicating the amount of risk in the shed load decision.

Break-even probability of a blackout, in which the two choices have equal risk, can be computed by setting the two equations equal to each another.

$$-\$512,000 = -\$10,600,000 \, (P)$$
$$\text{Solving for P: P} = -\$512,000 / -\$10,600,000 = .048 \text{ or } 4.8\%$$

The shed load decision gives the best outcome (minimal loss) when the chance of a blackout is 4.8% or more.

## New York City Blackout (Societal Costs)

### Data

|  |  | Blackout | No Blackout |
|---|---|---|---|
| Options | Shed load | –$1,000,000 | –$1,000,000 |
|  | Wait | –$310,000,000 | 0 |

### 1. Shed Load Cost Estimates

Cost to shed load is $1 million for law enforcement overtime costs and other charges to maintain order in affected area. It is assumed that law enforcement officials with adequate notification can contain looting and maintain order in the 5% of the city in which load would be shed for a time period of one and one-quarter hours.

### 2. Wait Cost Estimates

Societal blackout cost will include class action lawsuits that, in similar situations, produced an average of $10 million in damages. Damages are typically subsidized by utility rate increases. Other costs include

$120 million in rioting damage, $16.8 million for law enforcement to maintain order, and lost revenues for businesses estimated by congressional research to be $146.4 million, for a total of $310 million for similar civil unrest situations.

## Computations

Assigning P and 1 − P to represent the likelihood of a blackout and no blackout as above yields:

|           | Blackout         | No Blackout      |
| --------- | ---------------- | ---------------- |
|           | P                | 1 − P            |
| Shed load | −$1,000,000      | −$1,000,000      |
| Wait      | −$310,000,000    | 0                |

Shed = −1,000,000 (P) + −1,000,000 (1 − P) = −1,000,000
Wait = −310,000,000 (P) + 0 (1 − P) = −310,000,000 (P)

To plot, end points are established:

|         | Shed          | Wait          |
| ------- | ------------- | ------------- |
| P = 0   | −$1,000,000   | 0             |
| P = 1   | −$1,000,000   | −$310,000,000 |

These values are plotted on the bottom of Figure 8.1.

Breakeven is determined by setting the equations equal and solving for P:

$$-1,000,000 = -310,000,000 \text{ (P)}$$
$$P = 1 / 310 = .0032$$

The shed load decision is preferred when the chance of a blackout is 0.32% or more.

## AmeriFlora

### Data

|  |  | REVENUE FORECASTS | |
|---|---|---|---|
|  |  | Favorable | Unfavorable |
| OPTIONS | Hold Event | $6.1 million | −$27.8 million |
|  | Cancel | 0 | 0 |

### 1. Data Sources

The revenues for AmeriFlora are made up of gifts and sales. Gifts from private sponsorships and government funding were estimated to be $61 million. Sales included tickets sold and commissions and fees. Commissions and fees were estimated at $4.3 million. Ticket sales were placed at a worst case outcome of $22.9 million, and a best case outcome of $33.7 million. The sponsors hoped to break even. Critics said $8 million from private donors was all organizations could expect. Costs were estimated to be $93.0 million.

|  | Best Case | Worst Case | Actual |
|---|---|---|---|
| **Revenue Sources** | | | |
| Ticket Sales | $33.8 | $22.9 | $21.7 |
| Commissions | $4.3 | $4.3 | $5.3 |
| Government | $31.0 | $30.0 | $30.0 |
| Private | $30.0 | $8.0 | $8.0 |
| Total | $99.1 | $65.2 | $65.0 |
| | | | |
| Cost (Millions) | $93.0 | $93.0 | $95.0 |
| Difference | $6.1 | −$27.8 | −$30.0 |
| (all data in millions) | | | |

### Computations

The risk in the breakeven objective assumed by the AmeriFlora organizers is determined by comparing the best and worst case revenue streams offered by event proponents and found in public sources. The chance of a favorable outcome is set at P, and an unfavorable one at 1 − P, following the logic noted for the blackout. These values are assigned below:

|  | Favorable | Unfavorable |
|---|---|---|
|  | $\underline{P}$ | $\underline{1 - P}$ |
| Hold | 6.1 | −27.8 |
| Cancel | 0 | 0 |

Weighting the revenue less cost figures by their chance of being realized, and summing up the result value of each option,

Hold $= P (6.1) + (1 - P) (-27.8) = 33.9\ P - 27.8$
Cancel $= 0$

To plot the outcomes, assign the extreme values (never and certain) to each as before:

|  | Hold | Cancel |
|---|---|---|
| $P = 0$ | −27.8 | 0 |
| $P = 1$ | 6.1 | 0 |

These values are plotted on Figure 8.2.

Breakeven is determined as before:

$0 = 33.9\ P - 27.8$
$P = .82$

Breakeven for the event would be expected when the chance of realizing the optimistic revenues is 82% or greater.

## Telescope Consortium

### Data

|  |  | REVENUES | |
|---|---|---|---|
|  |  | Optimistic | Pessimistic |
| OPTIONS | Participate | −$4,400,000 | −$14,700,000 |
|  | Dropout | −$3,100,000 | −$3,100,000 |

Values come from the present worth of annual revenues less annual costs.

## 1. Costs and Revenues for Participate Option

Telescope costs include a $10.8 million one-time cost, an annual operating and space cost of $3.5 million, and new faculty annual costs of $0.5 million. Values represent present values of revenues less cost streams and then accounting for the $10.8 million one-time expenditure. Revenues were estimated at between $2 and 4 million annually.

## 2. Cost and Revenue for Dropout Decision

Present worth of revenues that have been $25,000 annually, less current annual expenses of $638,000.

## Computations

Risk in the telescope decision stems from the likelihood of producing revenue streams by grants. The astronomy department chair provided the estimate of a $2 million to $4 million per year increase in grant revenue. The present worth of these revenue streams, assuming a 20-year life and an interest rate of 10% (what T-bills were going for at the time), sets present worth of these revenues at $20.5 million to $10.2 million. The present worth of the cost stream for the "participate" option is $24.9 million. Revenues less cost for the "participate" option prompt losses of $4.4 million or $14.7 million. The current situation calls for $3.2 million in costs and produces $25,000 in grants (revenues), which creates $128,000 in present worth revenues. The present worth of the "dropout" option is a $3.1 million loss. Calling the chance of realizing the optimistic revenue P and the lower value 1 – P yields:

|  | Optimistic<br>P | Pessimistic<br>1 – P |
|---|---|---|
| Participate | –$4,400,000 | –$14,700,000 |
| Dropout | –$3,100,000 | –$3,100,000 |

Weighting each payoff for each option by its chance of being realized and summarizing:

Participate: $-4,400,000 \ (P) - 14,700,00 \ (1 - P)$
Dropout: $-3,100,000 \ (P) - 3,100,000 \ (1 - P)$

Reducing

| | | |
|---|---|---|
| Participate: | −10.3 P − 14.7 | |
| Dropout: | −3.1 | |

Plotting the values:

| | Participate | Dropout |
|---|---|---|
| P = 0 | −14.7 | −3.1 |
| P = 1 | −4.4 | −3.1 |

Breakeven never occurs because the dropout option produces a better outcome with fewer losses no matter what assumptions about grant revenue are made.

## Nationwide Arena

### Data

| | | ATTENDANCE | |
|---|---|---|---|
| | | Low | High |
| OPTIONS | Private Finance | −$3,100,000 | $38,800,000 |
| | Tax Subsidy | $6,500,000 | $11,500,000 |

### 1. Data for Tax Subsidy Option

Tax subsidy option estimates use present worth values of revenues less cost. Revenue is computed for 41 hockey games and 107 events to estimate parking, ticket, and concession revenues. Pessimistic attendance estimates call for 9,250 average attendance at hockey games and 50% attendance at 95 events, with the remainder of the events at 75%. Optimistic attendance estimates call for 16,650 in ticket sales for hockey games and 27 events half full, with the rest at 75% of capacity (Baim, 1996). Costs include $125 million construction costs less 35% to be covered by sales for personal seat licenses and luxury suites, leaving $73.1 million for Nationwide to cover. Annual construction cost based on a 9%, 12% real discount rate less 3% for inflation, discount rate and 99-year lease payment period to compute present value of construction costs. Other annual costs include $20 million for NHL payroll and taxes, less abatement of $9 million.

## 2. Data for Private Finance Option

Private finance option estimates also require present worth estimates. Revenues calculated as above, less the $17.5 from parking revenues to repay the city. Annual costs include NHL payroll of $20 million, arena rent of $700,000, and profit sharing and fees of $3 million, and taxes. A 15-year time frame was used in all calculations except the lease.

## Computations

Nationwide, as the key sponsor for the arena, was deciding whether to pursue a subsidy, in which the local sales tax would be increased to cover arena construction costs. The options and their outcomes are based on the decision to build with and without the tax subsidy. Nationwide preferred the tax subsidy option to reduce its risk. The company believed it would lose its investment if there was low attendance.

To estimate this risk, set P = to the low attendance outcome (at its lower revenue projection) and 1 − P for the high attendance outcome. This leads to:

|  | P = Low | 1 − P = High |
|---|---|---|
| Private | −3.1 | 38.8 |
| Subsidy | 6.5 | 11.5 |

Weighting the payoff for each option by its chance of occurring and adding the result:

Private Finance $= 3.1\,P + 38.8\,(1 − P) = -41.9\,P + 38.8$
Tax Subsidy $= 6.5\,P + 11.5\,(1 − P) = 5\,P + 11.5$

The extreme points for the graph in Figure 8.4:

|  | Private | Subsidy |
|---|---|---|
| P = 0 | 38.8 | −3.1 |
| P = 1 | 16.5 | 11.5 |

Breakeven:

$$-41.9\,P + 38.8 = 5\,P + 11.5$$

Solving:

   $P = .58$

Private finance risk is:

   $0 = -41.9\, P + 38.8$

Solving for P:

   $P = .926$

## EuroDisney

The option to locate near Paris has two unknowns, hotel occupancy and attendance. Not all park visitors stay overnight, so both can affect revenues. Data in present worth terms as shown below for these factors. (The no go option yields zero payoff and will not be considered.)

### Data (in millions)

|  |  | ATTENDANCE | |
|---|---|---|---|
|  |  | Low | High |
| HOTEL | Low | −$6 million | $9 million |
| OCCUPANCY | High | $77 million | $92 million |

Estimates for EuroDisney were based on an average ticket price of $33 per day, and an average in-park spending on food and other items of $28 per day. Hotel charges were set at $196 per day. There are 6 hotels with a total of 5,200 rooms for rental and the park is open every day of the year. The revenue is treated as an annuity discounted to the time when Disney spent $200 million for their share of the park. Disney was to receive 3% of the revenues as a management fee and 7.5% of the revenues as a royalty fee. The 3% management fee would increase to 6% after 10 years of operation.

Disney expected:
   76% hotel occupancy
   $15 million in park attendance
   $12.9 million in ticket sales revenues
These results proved to be wildly optimistic.

The actual values were:

37% hotel occupancy

11 million in park attendance (much due to discounted ticket prices)

$7.75 million in ticket sales revenues

The worst-case estimates were set: 60% hotel occupancy and $9 million in ticket sales. Disney spent $200 million in 1986. Revenues over a 20-year period are discounted by 8% to 1986.

Revenues were computed by:

.10 [attendance (33 + $28/day) + occupancy (8,200 * $196/day)]

The 10% is Disney's revenues share.

With optimistic attendance and hotel utilization: $292 million

With pessimistic attendance and optimistic hotel utilization: $277 million

With optimistic attendance and pessimistic hotel utilization: $209 million

With pessimistic attendance and pessimistic hotel utilization: $194 million

Each estimate has been reduced by the $200 million for the Disney share of the park cost in these values.

## Computations

The four possible outcomes with revenue projections are:

|  | REVENUES | |
| --- | --- | --- |
|  | 1 − P = Unfavorable | P = Favorable |
| Worst Case | −$6 million | −$6 million |
| Unfavorable Attendance | −$6 million | $77 million |
| Hotel Unfavorable | −$6 million | $9 million |
| Best Case | −$6 million | $92 million |

Solving:

Attendance Unfavorable:  $(1 - P) (-6) + P (77) = 83 P - 6$

Hotel Unfavorable:  $(1 - P) (-6) + P (9) = 15 P - 6$

Best Case:  $(1 - P) (-6) + P (92) = 97 P - 6$

|  |  | Build | Don't Build |
|---|---|---|---|
| Attendance | P = O | −6 | 0 |
|  | P = 1 | 77 | 0 |
| Hotel | P = 0 | −6 | 0 |
|  | P = 1 | 23 | 0 |
| Both | P = 0 | −6 | 0 |
|  | P = 1 | 103 | 0 |

## BeechNut Apple Juice

### Data

BeechNut's top management committed to disposing of its tainted inventory, valued at $3.5 million. This value is clear cut, but cost of litigation, fines, lost sales, and the like would be uncertain. This decision has the following outcomes:

|  |  | Caught | Escape |
|---|---|---|---|
| PAI | Cooperate | $3.5 million | $3.5 million |
| Lawsuit | Stonewall | $3.5 million + X | 0 |

X represents the unknown cost in fines and other penalties if caught.

The variable X represents the amount of loss that BeechNut would incur if caught. This value is estimated from figures revealed by court documents. The best case and actual losses appear below:

|  | Outcome |
|---|---|
| Best Case | $3.5 million |
| Worst Case | $7.0 million |
| Actual | $25.0 million |
| | (fines, legal fees, and class action lawsuits) |

Best case's $3.5 million is made up of $2.75 million in lost market share, $250,000 in fines, $500,000 for public relations and associated costs to explain company actions. Largest fines by FDA to date had been $330,000. The entire baby food industry at the time was $550 million and Beech-Nut's share was 15%, so a 2% loss in market share was assumed.

Worst case was estimated to be twice what BeechNut had estimated.

## Computations

To estimate values for Figures 8.6, each value for X is substituted in data below, setting the chance of getting caught at P and escaping at $1 - P$:

|  | $P = \text{Caught}$ | $1 - P = \text{Escape}$ |
|---|---|---|
| Cooperate | 3.5 | 3.5 |
| Stonewall | $3.5 + X$ | 0 |

Substituting values for X:

|  |  | Cooperate | Stonewall |
|---|---|---|---|
| $X = 3.5$ million | $P = 0$ | 3.5 | 0 |
|  | $P = 1$ | 3.5 | 7.0 |
| $X = 7.0$ million | $P = 0$ | 3.5 | 0 |
|  | $P = 1$ | 3.5 | 10.5 |
| $X = 25.0$ million | $P = 0$ | 3.5 | 0 |
|  | $P = 1$ | 3.5 | 28.5 |

Breakeven:

$$3.5 = P (3.5 + x)$$
$$P = 3.5 / (3.5 + x)$$

| Best | $X = 3.5$ | $P = 0.5$ |
|---|---|---|
| Worst | $X = 7.0$ | $P = 0.33$ |
| Actual | $X = 25.0$ | $P = 0.123$ |

## Ford Pinto Recall

Ford's top management was committed to resisting a recall and avoiding the $137 million in repair costs. This cost was clear, but cost to Ford of an accident that had fatal or disabling consequences to a Pinto driver and passengers was not. This decision has the following outcomes:

**Data (in millions)**

|  |  | An Accident | No Accident |
|---|---|---|---|
| Ford's | Fix | $137 | $137 |
| Options | Delay | $137 + X | 0 |

X represents unknown cost incurred if accident occurred and gas tank exploded, harming people in the vehicle.

The variable X represents an unknown loss that is quite difficult to determine. It can be estimated with best case and worst case values drawn from similar situations.

|  | Outcome |
|---|---|
| Best Case | $49.5 million |
| Worst Case | $247.5 million |
| Actual | 0 |

Court documents show that Ford had made estimates as follows: NHTSA set $200,000 as loss from each burn victim at the time and $67,000 each injury. The cost of the cars was set at $700. NHTSA estimates were 180 deaths and 180 serious injuries, or $49.5 millions in losses. NHTSA estimates were based on loss to society if person is injured or killed, so these values are low-end. Ford concealed tests of rear end collisions that showed 8 of 11 pintos had potentially catastrophic ruptures (Denhardt, 2000). Data are based on best case outcomes.

If Ford's duplicity is revealed, awards could skyrocket. Here it is assumed to be 5 times that amount, or $247.58 million. Ford's actual loss was limited because the jury found that Ford tried to recall the vehicle before the accident occurred. No lost sales data were available in the court records.

**Computations**

To estimate values for Figure 8.7, each value of X (litigation costs) was substituted in the data below, letting P = chance of an accident.

|  | $\underline{P = \text{Accident}}$ | $\underline{1 - P = \text{No Accident}}$ |
|---|---|---|
| Fix | 137 | 137 |
| Delay | 137 + X | 0 |

Fix Option = 137 (P) + 137 (1 – P) = 137
Delay Option = (137 + X) P + 0 (1 – P) = (137 + X) + P

Substituting for X:

|  |  | Fix | Delay |
|---|---|---|---|
| X = 49.5 million | P = 0 | 137 | 0 |
|  | P = 1 | 137 | 186.5 |
| X = 247.5 million | P = 0 | 137 | 0 |
|  | P = 1 | 137 | 384.5 |
| X = 0 | P = 0 | 137 | 0 |
|  | P = 1 | 137 | 137 |

Breakeven:

137 = (137 + X) P
P = 137 / (137 + X)

| Best | X = 79.5 | P = .735 |
|---|---|---|
| Worst | X = 247.5 | P = .356 |
| Actual | X = 0 | P = 1 |

# Appendix 3

# Citations for the Debacles

## AmeriFlora

AmeriFlora, Business Plan and Financial Statements, 1990.

AmeriFlora, Board of Trustees and Executive Committee (minutes from select meetings).

AmeriFlora, Community Relations Program, 1990.

Broron, M. Columbus Quincentennial Exposition. 1971.

Columbus "Eastsider," July 28, 1992.

*Columbus Monthly*, April 1990; April 1991; December 1992.

*Columbus Dispatch*, May 14, 1989; April 30, 1990.

*The Other Paper.* July 8, 1986.

## Barings Bank

Brilliant, David. "The Tone at the Top." *The Banker, 145*(837), November 1, 1995, 26–27.

Chernoff, Joel. "Barings Legacy: Tighter Controls." *Pensions and Investments, 23*(15), March 6, 1995, 1–3.

Fay, Stephen. "The Collapse of Barings." *Management Accounting, 74*(10), November 1, 1996, 14.

Guan, Lim Kian. "Barings Bankruptcy and Financial Derivatives." *Asia Pacific Journal of Management, 13*(1), April 1, 1996, 117–119.

Inspectors of Barings Futures. Singapore PTE LTD.

Investment Banking. "Out of Control." *The Banker, 145*(834), August 1, 1995, 15–16.

Leeson, Nick. *Rogue Trader: How I Brought Down Barings Bank and Shook the Financial World.* Boston: Little Brown, 1996.

*Living Marxism.* 1995. (Publisher unknown).

Ostro-Landau, Nilly. "It's Not Just Greed, Stupid." *International Business,* April 1, 1995, 18.

Overell, Stephen. "Barings Collapse Blamed on Lack of HR Strategy." *People Management, 1*(19), September 21, 1995, 8.

Reyes, Alejandro. "Uncovering The Cover-Up." *Asia Week,* October 27, 1995.

Senge, Peter. *The Fifth Discipline.* New York: Bantam Doubleday Dell, 1990.

Sraeel, Holly. "The Barings Report Lacks Cuts." *Bank System and Technology,* 32(9), September 1, 1995, 4.

## BeechNut

"Bad Apple for Baby." *Financial World,* June 27, 1989.

"Bad Apples in the Executive Suite." *Consumer Reports,* May 1989.

"Beech-Nut Bounces Up in the Baby Market." *Fortune,* December 24, 1984.

"Beech-Nut: The Case of the Ersatz Apple Juice." *Newsweek,* November 17, 1986.

"Beech-Nut Officers Sentences." *FDA Consumer,* September 1988.

"Beware of Corporate Criminal Conduct." *Design News,* November 7, 1988.

"Into the Mouth of Babes." *New York Times Magazine,* July 24, 1988.

"Juice Men, Ethics and the Beech-Nut Sentences." *Barrons,* June 20, 1988.

"Juice Sleuths." *Popular Science,* October 1988.

"Juiceless Baby Juice Leads to Full-Strength Justice." *FDA Consumer,* June 1988.

"What Led Beech-Nut Down the Road to Disgrace." *Business Week,* February 22, 1988.

## Challenger

"Countdown to a Thiokol Exit." *Time,* June 20, 1998, 52.

"Out of Court Settlement." *Time,* January 12, 1987, 35.

"Whistle-Blower." *Life,* March 1998, 17.

Burk, Charles. "When 'Can Do' Becomes 'Can't Fail'." *Fortune,* July 7, 1986, 8.

Jones, Sam L. "Thiokol Drops Bid for NASA Rocket Motor." *Metalworking News,* June 13, 1988, 5.

Kruglanski, Arie W. "Freeze-think and the Challenger." *Psychology Today*, August 1986, 48.

Lewis, Richard S. *Challenger: The Final Voyage*. New York: Columbia University Press, 1988.

Magnuson, Ed. "A Serious Deficiency; the Rogers Commission Faults NASA's 'Flawed' Decision-Making Process." *Time*, March 10, 1986, 38.

Magnuson, Ed. "NASA Takes a Beating; the Rogers Commission Blames the Agency for an Avoidable Accident." *Time*, June 23, 1986, 32.

Marbach, William D. "Pointing Fingers: NASA and Morton Thiokol Blame Each Other." *Newsweek*, March 10, 1986, 40.

McConnell, Malcolm. *Challenger: A Major Malfunction*. New York: Doubleday, 1987.

Mendes, Joshua. "Can Thiokol Rise from Challenger's Ashes?" *Fortune*, June 8, 1987, 152.

Milliken, Frances J., and Starbuck, Willliam. "Challenger: Fine-Tuning the Odds Until Something Breaks." *Journal of Management Studies*, July 1988, 319.

Perrow, C. *Normal Accidents: Living with High Risk Technologies*. New York: Basic Books, 1984.

Ronzek, B. and Dubnick, M. "Accountability in the Public Sector: Lessons From the Challenger Tragedy." *Public Administration Review, 47*, May/June 1987, 227–238.

Schwartz, Howard S. "On the Psychodynamics of Organizational Disaster: The Case of the Space Shuttle Challenger." *Columbia Journal of World Business*, Spring 1987, 59.

"Report to the President: Actions to Implement Recommendations of the Presidential Commission on the Space Shuttle Challenger Accident," Vol I. Washington DC; Government Printing Office, 1986.

Meyer, J. M. *A Major Malfunction*. Binghamton, NY: The Research Foundation of SUNY, 1990.

## Denver International Airport

Anderson, Darrell. "How Will DIA Fly?" *Colorado Business Magazine*, September 3, 1993, 53–56.

Auguston, Karen. "The Denver Airport: A Lesson in Coping with Complexity." *Modern Materials Handling*, 1994, 40–45.

Boyer, Robert. *International Air Transportation*. New York: American Society of Civil Engineers, 1992.

Denver International Airport. Annual Report. 1993.

Hedges, Stephen. "A Taj Mahal in the Rockies." *U.S. News & World Report,*. February 13, 1995, 48–53.

Meyer, Michael, and Glick, Daniel. "Still Late for Arrival." *Newsweek*, August 22, 1994, 38–40.

Moorman, Robert. "High Noon in Denver." *Air Transport World*, December 1991, 38–40.

Scheier, Robert. "Software Snafu Grounds Denver's High-tech Airport." *PC Week*, May 16, 1994, 1–3.

Smith, Eric. "The Promise of Colorado." *Colorado Business Magazine*, August 1988, 21–25.

Steers, Stuart. "DIA Resorts to Plan B." *Denver Business Journal*, July 22, 1993, 1A.

"Uncertain Ecnonomy Forces Scaling Back of International Airport's First Phase." *Aviation Week & Space Technology*, March 11, 1991, 48–49.

Wright, Gordon. "Denver Builds a 'Field of Dreams'." *Building Design & Construction*, 1994, 53–56.

## EuroDisney

Alexander, K. L. "Disney, Revisited." *USA Today*, December 14, 1999.

Corliss, Richard. "Viola! Disney Invades Europe. Will the French Resist?" *Time*, April 20, 1992.

"Disney's World." *Newsweek*, August 14, 1995.

Flower, Joe. *Prince of the Magic Kingdom*. New York: John Wiley & Sons, 1991.

Grover, Ron. *The Disney Touch*. Homewood, IL: Business One Irwin, 1991.

"EuroDisney Theme Park Near Paris Is Europe's Second Biggest Project." *Business America*, December 2, 1991.

Lawday, David. "Where All the Dwarfs Are Grumpy." *U.S. News & World Report*, May 28, 1990.

"Mouse Trapped in France." *New Statesman & Society*, August 20, 1993.

"No Fairy Tale." *The Economist*, November 13, 1993.

"Of Mice, Men and Money." *The Economist*, November 13, 1993.

Phillips, Andrew. "Where's the Magic?" *MacLeans*, May 3, 1993.

Rudnitsky, Howard. "Creativity with Discipline." *Forbes*, March 6, 1989.

Toy, Stewart. "Mouse Fever Is about to Strike Europe." *Business Week*, March 30, 1992.

Treichler, Robert. "Mickey Mouse Goes Continental." *World Press Review*, July 1991.

Turner, Richard. "Disney Proift, Revenue Set High in Period." *Wall Street Journal*, January 20, 1994.

"Waiting for Dumbo." *The Economist,* May 1, 1993.

Walt Disney Inc. Annual Reports/Archives. 1984–1999.

Wrubel, Howard. "Le Defi Mickey Mouse." *Financial World* Magazine, October 17, 1989.

## Ford Pinto

Deinhart, J. *Business, Institutions, and Ethics.* Oxford, UK: Oxford University Press, 2000.

Donaldson T., and Dunfee T. "Toward a Unified Conception of Business Ethics: Integrative Social Contracts Theory." *Academy of Management Review, 19*(2), 1994, 252–284.

Goia, D. "Pinto Fires and Personal Ethics," *Journal of Business Ethics, 1,* 1992, 379–380.

Johnson M. *Moral Imagination: Implications of Cognitive Science for Ethics.* Chicago: University of Chicago Press, 1993.

Trevino, L. "Ethical Decision-making in Organizations: A Person-Situation Interactionist Model." *Academy of Management Review, 11*:3 (1986), p. 603.

Trevino, L., and Nelson, K. *Managing Business Ethics: Straight Talk about How to Do It Right.* New York: Wiley, 1995.

Werhane, P. "Moral Imagination and the Search for Ethical Decision-Making in Management." Ruffin Lectures, 1994.

## Light Rail

Beimborn, Edward, and Horowitz, Alan. "Measurement of Transit Benefits." Center for Urban Transportation Studies, Milwaukee, WI. Prepared for the Urban Mass Transportation Administration, DOT-T-93-33, 1993.

Cohen, Harry S., Stowers, Jospeh R., and Petersilia, Michael. "Evaluating Urban Transportation Alternatives." Washington, DC: Systems Design Concepts Inc. U.S. Department of Transportation, 1978.

*COTA Long Range System Plan 1993.* Columbus, OH: Mid-Ohio Regional Planning Commission, Central Ohio Transit Authority, 1993.

Dickey, John W. *Metropolitan Transportation Planning* (2nd Ed.). New York: McGraw-Hill (Hemispherem), 1983.

Drake, Alvin W., Keeney, Ralph, and Morse, Philip (Eds.). *Analysis of Public Systems.* Cambridge MA: MIT Press, 1972.

Johnston, Robert, Sperling, Daniel, Deluchi, Mark, and Tracy, Steve. "Politics and Technical Uncertainty in Transportation Investment Analysis." *Transportation Research*, *21A*(6), 459–475, 1988.

"North Corridor Transit: Solutions for the Future." Columbus, OH: Mid-Ohio Regional Planning Commission, Central Ohio Transit Authority, 1985.

Parody, Thomas E. et al. "Characteristics of Urban Transportation Demand: An Updated and Revised Handbook." Washington DC:Transportation Research Record 1139, Transportation Research Board, 1987.

Pickrell, Don H. "Urban Rail Transit Projects: Forecasts versus Actual ridership and Costs."Cambridge, MA : Transportation Systems Center, Urban Mass Transportation Administration, DOT-T-91-04, 1990.

"Transportation System Management: State of the Art." Washington DC: U.S. Department of Transportation, Urban Mass Transportation Administration, February 1977.

## Nationwide Arena

Baim, Dean. *The Stadium as a Municipal Investment*. Westport, CO: Greenwood Press, 1996.

Cadawallader, Bruce. "Convention Authority Suing Nationwide Over Land." *Columbus Dispatch*, July 18, 1997.

Curtin, Mike. "Private Arena Proposal." *Columbus Dispatch*, June 2, 1997.

Edwards, Mary Mogan, LaLonde, Brent, and Wright, Steve. "Arena Abatement Deal in Sight." *Columbus Dispatch*, December 13, 1997.

Futty, John. "After Long Haul, Mayor Sees Fruits of City's Labor." *Columbus Dispatch*, June 26, 1997.

Futty, John, and LaLonde, Brent. "City to Get NHL Team." *Columbus Dispatch*, June 17, 1997.

Futty, John. "Council OK's Arena Proposal." *Columbus Dispatch*, June 3, 1997.

Futty, John. "NHL Hockey Franchise Dead, But Crew to Stay." *Columbus Dispatch*, May 7, 1997.

Futty, John. "Seat License, Suites to Help Pay for Arena." *Columbus Dispatch*, June 6, 1997.

Hunter, Bob. "With New Arena Plan, What's Left to Debate?" *Columbus Dispatch*, June 4, 1997.

LaLonde, Brent. "Arena Nearing Tax Break." *Columbus Dispatch*, December 16, 1997.

LaLonde, Brent. "City Urges Calm over Arena Tax Break." *Columbus Dispatch*, November 20, 1997.

LaLonde, Brent. "Hunt, Local Groups File Suits in Battle for City's NHL Team." *Columbus Dispatch*, June 24, 1997.

LaLonde, Brent. "School Board, Developers Hammer Out Arena Deal." *Columbus Dispatch*, December 24, 1997.

Mayhood, Kevin, and Wright, Steve. "Decision Day for Sales Tax." *Columbus Dispatch*, February 28,1997.

Merc, Craig. "Downtown Arena Has Surpassed Seat License Goal." *Columbus Dispatch*, November 14, 1997.

Rosentraub, Mark S. *Major League Losers: The Real Cost of Sports and Who's Paying for It.* New York: Basic Books, 1997.

Team Marketing Report. "NHL Ticket Prices / Fan Cost Index." *Columbus Dispatch*, October 31, 1997.

Wright, Steve. "Gift Meets Goal for Complex." *Columbus Dispatch*, January 28, 1997.

Wright, Steve. "Testa to Determine the Value of Nationwide Arena." *Columbus Dispatch*, December 13, 1997.

Wright, Steve. "Downtown Center Will Be Christened Nationwide Arena." *Columbus Dispatch*, September 9, 1997.

Wright, Steve. "Area Leaders Seek Arena Ideas." *Columbus Dispatch*, August 3, 1997.

Wright, Steve. "As Vote Nears, Arena-Stadium Sales Tax Still Trailing in Poll." *Columbus Dispatch*, May 5, 1997.

http://www.nationwide.com/nationwide/company/annual/anr96016.

## Nestle

Baer, E., and Margulies L. "Infant and Young Child Feeding: An Analysis of the WHO/UNICEF Meeting." *Studies in Family Planning*, 1980, 72–75.

Blodgett, T. B., and Banks, P. "Nestle—At Home Abroad." *Harvard Business Review*, November-December 1976, 80–88.

Ciocca, H. G. "The Infant Formula Controversy: The Nestle View." *Journal of Contemporary Business*, 7(4), 1979, 37–55.

Crain, R. "A Conversation with Nestle's Pierre Liotard-Vogt." *Advertising Age*, June 30, 1980, 31–34.

Gladwin, T., and Ingo, W. *Multinationals Under Fire: Lessons in the Management Conflict.* New York: Wiley, 1980.

Harrison, N., and Malone, C. B. "Nestle Alimantana S.A." *Harvard Business School Cases.* (Case #9-580-118). Cambridge, MA: Harvard Business School Press, 1980.

Johnson, D. "A Glimpse at Nestle's Anti-Boycott Strategy." *Business and Society Review*, Spring 1981, 65–67.

Manoff, R. M. "Learning a Lesson from Nestle." *Advertising Age*, February 13, 1984, 16, 20.

Salmon, C. L. "Milking Deadly Dollars from the Third World." *Business and Society Review*, 1989, 43–48.

Sethi, S. P. *Multinational Corporations and the Impact of Public Advocacy on Corporate Strategy: Nestle and the Infant Formula Controversy*. The Netherlands: Kluwer Academic Publishing, 1994.

Terpstra, V. *International Marketing* (3rd ed.). Chicago: Dryden Press, 1983.

## New York City Blackout

Behn, Robert D. "The Shed Load Decision." Institute of Policy Sciences and Public Affairs, Duke University, 1983.

"Con Ed Control Had 15 Minutes to Pull Switch." *New York Times*, July 18, 1977.

"The Hidden City." *NOVA*, No. 1611.

"The New York Blackout of July 13, 1977; Costs & Preventive Action." Committee on Interstate & Foreign Commerce House of Representatives Hearing, Second Session, Serial No. 95–148.

"The New York Blackout of July 13, 1977." Committee on Interstate & Foreign Commerce House of Representatives Hearing, Second Session, Serial No. 95–88.

"New York's Power Restored Slowly." *New York Times*. July 15, 1977.

"Second Phase Report: System Blackout & System Restoration, July 13–14, 1977." Con Edison Board of Review, August 24, 1977.

"Third Phase Report: System Blackout & System Restoration, July 13–16, 1977." Con Edison Board of Review, Vol I (Summary), December, 28, 1977.

"The Steep Price Tag on the Blackout." *Business Week*, August 1, 1977, 20–21.

Wilson, G. L., and Zarakas, P. "Anatomy of a Blackout." *IEEE Spectrum*, February, 1978, 38–46.

## Shell's Brent Spar

"Brent Spar." (Internal Brent Spar Communication). Barkers Trident Communications on Behalf of Shell UK, 1995.

"Brent Spar: A Scientific View." The Institute of Oceanographic Sciences Deacon Laboratory; The Plymouth Marine Laboratory; The British Geological Survey.

Det Norkse Veritas. "DNV Investigations of Brent Spar Inventory Concluded." October 18, 1995.

Shell UK Exploration and Production. "New DNV Study Finds No PCDs on Brent Spar." November 30, 1995.

Shell UK Exploration and Production. "21 Companies Take Up International Challenge for Brent Spar Solution." July 3, 1996.

Shell UK Exploration and Production. "Shell Publishes 'Long List' Outline Proposals for Brent Spar Disposal." August 15, 1996.

Shell UK Exploration and Production. "Brent Spar Short List: Six Top Contractor Groups to Develop Eleven Best Ideas." January 13, 1997.

University of Aberdeen. Removal and Disposal of the Brent Spar: A Safety and Environmental Assessment of the Options. Aberdeen: Author, January 1994.

http://www.greenpeace.org/~comms/toxics/dumping

http://www.greenpeace.org/~comms/brent/brent.html

http://www.shell.com/

http://www.shellexpro.brentspar.com/

http://www.cnn.com

http://www.pathfinder.com/fortune/

## Telescope Consortium

Report of the Ad Hoc Committee on the Columbus Project Chronology. March 24, 1992.

Report of the Ad Hoc Committee on the Columbus Project Chronology. (Executive Summary) March 31, 1992.

The Ohio State University, University Senate Archives.

## Quaker's Snapple Acquisition

"Distribution Is Altered for Beverages in Texas." Wall Street Journal, November 25, 1996.

"Sizing Up the Outstanding Mergers and Acquisitions of the Decade." Business Week, January 15, 1990.

"Snapple Continues to Lose Market Share." Wall Street Journal, October 8, 1996.

"Quaker's CEO, Led by Snapple Shakeup, Tells Outlets Time's Ripe for Fresh Start." Wall Street Journal, July 22, 1996.

"Quaker Oats Expects Snapple Line to Incur Major Losses Again." Wall Street Journal, June 27, 1996.

"Quaker Oats Co." Wall Street Journal, August 13, 1996.

"Is Stokely Worth Quaker's Lofty Bid?" Business Week, August 1, 1983.

"The Market Value Added List." *Fortune*, November 28, 1994.

"Moody's Reviews Debt of Quaker Oats, Cites Snapple, Cereal Woes." *Wall Street Journal*, August 5, 1996.

Beatty, Sally Goll. "Quaker Wants Snapple to Be No. 3, But Will the Strategy Bear Fruit?" *Wall Street Journal*, April 2, 1996.

Berner, Robert. "Quaker Oats Picks New Snapple Head, Hiring Schott from Nantucker Nectars." *Wall Strret Journal*, August 12, 1996.

Berrss, Marcia. "How Long Can You Twiddle Your Thumbs?" *Forbes*, September 11, 1995.

Bottrell, Ronald G., and Turner, Jim. "Snapple Assigns Texas Distribution to Dr. Pepper Bottling Co. of Texas." *PR Newswire*, November 22, 1996.

Bottrell, Ronald G. "Snapple to Make Halloween Debut on United Airlines." *PR Newswire*, September 9, 1996.

Bottrell, Ronald G. "Quaker Oats Announces Realignment of Snapple Beverage Management Structure." *PR Newswire*, July 19, 1996.

Bottrell, Ronald G. "Quaker Reports December-Quarter Loss; Takes Restructuring Charge to Improve Performance." *PR Newswire*, February 6, 1996.

Burns, Greg. "Food Processing: This New Recipe Is Proving Pretty Tasty." *Business Week*, January 9, 1995.

Burns, Greg. "Tea and Synergy?" *Business Week*, November 14, 1994.

Burns, Greg. "Will Quaker Get the Recipe Right?" *Business Week*, February 5, 1996.

Burns, Greg. "Putting the Snap Back into Snapple." *Business Week*, July 22, 1996.

Burns, Greg. "Crunch Time at Quaker Oats." *Business Week*, September 23, 1996.

Byrne, John A. "Deliver—Or Else." *Business Week*, March 27, 1995.

Byrne, John A., and Melcher, Richard A. "The Best & Worst Boards." *Wall Street Journal*, November 15, 1996.

Chura, Hillary. "Another Snapple Executive Leaves Amid Slow Sales." *Chicago AP*, July 19, 1996.

Done, Doug. "New Diet Snapple Campaign Launches: Another Bright Spot in Diet Snapple Momentum." *PR Newswire*, January 15, 1997.

Edwards, Cliff. "Snapple Continues to Drag on Quaker Profits." *Chicago Tribune*, Knight-Ridder/Tribune Information Services, October 24, 1996.

Edwards, Cliff. "Quaker Hires Nantucket Nectars Executive to Head Snapple Line—Apparently." *Chicago Tribune*, Knight-Ridder/Tribune Information Services, August 9, 1996.

Edwards, Cliff. "Quaker Taking $40 Million Charge in Snapple Restructuring." *Chicago Tribune*, Knight-Ridder/Tribune Information Services, December 21, 1995.

Gibson, Richard. "Quaker Oats Pops Chairman Smithburg; No Raise or Bonus after Snapple Deal." *Wall Street Journal*, April 3, 1996.

Gibson, Richard. "Heard on the Street: Quaker Oats Feeling Pressure for Big Changes in Wake of the Fizzled Snapple Acquisition." *Wall Street Journal*, July 25, 1996.

Gibson, Richard. "Snapple's Lowering of Profit Projection Underscores Continuation of Problems." *Wall Street Journal*, November 7, 1994.

Gibson, Richard. "Snapple May Hurt Profit for Quaker, Quaker Oats Says." *Wall Street Journal*, June 21, 1995.

Gibson, Richard. "Quaker Oats President Quits Post." *Wall Street Journal*, October 24, 1995.

Gibson, Richard. "Quaker Posts Better than Expected Net, But Disappoints with Snapple Inaction." *Wall Street Journal*, October 25, 1996.

Gibson, Richard. "At Quaker Oats, Snapple Is Leaving a Bad Aftertaste." *Wall Street Journal*, August 7, 1995.

Gibson, Richard. "Quaker Rejects the Notion of a Coastal Strategy for Snapple." *Wall Street Journal*, November 5, 1996.

Gibson, Richard. "Heard on the Street: Quaker Oats May Sell Its Beverage Business in Move that Would Boil Down Its Operations." *Wall Street Journal*, December 13, 1996.

Gibson, Richard. "Quaker to Cut Spending on Snapple Unit." *Wall Street Journal*, September 13, 1996.

Hammonds, Keith H. "In Business This Week: Et Cetera . . ." *Business Week*, November 6, 1995.

Hammonds, Keith H. "Snapped Up." *Business Week*, November 7, 1994.

Henkoff, Ronald, and Kover, Amy R. "Growing Your Company: Five Ways to Do It Right; This Implies, of Course, that You Can Do It Wrong Too. Here's How Some Shrewd Companies Avoid the Pitfalls." *Fortune*, November 25, 1996.

Heuslein, William. "The 47th Annual Report on American Industry: Food, Drink, & Tobacco." *Forbes*, January 2, 1995.

Heuslein, William. "The 48th Annual Report on American Industry: Food, Drink, & Tobacco." *Forbes*, January 1, 1996.

Holland, Kelley. "Can He Get Snapple Cracking?" *Business Week*, August 26, 1996.

Holland, Kelley. "In Business This Week: Et Cetera . . ." *Business Week*, July 8, 1996.

Jackson, Susan, Anderson Forest, Stephanie, and Bongioro, Lori. "Can Cadbury Dodge Big Cola's Bullets?" *Business Week*, August 12, 1996.

Jaffe, Thomas. "Endless Rumor." *Forbes*, May 22, 1995.

Jaffe, Thomas. "The Takeover that Wasn't." *Forbes*, February 13, 1995.

Kuntz, Mary, Weber, Joseph, and Dawley, Heidi. "The New Hucksterism." *Business Week*, July 1, 1996.

Lesly, Elizabeth. "A&W's Summer Plans: Hitting the Warpath." *Business Week*, April 12, 1993.

Marcial, Gene G. "Is Gatorade for Sale?" *Business Week*, August 26, 1996.

Marcial, Gene G. "Quaker May Start Feeling Its Oats." *Business Week*, August 28, 1995.

Marcial, Gene G. "Brio Takes Two Hefty Swings." *Business Week*, February 6, 1995.

McCarthy, Michael J. "Quaker Oats to Buy Snapple for $1.7 Billion." *Wall Street Journal*, November 3, 1994.

Moukheiber, Zina. "Quaker Contrarians." *Forbes*, January 22, 1996.

Moukheiber, Zina. "Was Quaker Oats Taken When It Paid $1.7 Billion for Snapple?" *Forbes*, January 1, 1996.

Munk, Nina. "Just Call Us Cockroaches." *Forbes*, August 26, 1996.

O'Brien, Timothy L. "Thomas H. Lee Cashes in on a Fad and a Fear." *Wall Street Journal*, November 9, 1994.

Oneal, Michael, Bremner, Brian, Levine, Jonathan B., Vogal, Todd, Schiller, Zachary, and Woodruff, David. "The Best and Worst Deals of the 80's." *Business Week*, January 15, 1990.

Oneal, Michael, Himelstein, Linda, Temes, Judy, and Scine, E. "Everybody's Talkin' at Us." *Business Week*, May 22, 1995.

Pare, Terrence P. "The New Merger Boom." *Fortune*, November 28, 1994.

Peterson, Thane. "In Business This Week: Et Cetera . . ." *Business Week*, July 3, 1995.

Puckett, Mary. "Lemonade Consumption Soars in July." *PR Newswire*, July 3, 1996.

Quaker Oats. 1995 Annual Report.

Quaker Oats Web Page: http://quakeroats.com.

Sanders, Lisa. "An Ice-Tea Tycoon Feels a Chill." *Business Week*, October 14, 1996.

Sellers, Patricia. "Can Coke and Pepsi Make Quaker Sweat." *Fortune*, July 10, 1995.

Therrien, Lois. "How Swallowing Gatorade Gave Quaker Oats a Boost." *Business Week*, April 29, 1996.

Tully, Shawn. "America's Best Wealth Creators." *Fortune*, November 28, 1994.

Verity, John. "Free E-Mail, But with a Catch." *Business Week*, February 14, 1994.

Yates, Ronald E. "Still No Snap from Snapple: Quaker to Take a Charge of $40 Million to Restructure Fizzled Beverage Unit." *Chicago Tribune*, February 1, 1993.

Zinn, Laura. "Pepsi's Future Becomes Clearer." *Business Week*, February 14, 1994.

Zinn, Laura. "Does Pepsi Have Too Many Products?" *Business Week*, October 20, 1995.

Zweig, Phillip L. "The Case against Mergers." *Business Week*, October 20, 1995.

## Waco Siege

Abaton, S. J. "Bentsen Signals Official's Ouster over Initial Raid on Cult in Texas." *New York Times*, April 29, 1993, A1.

Abaton, S. J. "FBI Cites Fresh Evidence that Cult Set Fatal Fire; Official's Accounts Clash." *New York Times*, April 21, 1993, A1.

Abaton, S. J. "Report on Siege in Texas Is Said to Blame Agents." *New York Times*, October 2, 1993, A1.

Abaton, S. J. "Report on Initial Raid on Cult Finds Officials Erred and Lied." *New York Times*, October 1, 1993, A1.

Dennis, Edward S. G. "Evaluation of the Handling of the Branch Davidian Stand-Off in Waco, Texas Feb 28 to April 19, 1993." Washington DC: U.S. Department of Justice, 1993.

*Frontline*. "Waco: The Inside Story." (transcript #1401), October 17, 1995.

Holmes, S. A., "Congressman Calls Raid Near Waco a Clinton Plot." *New York Times*, May 3, 1995, A8.

Johnston, D. "Doubt Recalled on Using Gas at Waco Siege." *New York Times*, July 28, 1995, A17.

Lewis, N. A. "FBI Overreacted in Waco, Witnesses Say." *New York Times*, July 26, 1995, A15.

Molotsky, I. "Official Balks at Releasing Waco Papers." *New York Times*, July 9, 1995.

Niebuhr, G. "Assault on Waco Sect Fuels Extremist's Rage." *New York Times*, April 26, 1995, A20.

Pear, R. "GOP Report Faults Reno in Texas Siege." *New York Times*, July 12, 1996.

Reavis, Dick J. "Statement: Congressional Waco Hearings." *New York Times*, July 19, 1995.

Reuters. "Bitter Defence in Cultist's Trial." *New York Times*, January 30, 1994.

Reuters. "Coalition Assails US Law Agencies." *New York Times*, January 11, 1994.

Stone, Alan A. "Report and Recommendations Concerning the Handling of Incidents Such as the Branch Davidian Standoff in Waco, Texas." Submitted to Deputy Attorney General Philp Haymann, November 10, 1993.

Verhover, S. H. "Tight Security Gets Tighter as a Sad Anniversary Nears." *New York Times*, April 15, 1996, A1.

Verhover, S. H. "11 in Texas Sect Acquitted of Key Charges." *New York Times*, February 27, 1994, A14.

Verhover, S. H. "Scores Die as Cult Compound Is Set Afire after FBI Sends in Tank with Tear Gas." *New York Times*, April 20, 1993, A1.

Voss, Cary R. W. "Students of the Seven Seals: An Organizational History." Communications Department, University of Kansas. [On-line] http://falcon.cc.ukans.edu/~

# References and Selected Readings

Abernathy, W., and Utterback, J. (1982). "Patterns of Industrial Innovations." In M. Tushman and W. Moore (Eds.), *Readings in Management Innovations*. Boston: Pitman.

Ackoff, R. (1981). *Creating the Corporate Future*. New York: Wiley.

Adizes, I. (1988). *Corporate Life Cycles: How and Why Corporations Grow and Die and What to Do about It*. Englewood Cliffs, NJ: Prentice-Hall.

Agar, W. (1986). *The Logic of Intuitive Decision-Making*. New York: Quorum.

Albert, S. (1984). "A Delete Design for Successful Transitions." In J. Kimberly and R. Quinn (Eds.), *Managing Organizational Transitions*. New York: Dow Jones-Irwin.

Alexander, L. (1986). "Successfully Implementing Strategic Decisions." In B. Mayon-White (Ed.), *Planning and Managing Change*. London: Harper and Row.

Allison, G. T. (1969). "Conceptual Models and the Cuban Missile Crisis." *American Political Science Review, 63,* 689–718.

Alter, C., and Hage, C. (1993). *Organizations Working Together*. Newbury Park, CA: Sage.

Amabile, T. (1996). *Creativity in Context: Update to Social Psychology of Creativity*. Boulder, CO: Westview.

Amabile, T., and Conti, R. (1999). "Changes in the Work Environment for Creativity During Downsizing." *Academy of Management Journal, 42*(6), 630–640.

Ansoff, H. I. (1988). *The New Corporate Strategy*. New York: Wiley.

Argyris, C. (1982). *Reasoning, Learning, and Action: Individual and Organizational*. San Francisco: Jossey-Bass.

Argyris, C., Putnam, R., and Smith, D. M. (1987). *Action Science*. San Francisco: Jossey-Bass.

Argyris, C., and Schon, D. (1978). *Organization Learning: A Theory of Action Perspective*, Reading, MA: Addison-Wesley.

Badaracco, J. L., Jr. (1997). *Defining Moments: When Managers Must Choose Between Right and Right*. Cambridge, MA: Harvard University Press

Baim, D. (1996). *The Sports Stadium as a Municipal Investment*. Westport, CO: Greenwood Press.

Bakhtin, M. (1981). *The Dialogic Imagination.* Austin: University of Texas Press.

Bardach, E. (1977). *The Implementation Game.* Cambridge, MA: MIT Press.

Bartlett, F. C. (1954). *Remembering: A Study in Experimental and Social Psychology.* Cambridge, MA: Harvard University Press.

Bass, B. M., and Avolio, B. J. (1990)."The Implications of Transactional and Transformational Leadership for Individual, Team, and Organizational Development." In R. W. Woodman and W. A. Pasmore (Eds.), *Research in Organizational Change and Development, Vol. 4* (pp. 231–272). Greenwich, CT: JAI Press.

Batson, G., and Batson, M. (1978). *Angels Fear.* New York: Macmillan.

Behn, R. D. (1991). *Leadership Counts: Lessons for Public Managers from the Massachusetts Welfare Training and Employment Program.* Cambridge, MA: Harvard University Press.

Bell, G., Bromley, P., and Bryson, J. (1997). "Spinning a Complex Web: Links Between Strategic Decision-Making Context, Content, Process, and Outcome." In V. Papadakis and P. Barwise (Eds.), *Strategic Decisions.* Boston, MA: Kluwer.

Bennis, W. (1989a). *On Becoming a Leader.* New York: Addison-Wesley.

Bennis, W. (1989b). *Why Leaders Can't Lead.* San Francisco: Jossey-Bass.

Bennis, W., and Nanus, B. (1985). *Leaders.* New York: Harper and Row.

Beyer, J. M., and Trice, H. M. (1982)."The Utilization Process: A Conceptual Framework and Synthesis of Empirical Findings." *Administrative Science Quarterly, 27* (4/5), 591–622.

Block, P. (1988). *The Empowered Manager.* San Francisco: Jossey-Bass.

Boal, K. B., and Bryson, J. M. (1987). "Representing and Testing Policy Implications of Planning Processes." *Strategic Management Journal, 8,* 211–231.

Bougon, M. G., and Komocar, J. M. (1987). "Directing Strategic Change in Social Systems: Sketch of a Dynamic Holistic Approach." Academy of Management national meeting, Boston, August 13–14.

Brilliant, David. (1995, November 1). "The Tone At The Top," *The Banker, 145*(837), 26–27.

Brunsson, N. (1982). "The Irrationality of Action and Action Rationality: Decisions, Ideologies, and Organization Action." *Journal of Management Studies, 19,* 29–44.

Bryman, A. (1992). *Charisma and Leadership.* London: Sage.

Bryson, J. M., Bromiley, P., and Jung, Y. S. (1990). "Influences of Context and Process on Project Planning Success." *Journal of Planning Education, 9*(3), 183–195.

Bryson, J. M., and Cullen, J. W. (1984). "A Contingent Approach to Strategy and Tactics in Formative and Summative Evaluation." *Evaluation and Program Planning, 7,* 267–290.

Burns, Greg. (1996, September 23). "Crunch Time at Quaker Oats," *Business Week.*

Burns, J. M. (1978). *Leadership.* New York: Harper and Row.

Burrell, G., and Morgan, G. (1979). *Sociological Paradigms and Organizational Analysis.* London: Heinemann.

Cameron, K. (1995). "Quality, Downsizing, and Performance." In R. Cole (Ed.), *The Death and Life of the American Quality Movement* (93–114). New York: Oxford University Press.

Cameron, K., Freeman, S., and Meshra, A. (1993)."Downsizing and Redesigning Organizations." In G. Huber and W. Click (Eds.), *Organizational Change and Redesign* (pp. 19–63). New York: Oxford University Press.

Carr, A. (1978, January-February). "Is Business Bluffing Ethical?" *Harvard Business Review, 1978,* 114.

Carton, B. (1983). "Ethical Postures and Ethical Posturing." *American Review of Public Management, 17*(2/3), 15–159.

Churchman, C. W. (1971). *On the Design of Inquiring Systems: Basic Concepts in Systems and Organizations.* New York: Basic Books.

Churchman, C. W. (1979). *The Systems Approach and Its Enemies.* New York: Basic Books.

Churchman, C. W., Ackoff, R., and Arnoff, L. (1957). *Operations Research.* New York: Wiley.

Coch, L., and French, J. (1948). "Overcoming Resistance to Change." *Human Relations, 1,* 512–532.

Cohen, M. D., March, J. P., and Olsen, J. P. (1976). "A Garbage Can Model of Organizational Choice." *Administrative Science Quarterly, 17,* 1–25.

Collins, B. E., and Guetzkow, H. (1964). *A Social Psychology of Group Processes for Decision Making.* New York: Wiley.

Collins, J. C., and Porras, J. I. (1994). *Built to Last: Successful Habits of Visionary Companies.* New York: Harper.

Conger, J. (1991). "Inspiring Others: The Language of Leadership." *Academy of Management Executive, 5* (1), 31–45.

Cooperrider, D, and Srivastva, S. (1987). "Appreciative Inquiry in Organizational Life." In R. W. Woodman and W. A. Pasnore (Eds.), *Research in Organizational Change and Development, Vol. 1.* Greenwich, CT: JAI Press.

Covey, S. (1989). *The Seven Habits of Highly Effective Leaders.* New York: Simon and Schuster.

Covey, S. R. (1990). *Principled Central Leadership.* New York: Summit.

Cyert, R. M., and March, J. G. (1963). *A Behavioral Theory of the Firm.* Englewood Cliffs, NJ: Prentice-Hall.

Dacey, J. S. (1989). *Fundamentals of Creative Thinking.* New York: Lexington Books.

Daft, R. (1995). *Organization Theory and Decision.* St. Paul, MN: West.

Daft, R., and Becker, S. (1980). *Innovation in Organizations.* New York: Wiley (Interscience).

Daft, R., and Weick, K. (1984). "Toward a Model of Organizations as Interpretive Systems." *Academy of Management Review, 9*(2), 284–295.

Damanpour, F. (1991). "Organizational Innovation: A Meta Analysis of Determinants and Moderators." *Academy of Management Journal, 34*(3) 555–590.

Daugherty, D., and Bowman, E. (1995). The Effects of Organizational Downsizing on Product Innovation." *CA Management Review, 37,* 28–44.

de Bono, E. (1970). *Lateral Thinking: Creativity Step by Step.* New York: Harper and Row.

de Bono, E. (1984). *Tactics: The Art and Science of Success.* Boston: Little Brown and Company.

Dean, J. (1976). *Blind Ambition: The White House Years.* New York: Simon and Schuster.

Dean, J., and Sharfman, M. (1996). "Does Decision Making Matter? A Study of Strategic Decision Making." *The Academy of Management Journal, 39*(2), 368–396.

Dearborn, D, and Simon H. (1958). "Selective Perception: A Note on the Departmental Identification of Executives." *Sociometry, 21,* 140–144.

Delbecq, A. (1989). *Sustaining Innovations as an American Competitive Advantage.* College Park, MD: Institute of Urban Studies, University of Maryland.

Delbecq, A. et al. (2002). *Discernment and Decision-Making.* Santa Clara, CA: University of Santa Clara.

Delbecq, A., Van de Ven, A., and Gustafson, D. (1986). *Group Techniques for Program Planning,* Middletown, WI: Greenbrier.

Denhardt, J. (2000). *Business, Institutions, and Ethics.* Oxford: Oxford University Press.

Dennis, Edward S. G. (1993). *Evaluation of the Handling of the Branch Davidian Stand-Off in Waco, Texas Feb 28 to April 19, 1993.* Washington DC: U.S. Department of Justice.

Denzin, N. K. (1989). *The Research Act.* Englewood Cliffs, NJ: Prentice-Hall.

Dewey, J. (1910). *How We Think.* New York: Heath.

Dierkes, M., Alexis, M., Antal, A., Stopfors, J, and Vonderstein, A., (Eds.). (2001). *The Annotated Bibliography of Organizational Learning and Knowledge Creation.* Berlin: edition sigma

Eden, C. and Radford, J. (1990). *Tackling Strategic Problems.* London: Sage.

Eichholtz, G., and Rodgers, M. (1964). "Resistance to the Adoption of Audio-Visual Aids by Elementary Teachers." In M. Miles (Ed.), *Innovations in Education.* New York: Columbia University Teachers College Press.

Eisenhardt, K. (1989). "Making Fast Strategic Decisions in High Velocity Environments." *Academy of Management Journal, 32,* 543–-576.

Eisenhardt, K. (1997). "Strategic Decision Making as Improvisation." In V. Papadakis and P. Barwise (Eds.), *Strategic Decisions.* London: Kluwer.

Eisenhardt, K., and Zbaracki, M. (1992). "Strategic Decision Making." *Strategic Management Journal, 13*, 17–37.

El Sawy, O. A. (1985, May). *Exploring Temporal Perspectives as a Bias to Managerial Attention.* Los Angeles, CA: Center for Futures Research, Graduate School of Business Administration, University of Southern California.

Fay, Stephen. (1996, November 1). "The Collapse of Barings," *Management Accounting, 74*(10), 14.

Fisher, D., and Torbert, W. (1991). "Transforming Management Practice: Beyond the Achiever Stage." *In Research in Organizational Development, Vol. 5* (pp. 143–173). Greenwich, CT: JAI Press.

Fisher, R., and Brown, S. (1988). *Getting Together: Building a Relationship that Gets to Yes.* Boston: Houghton Mifflin.

Fishhoff, B. (1975). "Hindsight-Foresight: The Effect of Outcome Knowledge on Judgment Under Uncertainty." *Journal of Experimental Psychology, Human Perception, and Performance, 1*, 288–199.

Fiske, S., and Taylor, S. (1991). *Social Cognition.* New York: McGraw-Hill.

Frederickson, J. W. (1985). Effects of Decision Motive and Organizational Performance on Strategic Decision Processes." *Academy of Management Journal, 28*, 821–843.

Freeman, R. (1984). *Strategic Management: A Stakeholder Approach.* New York: Pitman.

French, J., and Raven, B. (1959). "The Basis of Social Power." In D. Cartright (Ed.), *Studies in Social Power.* Ann Arbor, MI: University of Michigan Press.

*Frontline.* (1995, October 17). "Waco: The Inside Story." (transcript #1401).

Gailbreth, C., and Schendel, D. (1983). "An Empirical Analysis of Strategic Types." *Strategic Management Journal, 4*, 153–173.

Galbraeth, J. R., Lawler, E. E. III, and Associates. (1993). *Organizing for the Future.* San Francisco: Jossey-Bass.

Glieck, J. (1987). *Chaos: The Making of a New Science.* New York: Viking.

Goldberg, P. (1983). *The Intuitive Edge.* Los Angeles, CA: Tarcher.

Gordon, W. J. J. (1971). *Synetics.* New York: Harper and Row.

Guilford, A. (1967). *The Nature of Human Intelligence.* New York: McGraw-Hill

Habermas, J. (1970). *Toward a Rational Society.* Boston: Beacon Press.

Hackman, J. R. (1990). *Groups that Work (and Those that Don't): Creating Conditions for Effective Teamwork.* San Francisco: Jossey-Bass.

Hage, J., and Aiken, H. (1970). *Social Change in Complex Organizations.* New York: Random House.

Hall, P. (1984). *Great Planning Disasters.* Berkeley: University of California Press.

Hall, R. (1962). "The Concept of Bureaucracy: An Empirical Assessment." *American Journal of Sociology, 69,* 32–40.

Hall, R. (1984). "The Natural Logic of Management Policy-Making: Its Implications for the Survival of an Organization." *Management Science, 30,* 905–927.

Hambrick, D., and D'Aveni, R. (1988). "Large Corporate Failures as Downward Spirals." *Administrative Science Quarterly, 33,* 1–23.

Hamel, G., and Prahalad, C. K. (1994, July-August). "Competing for the Future." *Harvard Business Review,* 122–128.

Hammond, S. A. (1998). *The Thin Book of Appreciative Inquiry.* Plano, TX: The Thin Book Publishing Co.

Hampden-Turner, C. M. (1981). *Maps of the Mind.* New York: Macmillian.

Hampden-Turner, C. M. (1990). *Charting the Corporate Mind.* New York: The Free Press.

Harmon, M. M. (1980). *Action Theory for Public Administration.* New York: Longmont.

Harrison, E. F. (1999). *The Managerial Decision-Making Process.* New York: Houghton-Mifflin.

Harrison, M., and Phillips, B. (1991). "Strategic Decision-Making: An Integrated Explanation." *Research in the Sociology of Organizations, 9,* 319–358.

Hart, G. P., and Bogan, A. (1993). *The Baldrich Prize.* New York: McGraw-Hill.

Hassard, J., and Parker, M. (1993). *Postmodernism and Organizations.* London: Sage.

Havelock, R. (1973). *Planning for Innovation through Dissemination and Utilization of Scientific Knowledge.* Ann Arbor,MI: CRUSK, The Center for Research Utilization of Scientific Knowledge.

Henderson, B. (1979). *Henderson on Corporate Strategy.* Cambridge, MA: MIT Press.

Hickson, D., Butler, R., Gray, D., Mallory, G., and Wilson, D. (1986). *Top Decisions: Strategic Decision Making in Organizations.* San Francisco: Jossey-Bass.

Hogarth, R. (1980). *Judgment and Choice.* New York: Wiley.

Huber, G. (1991). Organizational Learning: An Examination of the Contributing Processes and Literatures." *Organization Science, 2,* 88–115.

Huse, E. F., and Cummings, T. (1990). *Organizational Change and Development* (4th ed.). St. Paul, MN: West.

Ichazo, O. (1982). *Between Meta Physics and Protoanalysis.* New York: Arica Institute Press.

Janis, I. (1989). *Crucial Decisions.* New York: The Free Press.

Janis, I., and Mann, L. (1977). *Decision-Making: A Psychological Analysis of Conflict, Choice, and Commitment.* New York: The Free Press

Jantsch, E. (1975). *Design for Evolution: Self Organization and Planning in the Life of Systems.* New York: Brasilia.

Johnson, M. (1993). *Moral Imagination*. Chicago: University of Chicago Press.

Kelley, R. (1992). *The Power of Followership*. New York: Doubleday.

Kimberly, J., Miles, R. H., and Associates. (1980). *The Organizational Lifecycle*. San Francisco: Jossey-Bass.

Kimberly, J., and Quinn, R. (1984). *Managing Organizational Transitions*. Homewood, IL: Irwin.

King, W. R. (1982). "Using Strategic Issue Analysis." *Long Range Planning, 15*(4), 45–49.

Kolb, D. A. (1983). "Problem Management: Learning from Experience." In S. Srivastva (Ed.), *The Executive Mind* (pp. 109–143). San Francisco: Jossey-Bass.

Kotter, J. (1982). *A Force for Change*. New York: The Free Press.

Kotter, J. (1996). *Leading Change*. Cambridge, MA: HBS Press.

Kouzes, J. M., and Posner, B. Z. (1987). *The Leadership Challenge*. San Francisco: Jossey-Bass.

Kouzes, J. M., and Posner, B. Z. (1993). *Credibility*. San Francisco: Jossey-Bass.

Land, G., and Jarman, B. (1992). *Breakpoint and Beyond: Mastering the Future Today*. New York: HarperCollins.

Langley, A. (1989). "In Search of Rationality: The Purposes Behind the Use of Formal Analysis in Organizations," *Administrative Science Quarterly, 34*,(4), 598–631.

Langley, A., Minzberg, H., Pitcher, P., Posada, E., and Saint-Macary, J. (1995). "Opening Up Decision-Making: The View from the Black Stool." *Organization Science, 6*(3), 279–360.

Lawler, E. (1986). *High Involvement Management*. San Francisco: Jossey-Bass.

Lawrence, P. R., and Dyer, D. M. (1983). *Renewing American Industry*. New York: The Free Press.

Leavitt, H. J. (1986). *Corporate Pathfinders*. Homewood, IL: Dow Jones, Irwin.

Leeson, Nick. (1996). *Rogue Trader: How I Brought Down Barings Bank and Shook the Financial World*. Boston: Little Brown.

Levine, C. H. (1978). "Organizational Decline and Cut-Back Management." *Public Administration Review, 38*, 316–325.

Levine, C. H. (1980). *Managing Fiscal Stress: The Crisis in the Public Sector*. Chatham, NJ: Chatham House.

Levy, A. (1978). "Second-Order Planned Change: Definition and Conceptualization." *Organizational Dynamics, 5*(20).

Levy, A., and Merry, U. (1986). *Organizational Transformation: Approaches, Strategies and Theories*. New York: Prager.

Lewin, K. (1958). "Group Decisions and Social Change." In J. E. Maccoby, T. W. Newcomb, and E. Hartley (Eds.), *Readings in Social Psychology*. New York: Holt, Rinehart and Winston.

Likert, R. (1967). *The Human Organization*. New York: McGraw-Hill.

Lincoln, Y., and Guba, E. (1985). *Naturalistic Inquiry*. Beverly Hills, CA: Sage.

Lindblom, C. (1965). *The Intelligence of Democracy: Decision Process through Adjustment*. New York: The Free Press.

Linden, R. (1994). *Seamless Government: Re-engineering the Public Sector*. San Francisco: Jossey-Bass.

Linstone, H. (1984). *Multiple Perspectives for Decision Making: Bridging the Gap Between Analysis and Action*. New York: North Holland.

Machiavelli, N. (1952). *The Prince*. Oxford: Oxford University Press. (Original translation by L. Ricci, 1903)

March, J. G. (1981). "Footnotes to Organizational Change." *Administrative Science Quarterly, 26*(4), 563–577.

March, J. G. (1994). *A Primer on Decision Making: How Decisions Happen*. New York: The Free Press.

March, J. G., and Simon, H. A. (1958). *Organizations*. New York: McGraw-Hill.

Maruyama, M. (1983). "Second Order Cybernetics: Deviation Amplificating Mutual Causal Processes." *American Scientist, 51*, 1–24.

Mason, R. O., and Mitroff, I. I. (1981). *Challenging Strategic Planning Assumptions*. New York: Wiley (Interscience).

Mausch, M., and LaPonin, P. (1989). "Beyond Garbage Cans: An AI Model of Organizational Choice." *Administrative Science Quarterly, 34*, 38–67.

McConnell, Malcolm. (1987). *Challenger: A Major Malfunction*. New York: Doubleday.

McGrath, J. E. (1988). *The Social Sociology of Time: New Perspectives*. Beverly Hills, CA: Sage.

McKie, D. (1973). *A Sadly Mismanaged Affair: The Political History of the Third London Airport*. London: Croom Helm.

McKinley, W. (1993). "Organizational Decline and Adaptation: Theoretical Controversies." *Organizational Science, 4*(1).

Meindl, J., Ehrich, S., and Dukerich, J. (1985). "The Romance of Leadership." *Administrative Science Quarterly, 30*, 78–102.

Meyer, A. (1982). "Adapting to Environmental Jolts." *Administrative Science Quarterly, 27*, 515–537.

Meyer, J., and Rowan, B. (1977). "Institutional Organizations: Formal Structure as Myth and Ceremony." *American Journal of Sociology, 83*, 340–363.

Meyer, M. W., and Zucker, L. G. (1989). *Permanently Failing Organizations*. Newbury Park, CA: Sage.

Miles, M., and Huberman, A. (1994). *Qualitative Data Analysis: An Expanded Source Book* (2nd ed.). Thousand Oaks, CA: Sage.

Miller, D. (1990). *The Icarus Paradox: How Excellent Companies Bring about Their Own Downfall*. New York: Harper.

Miller, D., and Friesen, P. (1995). *Organizations: A Quantum View*. Englewood Cliffs, NJ: Prentice-Hall.

Mintzberg, H. (1985). *Structure in Fives*. Englewood Cliffs, NJ: Prentice-Hall.

Mintzberg, H. (1994). *The Rise and the Fall of Strategic Planning*. New York: The Free Press.

Mintzberg, H., Raisinghani, D., and Theoret, A. (1976). "The Structure of Unstructured Decisions," *Administrative Science Quarterly, 21*(2), 246–275.

Mintzberg, H., and Westley, F. (2000, August). *Decision-Making: Its Not What You Think*. Unpublished manuscript. McGill University, Montreal, Quebec.

Mitroff, I. I., and Emshoff, J. R. (1979). "On Strategic Assumption-Making: A Dialectical Approach to Policy & Planning." *Academy of Management Review, 4*(1), 1–12.

Mitroff, I. I., Moherman, S., and Little, G. (1987). *The Global Solution: The New Rules for Doing Business in a World Economy*. San Francisco: Jossey-Bass.

Mitroff, I. I. and Pauchant, T. (1990). *We're So Big and Powerful Nothing Bad Can Happen to Us*. New York: Buchtone.

Mohr, L. (1985). *Explaining Organizational Behavior*. San Francisco: Jossey-Bass.

Morgan, G. (1984). "Opportunities Arising from Paradigms Diversity." *Administration and Society, 16*(3), 306–327.

Morgan, G. (1986). *Images of Organizations*. Beverly Hills, CA: Sage.

Morgan, G. (1988). *Riding the Waves of Change*. San Francisco: Jossey-Bass.

Morgan, G. (1993). *Imaginization*. Newbury Park, CA: Sage.

Nadler, D. A., Gerstein, M. S., Shaw, R. B., and Associates. (1992). *Organizational Architecture*. San Francisco: Jossey-Bass.

Nadler, G. (1981). *The Planning and Design Approach*. New York: Wiley.

Nadler, G., and Hibino, S. (1990). *Breakthrough Thinking*. Rocklin, CA: Prima.

Nanus, B. 1989). *The Leader's Edge*. Chicago: Contemporary Books.

Neuman, J. E. (1989). "Why People Don't Participate in Organizational Change." In R. W. Woodman and W. A. Pasmore (Eds.), *Research in Organizational Change and Development, Vol. 3* (pp. 181–212). Greenwich, CT: JAI Press.

Nisbett, R., and Ross, L. (1989). *Human Inferences: Strategies and Shortcomings of Human Judgments* (rev. ed.). New York: Wiley.

Nutt, P. C. (1989). *Making Tough Decisions*. San Francisco: Jossey-Bass.

Nutt, P. C. (1992). *Managing Planned Change*. New York: Macmillan.

Nutt, P. C., and Backoff, R. W. (1992). *The Strategic Management of Public and Third Sector Organizations*. San Francisco: Jossey-Bass.

Nutt, P. C., and Backoff, R. W. (1993). "Strategic Issues as Tensions." *Journal of Management Inquiry, 2*(1), 28–43.

Nutt, P. C., and Backoff, R. W. (1997a). "Crafting Vision." *Journal of Management Inquiry, 6*(4), 308–328.

Nutt, P. C., and Backoff, R. W. (1997b). "Facilitating Transformational Change." *Journal of Applied Behavioral Science, 33*(4), 488–506.

Nystrom, P., and Starbuck, W. (1984). "To Avoid Organizational Crises, Unlearn." *Organizational Dynamics, 12*(4), 53–65.

Oakley, E., and Krug, D. (1993). *Enlightened Leadership.* New York: Simon and Schuster.

Osborn, D., and Gaebler, T. (1992). *Reinventing Government.* Reading, MA: Addison-Wesley.

Overell, Stephen. (1995, September 21). "Barings Collapse Blamed on Lack of HR Strategy," *People Management, 1*(19), 8.

Pacanowski, M. (1988). "Communication in the Empowering Organization." In J. Anderson (Ed.), *International Communications Association Yearbook* (pp. 356–379). Beverly Hills, CA: Sage.

Papadakis, V., and Barwise, P. (1997). *Strategic Decisions.* London: Kluwer.

Pascale, T. T. (1990). *Managing on the Edge.* New York: Simon and Schuster.

Patton, M. E. (1990). *Qualitative Evaluation and Research Methods.* Los Angeles, CA: Sage.

Pauchant, T. C., and Mitroff, I. I. (1992). *Transforming the Crisis Prone Organization.* San Francisco: Jossey-Bass.

Pelz, D. C. (1978). "Some Expanded Perspectives on Use of Social Science in Public Policy." In M. Yinger and S. J. Cutler (Eds.), *Major Social Issues: A Multidisciplinary View* (pp. 346–357). New York: The Free Press.

Peters, T. J., and Waterman, R. H. (1982). *In Search of Excellence: Lessons from America's Best Run Companies.* New York: Harper and Row.

Pettigrew, A. (1987). "Context and Action in the Transformation of a Firm." *Journal of Management Studies, 11*(2), 31–48.

Pettigrew, A. (1987). *The Management of Strategic Change.* Oxford: Oxford University Press.

Pfeffer, J. (1992). *Managing with Power: Politics and Influence in Organizations.* Boston: MA: Harvard University Press.

Pickrell, Don H. (1990). *Urban Rail Transit Projects: Forecasts versus Actual Ridership and Costs.* Cambridge, MA: Transportation Systems Center, Urban Mass Transportation Administration, DOT-T-91-04.

Pinchot, G. (1985). *Intrapreneuring.* New York: Harper and Row.

Polanyi, M. (1967). *The Tacit Dimension.* Garden City, NJ: Doubleday.

Pondy, L. R., Boland, R. J. Jr., Thomas, H. (1988). *Managing Ambiguity and Change.* New York: Wiley.

Popper, K. P. (1959). *The Logic of Scientific Discovery.* New York: Basic Books.

Porter, M. (1985). *Competitive Advantage.* New York: The Free Press.

Pribam, K. I. (1983). "The Brain, Cognitive Commodities, and the Enfolded Order." In K. Boulding and L. Senesch, (Eds.), *The Optimum Utilization of Knowledge.* Boulder, CO: Westview.

Prigogine, I., and Stengers, I. (1984). *Order Out of Chaos.* New York: Bantam.

Quinn, J. B. (1990). "Managing Strategic Change." In A. A. Thompson Jr., W. E. Fulmer, and A. J. Strikland III (Eds.), *Strategic Management* (pp. 10–32). Homewood, IL: Irwin.

Quinn, R. E., Faerman, S. R., Thompson, M. P., and McGrath, M. R. (1990). *Becoming a Master Manager.* New York: Wiley.

Quinn, R. E. (1988). *Beyond Rational Management: Mastering the Paradoxes and Competing Demands of High Performance.* San Francisco: Jossey-Bass.

Quinn, R. E., and Cameron, K. (1988). *Paradox and Transformation.* Cambridge, MA: Ballinger.

Rasmussen, J., and Batson, R. (1991). *Toward Improved Safety and Risk Management.* Washington, DC: World Bank.

Rainey, H. E. (1991). *Understanding and Managing Public Organizations.* San Francisco: Jossey-Bass.

Ray, M., and Myers, R. (1989). *Creativity in Business.* New York: Doubleday.

Reyes, Alejandro. (1995, October 27). "Uncovering the Cover-Up," *Asia Week.*

Ritti, R., and Funkhouser, G. (1987). *The Ropes to Skip and the Ropes to Know.* New York: Wiley.

Rodrigues, S., and Hickson, D. (1995). "Success in Decision-making: Different Organizations, Different Reasons for Success." *Journal of Management Studies, 32*(5) 654–679.

Rosenau, P. (1992). *Post-Modernism and the Social Sciences.* Princeton, NJ: Princeton University Press.

Rothenburg, A. (1979). *The Emerging Goddess,* Chicago: University of Chicago Press.

Ruelle, D. (1990). *Chance and Chaos.* Princeton NJ: Princeton University Press.

Ruvolu, A., and Marcus, H. (1992). "Possible Selves and Performance: The Power of Self-Relevant Imagery." *Social Cognition, 10*(1), 95–124.

Sashkin, M., and Kisner, K. J. (1993). *Putting Total Quality Management to Work.* San Francisco: Berrett-Koehler.

Schein, E. (1967). *Process Consultation.* Reading, MA: Addison-Wesley.

Schon, D. A. (1983). *The Reflective Practitioner: How Professionals Think in Action.* New York: Basic Books.

Schon, D. A. (1987). *Educating the Reflective Practitioner.* San Francisco: Jossey-Bass.

Schwartz, P. (1991). *The Art of the Long View.* New York: Doubleday.

Senge, P. (1990). *The Fifth Discipline: The Art and Management of the Learning Organization.* New York: Doubleday.

Shamir, B., House. R., and Arthur, M. (1993). "The Motivational Effects of Charismatic Leadership: A Self-Concept Theory." *Organizational Science,* 4(4), 577–594.

Shapiro, G., and Sica, A. (1984). *Hermeneutics: Questions and Prospects.* Amherst: University of Massachusetts Press.

Shortell, S., Morrison, E. M., and Friedman, B. (1988). *Strategic Choice for America's Hospitals: Managing Change in Turbulent Times.* San Francisco: Jossey-Bass.

Shull, F., Delbecq, A., and Cummings, L. (1970). *Organizational Decision Making.* New York: McGraw-Hill.

Simon, H. A. (1969). *The Sciences of the Artificial.* Cambridge, MA: MIT Press.

Simon, H. A. (1977). *The New Science of Management Decision* (rev. ed.). Englewood Cliffs, NJ: Prentice-Hall.

Sims, R. (1991). *Ethics and Organizational Decision Making: A Call for Renewal.* New York: Quorum Books.

Snyder, R. C., and Page, G. D. (1958). "The United States Decision to Resist Aggression in Korea: The Application of an Analytical Scheme." *Administrative Science Quarterly,* 3, 341–378.

Soleberg, P. O. (1967, Spring). "Unprogrammed Decision Making." *Industrial Management Review,* 19–29.

Spradley, J. P. (1980). *Participant Observation.* New York: Holt, Rinehart, and Winston.

Spreitzer, G. M., and Quinn, R. E. (2001). *A Company of Leaders: Five Disciplines for Unleashing the Power in Your Workforce.* San Francisco: Jossey-Bass.

Sraeel, Holly. (1995, September 1). "The Barings Report Lacks Cuts," *Bank System and Technology,* 32(9), 4.

Starbuck, W. H. (1983). "Organizations as Action Generators." *American Sociological Review,* 48, 91–102.

Staw, B., Sandelands, L., and Dutton, J. (1981). "Threat-Rigidity Effects on Organization Behavior." *Administrative Science Quarterly,* 26, 501–524.

Stein, M. I. (1975). *Stimulating Creativity: Volume 2 Group Procedures.* New York: Academic Press.

Stogdill, R. M. (1974). *Handbook of Leadership: A Survey of Theory and Research.* New York: The Free Press.

Stone, Alan A. (1993, November 10). "Report and Recommendations Concerning the Handling of Incidents Such as the Branch Davidian Standoff in Waco, Texas."

Submitted to Deputy Attorney General Philp Haymann.

Theitart, R., and Forgues, (1995). "Chaos Theory and Organization." *Organization Science, 6*(1), 19–31.

Thompson, J. D. (1967). *Organizations in Action.* New York: McGraw-Hill.

Tichy, N., and Devanna, M. (1986). *The Transformational Leader.* New York: Wiley.

Tichy, N., and Devanna, M. (1990). *Revisiting the Transformational Leader.* New York: Wiley.

Torbert, W. R. (1989). "Leading Organizational Transformation." In R. W. Woodman and W. A. Pasmore (Eds.), *Research in Organizational Change and Development, Vol. 3* (pp. 83–116). Greenwich, CT: JAI Press.

Toulmin, S. (1979). *Knowing and Understanding: An Invitation to Philosophy.* New York: Macmillan.

Toulmin, S, Rieke, R., and Janik, A. (1979). *An Introduction to Reasoning.* New York: Macmillan.

Trevino, L. (1986). "Ethical Decision-Making in Organizations: A Person–Situation Interactionist Model." *Academy of Management Review, 13*(3), 601–617.

Tversky, A., and Kahneman, D. (1973). "Availability: A Heuristic for Judging Frequency and Probability." *Cognitive Psychology, 5,* 207–232.

Tversky, A., and Kahneman, D. (1981). "The Framing of Decisions and the Psychology of Choice." *Science, 211,* 453–458.

Utterback, J. M. (1974). "Innovation in Industry and the Differentiation of Technology." *Science, 183,* 620–626

Vail, P. B. (1989). *Managing as a Performing Art.* San Francisco: Jossey-Bass.

Van de Ven, A., Angle, V., and Poole, M. S. (2000). *Research on the Management of Innovation.* Oxford: Oxford University Press.

Van de Ven, A., Polley, D. E., Garud, R., and Venkataraman, S. (1999). *The Innovation Journey.* New York: Oxford University Press.

Van de Ven, A., and Poole, M. S. (1995). "Explaining Development and Change in Organizations." *Academy of Management Review, 20*(3), 510–540.

Van Gundy, A. (1981). *Techniques of Structured Problem Solving.* New York: Van Norstrom, Reinhold, Winston.

Voss, Cary R. W. (1997). "Students of the Seven Seals: An Organizational History." Communications Department, University of Kansas. [on-line] http://falcon.cc.ukans.edu/~

Vroom, V., and Jago, A. (1988). *The New Leadership: Managing Participation in Organizations.* Englewood Cliffs, NJ: Prentice-Hall.

Vroom, V., and Yetton, P. (1973). *Leadership and Decision-Making.* Pittsburgh. PA: University of Pittsburgh Press.

Wall, B., Solum, R., and Sobol, M. (1992). *The Visionary Leader*. Rocklin, CA: Prima.

Walton, R. E. (1985, March-April). "From Control to Commitment in the Workplace." *Harvard Business Review*, 77–94.

Watzawick, P., Weakland, J., and Frisch, R. (1974). *Change*. New York: Norton.

Weick, K. (1979). *The Social Psychology of Organizing*. Reading: MA: Addison-Wesley.

Weick, K. (1989). "Cognitive Processes in Organizations." In B. Staw (Ed.), *Research in Organizational Behavior* (Vol. 1, pp. 41–74). Greenwich, CT: JAI Press.

Weick, K. (1994). "The Collapse of Sense-Making in Organizations: The Manngulch Disaster." *Administrative Science Quarterly*, *38*(4/5), 628–652.

Weinberg, G. (1985). *An Introduction to Systems Thinking*. New York: Wiley.

Weisbord, M. R. (1988). "Towards a New Practice Theory of OD: Notes on Snap-shooting and Movie Making." In R. W. Woodman and W. A. Pasmore (Eds.), *Research in Organizational Change and Development, Vol. 2* (pp. 59–96). Greenwich, CT: JAI Press.

Werhane, P. H. (1999). *Moral Imagination and Managerial Decision-Making*. New York: Oxford University Press.

Wheatley, M. J. (1992). *Leadership and the New Science*. San Francisco: Berrett-Koehler.

Wilber, K. (Ed.). (1982). *The Holographic Paradigm and Other Paradoxes*. Boulder, CO: Shambala.

Wildavsky, A. (1979). *Speaking Truth to Power*. Boston: Little Brown.

Witte, E. (1972). "Field Research on Complex Decision Making Process—The Phase Theory." *International Studies of Management and Organization*, *56*, 156–182.

Woodman, R. W. (1989). "Evaluation Research and Organizational Change: Arguments for a 'Combined Paradigm' Approach." In R. W. Woodman and W. A. Pasmore (Eds.), *Research in Organizational Change and Development, Vol. 3* (pp.161–180). Greenwich, CT: JAI Press.

Woodman, R. W., Sawyer, J., and Griffen, R. (1993). "Toward a Theory of Organizational Creativity." *Academy of Management Review*, *18*(2), 293–321.

Woodward, J. (1965). *Industrial Organization: Theory and Practice*. New York: Oxford University Press.

Yin, R. K. (1981). "The Case Study Crisis: Some Answers," *Administrative Science Quarterly*, *26*(10), 58–65.

Yin, R. K. (1993). *Applications of Case Study Research*. Beverly Hills, CA: Sage.

Zaltman, G. R., Duncan, R., and Holbook, J. (1973). *Innovation and Organizations*. New York: Wiley (Interscience).

Zukav, G. (1989). *The Seat of Soul*. New York: Simon and Schuster.

# Index

# About the Author

Paul C. Nutt is a professor of Management Sciences and Public Policy and Management in the Fisher College of Business at The Ohio State University. He received his Ph.D. (1974) from the University of Wisconsin–Madison and a B.S. and M.S. from the University of Michigan (1962, 1963), all in Industrial Engineering. He has written more than one hundred articles and six books. His current research interests include organizational decision making and radical change.

The decision-making stream of work, drawn upon to write this book, is taken from more than two decades of research into the decision-making practices used by people in organizations and how to improve them. Articles first appeared in 1984 and have continued at a steady pace since then, with several currently in press. In all, thirty-eight articles have appeared or will appear in referred journals and more are planned. This work has received numerous awards including two best theoretical/empirical paper awards from the Decision Sciences Institute, its top award, and several from the Academy of Management. His other work in decision making involves decision analysis, risk measurement, using MBTI and the Enneagram to identify a person's decision style, Multiattribute Utilities, ethics, and learning.

The radical change stream of work investigates the nature of and means to create organizational transformation, the role of vision and how to create it, finding organizations susceptible to radical change, strategic management, change leadership, and de-development—an alternative to downsizing. This work has also received numerous awards, including two best paper awards from the Academy of Management.

He has received awards for his articles, books, and teaching in other areas from the International Federation of Operations Research and Management Science (IFORMS), the Center for Creative Leadership, the American College of Health Care Executives, the Decision Sciences Institute, the Academy of Management, and others. He is a Fellow in the Decision Sciences Institute. Other recent books include *The Strategic Management of Public and Third Sector Organizations* and *Making Tough Decisions* (Jossey-Bass, 1992 and 1989) and *Managing Planned Change* (Macmillan, 1992). He serves on several editorial review boards, including that of the *Strategic Management Journal*, and regularly consults and provides executive education for public, private, and nonprofit organizations.

## Berrett-Koehler Publishers

BERRETT-KOEHLER is an independent publisher of books, periodicals, and other publications at the leading edge of new thinking and innovative practice on work, business, management, leadership, stewardship, career development, human resources, entrepreneurship, and global sustainability.

Since the company's founding in 1992, we have been committed to supporting the movement toward a more enlightened world of work by publishing books, periodicals, and other publications that help us to integrate our values with our work and work lives, and to create more humane and effective organizations.

We have chosen to focus on the areas of work, business, and organizations, because these are central elements in many people's lives today. Furthermore, the work world is going through tumultuous changes, from the decline of job security to the rise of new structures for organizing people and work. We believe that change is needed at all levels— individual, organizational, community, and global—and our publications address each of these levels.

We seek to create new lenses for understanding organizations, to legitimize topics that people care deeply about but that current business orthodoxy censors or considers secondary to bottom-line concerns, and to uncover new meaning, means, and ends for our work and work lives.

See next page for other publications
from Berrett-Koehler

### The Answer to How Is Yes
#### Acting on What matters

Peter Block

Peter Block puts the "how-to" craze in perspective. He presents a guide to the difficult and life-granting journey of bringing what we know is of personal value into an indifferent or even hostile corporate and cultural landscape and teaches individuals, workers, and managers how to reclaim their capacity to create a world they want to live in.

Hardcover, 200 pages • ISBN 1-57675-168-6
Item #51686-408 $24.95

### Stewardship
#### Choosing Service Over Self-Interest

Peter Block

Peter Block shows how to recreate our workplaces by replacing self-interest, dependency, and control with service, responsibility, and partnership. He shows how redistribution of power, privilege, and wealth will radically change all areas of organizational governance.

Paperback, 288 pages• ISBN 1-881052-86-9
Item # 52869-408 $16.95

Hardcover • ISBN 1-881052-28-1 • Item #52281-408 $24.95

Audiotape, 2 cassettes • ISBN 1-57453-147-6
Item #31476-408 $17.95

### The New SuperLeadership
#### Leading Others to Lead Themselves

Charles C. Manz and Henry P. Sims, Jr.

"SuperLeadership" describes a style of leadership that focuses on "leading others to lead themselves." Based on the same concepts as the authors' previous bestselling book, this edition is thoroughly revised throughout and emphasizes a pragmatic, how-to approach and features contemporary examples and profiles, many from the high-tech and knowledge-based business sectors.

Hardcover, 280 pages • ISBN 1-57675-105-8
Item #51058-408 $27.95

**Berrett-Koehler Publishers**
PO Box 565, Williston, VT 05495-9900
Call toll-free! **800-929-2929** 7 am-12 midnight

Or fax your order to 802-864-7627
For fastest service order online: **www.bkconnection.com**

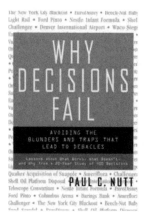